THE
DEFINITIVE
GUIDE
TO
BETTING ON THE
ALL-WEATHER

RACING POST

THE
DEFINITIVE GUIDE
TO
BETTING ON THE
ALL-WEATHER

David Bellingham

First published by Pitch Publishing on behalf of Racing Post, 2022

Pitch Publishing
9 Donnington Park,
85 Birdham Road,
Chichester,
West Sussex,
PO20 7AJ

www.pitchpublishing.co.uk
info@pitchpublishing.co.uk
www.racingpost.com/shop

A CIP catalogue record is available for this book
from the British Library.

ISBN 9781839501111

Typesetting and origination by Pitch Publishing

Printed and bound by TJ Books

CONTENTS

INTRODUCTION

It was the evening of 6 January 1994, and I was lounging about in my room at the Towcester Travelodge in Northamptonshire, just south of the town on the A43. My original plan had been to attend the jumps fixture at Towcester the following day and then drive down on the morning of 8 January for what is now known as the Tolworth Hurdle meeting at Sandown. However, the weather intervened, and the Towcester meeting was likely to be frozen off, but I was desperate for some horse action so had decided that if my original destination was unable to race, I would grab the bull by the horns and go up to attend the All-Weather fixture at Southwell instead.

Even though All-Weather racing had been going for over four years I had never been to a meeting before, not that I had anything against it (I had already witnessed racing on non-grass surfaces at first hand when attending the Breeders' Cups of 1991, 1992 and 1993). It was just that there was usually a Flat turf or jumps fixture taking place closer to where I live, but I had always intended to go to an All-Weather meeting at some point and this might turn out to be an opportunity.

Just in case it turned out that I was indeed going to end up at Southwell, I decided to sit down on the floor of my room at the Travelodge and try to calculate some 'speed figures' for the meeting. I had kept the results from the pull-out section of the *Sporting Life Weekender*, both for the Flat and the jumps, and had them filed away in a rather snazzy green folder with gold leaf provided by the publishers, which I had fortunately brought along with me. I also had a calculator close at hand, without which I would have been well and truly lumbered. I was fascinated to see how these speed figures would perform at a British All-Weather fixture, knowing how important they were for bettors in the US, particularly on dirt. I'm not going to pretend these figures were anything elaborate as this was going to be an unintended visit if it turned out that way, but at least they would be something and without them I would have been totally in the dark.

With Towcester duly having been called off and after consulting the road map in my car, I made my way up the M1 and somehow managed to arrive at Southwell racecourse. Don't ask me how, as the route I took then isn't one I would entertain now, but I was there safe and sound and that was the main thing. In those days meetings at this time of year counted towards the Flat Jockeys' Championship. I still think they should do so now, but that's a completely different subject. However, for that reason some big-name jockeys were riding at this fixture, not least Frankie Dettori and Jason Weaver. Frankie would go on to ride 233 winners that year to clinch the title, while Jason rode 200. That's quite a feat for someone to achieve that milestone and yet still not be champion jockey. Other notable riders at this meeting were Jimmy Quinn and Joe Fanning, the only others apart from Frankie to still be riding now, while Chris Rutter, Dale Gibson and Nicky Carlisle have all gone on to high office.

Frankie rode the first winner on the card, a horse named Akabusi (trained by Lord Huntingdon) in the first division of the 7f maiden. It was also the perfect start for the speed figures as they had him well out in front, so I was feeling quite pleased with myself. Things got even better when Just Harry won the following 1m handicap under Darren Biggs, but despite now being two from two punting-wise I never thought for one moment this game was going to be easy (experience had told me how futile such thoughts can be). I was now approaching this new game with a degree of confidence, though, and that was always going to be important.

The third race on the card was a 1m claimer and even though I thought No Submission would win, I decided to sit the race out. I didn't like claimers then and I still don't. I just find them too hard to fathom and usually they are uncompetitive races from the punter's point of view. The eight-year-old duly won easily under Frankie, but although I had stuck to my guns and decided not to invest in this contest, part of me was a little sore that I had missed a 3-1 winner! No Submission would go on the win 19 times on the All-Weather in his career, 15 of those at Southwell, and it was watching him rack up so many wins at Southwell which first brought home to me the whole concept of an All-Weather track specialist.

I had my punting boots back on in time for Rad to win the second division of the 7f maiden under Wendyll Woods, while the winning run continued when Warwick Warrior easily landed the 6f handicap under Jason Weaver. The sixth race was a no-bet contest for me as not only was it a 1m3f claimer, but it was also a 1m3f *amateur-riders'* claimer! I don't think I would have backed the 50-1 winner Sporting Spirit in any case.

The best was yet to come, however, as somehow Royal Citizen managed to get back up after looking beaten in the concluding 1m4f handicap, thereby completing a treble on the day for Dettori. I was more than delighted with his 7-1 odds, and even more delighted when a swift count of the cash after racing had revealed that I had made a profit of well over £700 on the day! That was no mean feat considering that my average stake was a bit smaller then than it is now. I remember driving away from the track with a real sense of satisfaction, not only because of the financial benefit but because I had a most enjoyable experience. Incidentally, the Sandown meeting I was due to attend on the Saturday was also abandoned and I ended up going to the jumps fixture at Warwick instead.

I vowed that I would be back at Southwell as soon as possible, despite the course being over 100 miles from my home, and that I would also try to get to Lingfield and Wolverhampton (the latter had only just become an All-Weather track). There is no doubt that because of what happened on that cold winter's day back in 1994 I became hooked on All-Weather racing, and it's a passion I have retained to this day.

In 1997 I was fortunate to realise a lifetime's dream when I landed a job with *Raceform* (soon to become part of the *Racing Post*), where I stayed until 2018, though I still do work for them on a freelance basis (Spotlights, analysis and close-ups). It wasn't long after joining the company that I began to write under the pseudonym of 'King Of The Sand' in the *Racing and Football Outlook*, and soon after that I took over compiling *Raceform's* Split Second speed ratings. These two jobs became very closely knit, as speed figures were a vital part in coming up with my weekly selections as 'KOTS' and they still play a big part in my betting now. That will become very clear throughout these pages.

The idea for writing this book was first discussed at the start of 2020, the plan being to publish in the autumn of that year. It had been 12 years since my last book, but I had been keen not to write another one until things had changed sufficiently to make another volume worthwhile. I felt that now was the time as not only had Newcastle become an All-Weather venue, but Wolverhampton had changed its surface for a second time and Great Leighs had reinvented itself as Chelmsford City.

However, soon after the idea for the book was first mooted Covid happened and everything changed, hence the two-year delay. Another major change occurred when Southwell ditched its Fibresand surface in favour of Tapeta at the end of 2021, so there was something else new to discuss.

As I said in the last book, horseracing should be fun, but it can be an opportunity to make money if you put a little work in and know what you are doing. Hopefully, how to spot those opportunities will come across within these pages.

CHELMSFORD

It had been a long time coming (indeed I never thought it would happen) but here we were about to see the revealing of a brand-new racetrack, the first in England since Taunton opened its doors in 1927. There had been a series of frustrating delays over the previous couple of years, but now we were on the cusp of a new adventure, or so it seemed.

It was 18 April 2008 and at that time I was working for *Racing Post/Raceform* as a race analyst and compiler of the *Raceform* Split Second speed ratings. I was also writing the 'King Of The Sand' column in the *Racing and Football Outlook* and it was in that capacity that I had received an invitation to attend the opening fixture, which was due to take place two days later. I was given details on where to go and what I was likely to see and it was made quite clear this wouldn't be the sort of normal race day experience I was used to. For one thing, although the racing infrastructure was now complete and had met all the criteria required to stage a proper race meeting, the public infrastructure was not. Therefore, attendance at this meeting would be by invitation only and I remember feeling privileged that I had been included in that group. The anticipation grew when, after a near two-hour drive, those stirrup-shaped floodlights suddenly loomed on the horizon.

It was a rather strange environment for a race meeting to take place in. Apart from Cartmel, I had never been to a racecourse where all the facilities were on the inside of the track, but that was the situation here and it remains the case at the time of writing. I also remember the mud, lots of it, because I was basically viewing racing from a building site. Many of my press colleagues had taken advantage of the blue plastic coverings you could place over your

They have just over a circuit to go in the staying event at Chelmsford (Megan Rose Photography).

shoes to keep the mud off them, but for some reason I didn't use them, something I quickly regretted. These were all trivial matters in the overall scheme of things, though, and having been given a guided tour of the facilities, including all the areas the public would eventually be able to use, it was now time for history to be made.

The first race on the card was a 6f fillies' maiden which was won easily by the 7-4 favourite Temple Of Thebes (Ed Dunlop/Stevie Donohoe) and the initial feedback was positive, about the track itself at least. Things appeared to go well in the following few weeks including the first fixture open to the public on 28 May (another meeting I had the pleasure of attending). In September of that year the track even staged a fixture that was advertised as a Breeders' Cup Trials meeting and even though events here would be unlikely to have much bearing on what was due to happen on the other side of the Atlantic later in the autumn, this was still a notable meeting with plenty of good horses and good prize money on offer, including four valuable conditions events. Even internationally renowned South African trainer Mike de Kock had a few runners on the card, and he didn't leave empty-handed, winning the concluding contest over 1m1f with Lucky Find, albeit the gelding was the least fancied of his two runners!

It was therefore sad, especially for someone like me who personally witnessed the track's early development, when Great Leighs was placed into administration the following January (the last fixture took place on 11 January) and everything suddenly ground to a halt, just nine months after the optimism and excitement of that very first fixture. However, despite several false dawns the track eventually reopened on 11 January 2015, not as Great Leighs but as Chelmsford City Racecourse.

Happily, the track has established itself since then with good prize money and often a nice type of horse. For instance, Highfield Princess's record at the track read 1121213 before her meteoric rise in the summer of 2022, while after Newbury was abandoned on 16 April 2016 due to waterlogging the meeting was transferred to Chelmsford including the three Group 3 contests, the Greenham, Fred Darling and John Porter. It wasn't long before the track was staging classier contests in its own right with the introduction of two Listed races for fillies and mares, the Queen Charlotte Stakes in 2018 and the Chelmer Stakes in 2019. The former event has already established an attractive Roll Of Honour, having been won by the dual Group 1 winner Billesdon Brook in 2019 while Highfield Princess herself won it in 2021.

Chelmsford has always had a Polytrack surface (silica sand with fibres made from various components and covered with wax) and was a floodlit track ever since the Great Leighs days. The circuit is just over 1m round with separate starting chutes for races over 7f and 1m, while the back and home straights are around 2f in length. It's also a wide track, 22 metres in width with two sweeping bends of more than 135 metres in radius. Therefore, you often find that the field fans right out on the entrance to the home straight and the real question here is whether those who stay inside (and therefore cover less ground) are favoured or whether those who come wider find themselves on the faster part of the track.

Unfortunately, it isn't a question that can be answered beforehand. As with the other tracks you may need to wait until a few races have been run to see what is happening, but it can be worth the wait as on many occasions a bias (towards or against the inside rail) can be identified. Of course, it's no good to you if you have already placed a bet as you don't know what the jockey's intentions are, and even if they already had a plan in mind it might have to change subject to circumstances. My own view is that (and this is true of a couple of the other tracks as well) attempting to put in a sustained effort from off the pace close to the inside rail is difficult. It may not be true at every fixture of course, hence the need for a little patience.

Such biases can be useful to in-running players, but also to those of us who analyse a contest post-race with a view to the future. In other words, was the horse helped or hindered by where they raced, especially when making their final efforts? Were they flattered or can their performance be forgiven and even be marked up? When the horse in question runs again you will be in possession of the sort of information many other punters aren't. Therefore, taking the time to do this is time well spent.

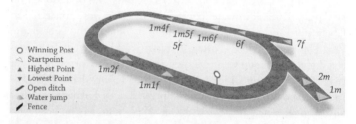

FIVE-SEASON TOP JOCKEY, TRAINER AND SIRE STATISTICS FOR CHELMSFORD

Below are the top jockeys, trainers, and sire statistics at Chelmsford since the start of 2018 to the end of June 2022. To qualify for the listing and to provide a more meaningful sample, a jockey must have had at least 20 rides at the track within that period and a trainer at least 20 runners. Both must have had at least 10 winners and a strike rate of at least 10 per cent. There is a little more flexibility when it comes to sires. Again, they must have had at least 20 runners during the period but need to have had five winners or more and a strike rate of at least 15 per cent. As is shown, the profit or loss is to a £1 level stake.

JOCKEYS

%	RIDES	WNS	P/L (£1)	NAME
50	26	13	+6.43	FRANKIE DETTORI
29	135	39	+23.43	JIM CROWLEY
27	94	25	+10.46	RYAN MOORE
25	156	39	-49.32	JAMES DOYLE
24	244	59	-12.46	OISIN MURPHY
21	47	10	+53.63	FINLEY MARSH
20	97	19	-5.63	WILLIAM BUICK
19	176	33	+38.17	R. KINGSCOTE
19	90	17	-14.66	ANDREA ATZENI

18	271	49	-40.36	ADAM KIRBY
18	197	36	+38.17	P.J. MCDONALD
18	114	21	-8.02	MARTIN HARLEY
18	113	20	-47.87	JAMIE SPENCER
17	169	29	-55.82	S. DE SOUSA
17	150	26	+2.89	JASON HART
17	133	23	+43.93	RAY DAWSON
16	148	23	+19.99	JOE FANNING
15	310	45	-97.01	ROBERT HAVLIN
15	247	38	-16.53	JACK MITCHELL
15	200	29	-31.71	JASON WATSON
15	151	22	+4.93	KIERAN SHOEMARK
15	101	15	-13.33	PAT COSGRAVE
15	93	14	-24.08	ROBERT WINSTON
14	330	47	+102.77	CALLUM SHEPHERD
14	267	38	-26.89	FRANNY NORTON
14	205	28	-37.05	ROSSA RYAN
14	161	23	-15.88	CIEREN FALLON
14	144	20	-24.50	BEN CURTIS
14	131	18	+0.63	MARTIN DWYER
14	74	10	-22.43	NICKY MACKAY
13	166	22	+79.48	SEAN LEVEY
13	159	21	-37.46	MARCO GHIANI
13	156	20	-50.88	DYLAN HOGAN
13	120	15	-52.51	CHARLES BISHOP
12	332	40	-43.48	HOLLIE DOYLE
12	83	10	-31.88	HARRY BENTLEY
11	341	38	-152.60	TOM MARQUAND
11	205	23	-77.56	STEVIE DONOHOE
11	184	21	-48.04	DAVID EGAN
11	170	19	-24.72	A. RAWLINSON
11	171	18	-35.20	HAYLEY TURNER
11	170	18	+7.63	ROB HORNBY
11	141	16	-38.68	GEORGE ROOKE
11	132	15	-77.36	HECTOR CROUCH
10	645	65	-163.29	LUKE MORRIS
10	374	37	-159.51	DAVID PROBERT
10	267	26	-76.93	DANIEL MUSCUTT
10	172	17	+27.25	DOUGIE COSTELLO
10	130	13	-43.38	PADDY MATHERS
10	97	10	+8.38	GABRIELE MALUNE

TRAINERS

%	RNRS	WNS	P/L (£1)	NAME
29	75	22	-25.68	CHARLIE APPLEBY
26	221	58	-42.92	J. & T. GOSDEN
25	93	23	+39.67	RALPH BECKETT
23	162	37	-30.92	SAEED BIN SUROOR
23	125	29	-35.05	SIR M. STOUTE
22	68	15	+0.28	JOHN QUINN
22	67	15	+20.20	OWEN BURROWS
20	117	23	-26.19	JAMES TATE
20	207	41	+38.18	RICHARD HUGHES
19	78	15	-3.56	CHARLES HILLS
19	115	22	+0.70	IAN WILLIAMS
19	136	26	+62.44	MICHAEL BELL
19	127	24	-45.07	ROGER VARIAN
18	160	28	-71.66	WILLIAM HAGGAS
17	435	76	-32.42	C. & M. JOHNSTON
17	122	21	-19.06	S. & E. CRISFORD
16	279	46	-50.67	DAVID SIMCOCK
16	137	22	-62.62	HUGO PALMER
15	66	10	-3.43	JOSEPH TUITE
15	78	12	+6.58	MICK CHANNON
14	220	30	-29.68	HENRY SPILLER
14	140	20	+29.44	MARK USHER
13	203	27	-84.84	ANDREW BALDING
13	207	27	-41.28	ARCHIE WATSON
13	102	13	-25.19	C. FELLOWES
13	143	18	-44.20	SIR M. PRESCOTT
13	378	50	-141.16	STUART WILLIAMS
12	85	10	-40.65	JAMES FANSHAWE
12	198	24	+15.23	J. CHAPPLE-HYAM
12	558	68	-92.54	MICHAEL APPLEBY
12	124	15	-10.63	MIKE MURPHY
12	179	22	+19.96	ROBERT COWELL
11	186	20	-30.72	DAVID O'MEARA
11	198	22	-43.28	ED DUNLOP
11	101	11	-1.38	GAY KELLEWAY
11	90	10	+0.58	GEORGE SCOTT
11	208	23	-58.15	JAMIE OSBORNE
11	204	23	-61.04	MARCO BOTTI
11	105	12	-39.20	RAE GUEST

11	106	12	+13.88	SHAUN KEIGHTLEY
11	113	12	-14.63	SIMON DOW
10	124	12	-3.25	AMY MURPHY
10	266	27	-49.38	CHARLIE WALLIS
10	277	28	-80.65	DEAN IVORY
10	157	16	+35.63	IVAN FURTADO
10	163	17	-12.50	TONY CARROLL

Note: In the case of trainers who hold a joint licence, the statistics for the individual who held it previously have been incorporated into those for the joint licence.

SIRES

%	RNRS	WNS	P/L (£1)	NAME
35	23	8	+12.32	THEWAYYOUARE
30	27	8	+82.96	THE GURKHA
23	26	6	-0.38	KODI BEAR
22	82	18	+7.00	WAR FRONT
21	61	13	-18.38	DECLARATION OF WAR
21	112	24	-28.01	FRANKEL
21	56	12	+13.97	POWER
21	61	13	+9.85	SPEIGHTSTOWN
20	64	13	+6.45	ROCK OF GIBRALTAR
20	65	13	+88.00	WAR COMMAND
19	74	14	+5.28	ARCANO
19	27	5	+8.08	BLAME
19	174	33	-50.82	DUBAWI
19	31	6	-3.54	KITTEN'S JOY
19	199	37	-12.54	LOPE DE VEGA
18	28	5	+0.43	ANJAAL
18	40	7	+25.83	BIG BAD BOB
18	91	16	-4.43	CHARM SPIRIT
18	73	13	+13.01	GLENEAGLES
17	35	6	-0.20	AUSSIE RULES
17	30	5	-1.62	FARHH
17	70	12	+4.33	FASTNET ROCK
17	102	17	+16.74	NEW APPROACH
17	82	14	-27.56	SIYOUNI
16	401	64	-29.43	DARK ANGEL
16	44	7	+41.00	EXCELLENT ART
16	49	8	+4.94	KENDARGENT
16	32	5	-3.50	MAKFI
16	100	16	-24.89	SEA THE STARS

15	135	20	-18.24	CAPE CROSS
15	53	8	-0.25	DICK TURPIN
15	67	10	-24.23	DRAGON PULSE
15	111	17	+45.48	FOXWEDGE
15	53	8	+10.30	GOLDEN HORN
15	102	15	+57.45	HOLY ROMAN EMPEROR
15	213	31	-56.53	INVINCIBLE SPIRIT
15	60	9	-11.67	LEROIDESANIMAUX
15	144	22	-11.30	LETHAL FORCE
15	52	8	-2.64	MEHMAS
15	46	7	-4.00	MORPHEUS
15	33	5	-9.50	MULTIPLEX
15	111	17	+36.50	NATHANIEL
15	41	6	-12.30	SCAT DADDY
15	73	11	+42.63	SLADE POWER
15	47	7	-1.75	TWILIGHT SON

These types of statistics are widely available (albeit less so with the sires) and constantly updated elsewhere, but when I first generated them for this book a couple of things struck me, especially among the jockeys. The top three riders in terms of the percentage of winners-to-rides are big names, those you would expect at most racecourses not just at Chelmsford, but you would also expect them to have a level-stake loss given how often these riders are backed blind. Not in this case, though, and given the total number of rides during the period (especially in the case of Dettori and Moore) it seems clear to me that when they turn up at Chelmsford they do so for fancied rides. It's certainly true of Dettori, hence a 50 per cent strike rate! Clearly with Frankie the only way is Essex.

It's well worth looking further down the list too, as although their strike rates aren't as high as the previously mentioned trio, the likes of Callum Shepherd and Sean Levey do rather better around here than the betting market would have indicated. They aren't the only ones, though, so if you like one ridden by one of those jockeys who show a good profit such as Messrs Shepherd and Levey, it should fill you with a bit more confidence.

CHELMSFORD DRAW AND PACE STATISTICS

Below are the draw and pace statistics for each distance at Chelmsford from 1 January 2020 up to 30 June 2022. The statistics for pace (next to Front-Runners, Prominent Horses and

Hold Up Horses) are shown as an Impact Value, with an IV of 1.0 meaning average. The way these IV figures are arrived at is explained in more detail in the 'Track and Pace Bias' chapter, but for now suffice to say the higher the figure the more that group is favoured over the trip.

The draw statistics are fairly self-explanatory. Next to the draw are the number of horses to have started from that stall within the period, followed by the number of winners from the stall and then the percentage of winners to runners from that draw, not the percentage of winners to the number of races.

5f

Front-Runners   1.7
Prominent Horses 1.4
Hold Up Horses   0.6

STALL	RUNNERS	WINNERS	%W/R
1	83	13	16
2	84	15	18
3	82	13	16
4	81	10	12
5	76	12	16
6	76	5	7
7	64	9	14
8	51	1	2
9	37	5	14
10	26	2	8
11	15	1	7
12	9	0	0

6f

Front-Runners   2.2
Prominent Horses 1.2
Hold Up Horses   0.6

STALL	RUNNERS	WINNERS	%W/R
1	142	22	15
2	143	25	17
3	151	16	11
4	147	15	10
5	147	7	5
6	138	19	14
7	122	16	13
8	106	11	10

9	92	9	10
10	69	8	12
11	51	4	8
12	42	1	2
13	18	0	0
14	12	1	8

Apart from early speed being an advantage over the sprint trips, so is a low draw and this is a theme that will be repeated at most of the All-Weather tracks, particularly those that stage sprint races around a bend and this bias will be of more significance at some tracks than others. The layout of the course is very much a contributory factor with a left-hand bend soon to be negotiated. Clearly a wide draw is a major disadvantage over these distances, as on many occasions a horse will be stuck out wide while rounding a long sweeping bend and the ground loss would be significant.

7f

Front-Runners	2.3
Prominent Horses	1.2
Hold Up Horses	0.6

STALL	RUNNERS	WINNERS	%W/R
1	179	25	14
2	181	19	10
3	177	26	15
4	176	16	9
5	176	16	9
6	169	20	12
7	153	19	12
8	133	9	7
9	120	13	11
10	92	6	7
11	78	3	4
12	53	7	13
13	33	5	15
14	32	3	9
15	13	0	0
16	9	0	0

1m

Front-Runners	2.1
Prominent Horses	1.1
Hold Up Horses	0.7

STALL	RUNNERS	WINNERS	%W/R
1	141	26	18
2	142	21	15
3	141	11	8
4	142	18	13
5	143	12	8
6	131	19	15
7	116	11	9
8	100	9	9
9	85	4	5
10	68	7	10
11	54	4	7
12	37	1	3
13	23	4	17
14	18	0	0
15	10	1	10
16	3	0	0

The draw becomes less significant over 7f and 1m, but it doesn't disappear completely as a very high draw is still a potential stumbling block. A handy early position is at least as much of an advantage as it is for the shorter trips.

1m2f

Front-Runners	1.6
Prominent Horses	1.4
Hold Up Horses	0.7

STALL	RUNNERS	WINNERS	%W/R
1	164	28	17
2	159	25	16
3	156	17	11
4	163	22	13
5	159	17	11
6	148	21	14
7	131	15	11
8	110	7	6
9	90	5	6
10	80	3	4
11	62	6	10
12	44	1	2
13	32	1	3
14	17	0	0
15	12	0	0
16	4	1	25

1m5f 66yds

Front-Runners	0.6
Prominent Horses	1.2
Hold Up Horses	1.0

STALL	RUNNERS	WINNERS	%W/R
1	21	0	0
2	20	4	20
3	22	3	14
4	21	0	0
5	18	3	17
6	17	5	29
7	13	2	15
8	12	2	17
9	10	1	10
10	8	1	13
11	3	0	0
12	3	1	33
13	3	0	0
14	1	0	0

The draw statistics for races over 10f are revealing and for quite some time now it has made my life rather easier, especially for those races run over this trip with bigger fields. When doing a tipping piece of some sort, either for the *Racing Post* Spotlight or for the Sandform website, I could basically ignore those drawn in the top half of the field and even if a horse had attractive credentials on several other fronts, experience told me to resist the temptation to recommend them. It wasn't easy but doing so spared me plenty of heartache.

1m6f

Front-Runners	1.0
Prominent Horses	1.3
Hold Up Horses	0.9

STALL	RUNNERS	WINNERS	%W/R
1	43	4	9
2	43	8	19
3	42	5	12
4	40	6	15
5	37	10	27
6	36	6	17
7	24	4	17

8	21	1	5
9	19	1	5
10	12	0	0
11	5	0	0
12	4	1	25
13	1	0	0

2m

Front-Runners	2.0
Prominent Horses	0.9
Hold Up Horses	0.7

STALL	RUNNERS	WINNERS	%W/R
1	21	4	19
2	21	2	10
3	21	3	14
4	20	3	15
5	18	2	11
6	15	2	13
7	8	2	25
8	4	3	75
9	2	0	0

The statistics for races of 1m5f and further are shown for information purposes, but they are from a limited sample so I wouldn't draw any hard and fast conclusions from them.

DUNDALK

I don't get to Dundalk as often as I would like and that is something I need to put right in the future as it's a great place to visit and the backdrop is worth the entrance fee alone! Racing on sand in Ireland is hardly new as they have been racing on the beach at Laytown since 1868, but All-Weather racing as we understand it didn't take place in Ireland until Dundalk staged its first fixture on its Polytrack surface in August 2007 and the venture has been an unqualified success. Certainly, the immediate feedback was positive from jockeys and trainers and there was clearly an appetite for such a track to appear in Ireland. There are always plenty of runners with many meetings having eight races and the track also stages contests of real quality, with several Listed contests taking place during the year plus two Group 3 events, the Mercury Stakes over 5f and the Diamond Stakes over the extended 1m2f. As you will be able to see later in the book, the track has also seen the debuts of horses who have gone on to success at the highest level.

The track is a left-handed oval of around 10f with a home straight of just under 3f. In 2013 came the introduction of a false rail on the inside of the track on the home bend, which had the effect of fanning the horses out and reducing the likelihood of crowding against the inside rail (a similar false rail was introduced at Southwell in December 2021). The 5f track is quite a strange one and those with long memories may remember the old sprint track at Haydock on which the Vernons Sprint Cup (now the Betfair Sprint Cup) was run. The start was on a chute which joined the round course on the turn out of the back straight, with the field running straight for over a furlong before a dogleg turn which brought them into the home stretch. The sprint track at Dundalk is rather like that. There is also a small chute at the entrance to the back straight for races over 1m and there is no doubt that Dundalk is a galloping track.

A good time is being had by all at an evening fixture at Dundalk (RP Photos).

Although Dundalk does stage a few fixtures in the summer, the focus is between the autumn and the following spring. Windsor has its Monday evening fixtures, Kempton its Wednesdays, Wolverhampton its Saturdays, and Dundalk its Fridays. However, during the winter months the traditional Friday evening fixtures have now been joined by a Wednesday afternoon meeting, thereby opening up still further the opportunities for those horses who show an aptitude for an artificial surface. There is one subtle difference between Dundalk and its British counterparts, though.

British trainers have the option of running their All-Weather horses at six different venues, but unless Irish trainers are willing to travel their horses over the water (which they have done with great success) then at the time of writing Dundalk is their only option. This has an interesting result in that, especially during the winter, the same horses will return on a regular basis so you will see many familiar names among those taking part. This may not be ideal for the professionals, but for the All-Weather punter it's not a bad situation as with these horses meeting each other week in and week out and the field sizes often at their maximum (especially in the handicaps), the form has a certain uniform structure to it. There is certainly room for at least one more All-Weather track in Ireland, though, and hopefully before long that will come to fruition.

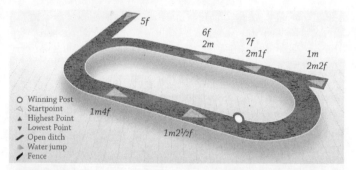

○ Winning Post
◁ Startpoint
▲ Highest Point
▼ Lowest Point
✎ Open ditch
🔻 Water jump
✐ Fence

FIVE-SEASON TOP JOCKEY, TRAINER AND SIRE STATISTICS FOR DUNDALK

With a smaller sample to choose from, trainers and jockeys must have had at least ten rides/runners but only need to have had at least five winners. Sires must have a strike rate of 12 per cent or more.

JOCKEYS

%	RIDES	WNS	P/L (£1)	NAME
26	118	31	-14.01	D.A. O'BRIEN
21	38	8	-7.92	PAT SMULLEN
17	508	85	+6.10	RONAN WHELAN
15	636	98	-131.39	COLIN KEANE
13	461	61	-143.23	DECLAN MCDONOGH
13	254	32	-16.00	MIKEY SHEEHY
13	351	46	-104.90	SHANE CROSSE
13	378	50	-37.12	W.J. LEE
12	637	75	-126.04	CHRIS HAYES
12	60	7	-8.13	DANIEL KING
12	376	45	-24.34	GAVIN RYAN
12	50	6	-24.42	HUGH HORGAN
12	245	30	-37.05	SAM EWING
10	326	33	-33.75	CONOR HOBAN
10	347	35	-59.47	DONAGH O'CONNOR
10	104	10	-52.11	JAKE COEN
10	333	33	-72.17	OISIN ORR
10	84	8	-1.01	ROBBIE DOWNEY
10	300	31	-88.13	S. HEFFERNAN

TRAINERS

%	Rnrs	Wns	P/L (£1)	Name
27	143	38	+9.76	A.P. O'BRIEN

26	34	9	+6.87	D.A. O'BRIEN
23	22	5	+43.00	W. ROSS
22	27	6	+19.13	SHANE CRAWLEY
19	293	56	-50.77	G.M. LYONS
18	28	5	+21.50	J. LARKIN
18	101	18	+42.20	K. PRENDERGAST
17	47	8	+14.25	D.P. COAKLEY
17	35	6	-2.95	P.J. PRENDERGAST
16	814	128	-507.09	JOSEPH P. O'BRIEN
16	503	81	-22.76	M. HALFORD
14	140	19	-12.65	A. OLIVER
14	231	32	-35.01	EDWARD LYNAM
14	94	13	-3.28	P.J.F. MURPHY
13	77	10	-4.55	JOHN J. MURPHY
12	68	8	-17.50	ANDREW MCNAMARA
12	117	14	-32.59	H. DE BROMHEAD
12	59	7	-9.97	J.G. COOGAN
12	73	9	-22.08	JOHN GEOGHEGAN
12	193	23	-39.93	J.P. MURTAGH
12	129	15	-19.29	PATRICK J. FLYNN
12	120	14	-52.58	SARAH LYNAM
11	710	80	-178.77	A. MCGUINNESS
11	47	5	-14.25	A. MULHOLLAND
11	206	23	-50.96	JOHN JAMES FEANE
11	153	17	-44.68	J.S. BOLGER
11	136	15	-21.70	NOEL MEADE
11	161	18	+6.83	R.J. O'BRIEN
11	47	5	+50.00	THOMAS MULLINS
10	88	9	-28.63	GORDON ELLIOTT
10	171	17	-47.47	KIERAN P. COTTER
10	115	11	+163.95	LEE SMYTH
10	67	7	0.00	MARK FAHEY
10	168	16	-52.58	MS SHEILA LAVERY
10	86	9	-16.24	NOEL C. KELLY
10	68	7	+37.50	SHANE NOLAN

SIRES

%	RNRS	WNS	P/L (£1)	NAME
28	25	7	+5.48	CHAMPS ELYSEES
25	20	5	+6.50	BRAZEN BEAU
25	20	5	+3.13	SAMUM

24	21	5	-0.90	CARAVAGGIO
24	59	14	+18.99	FRANKEL
23	74	17	+4.47	DECLARATION OF WAR
22	23	5	+5.83	GETAWAY
21	56	12	+32.75	HARBOUR WATCH
21	29	6	+36.10	VERGLAS
18	28	5	-7.63	KENDARGENT
18	99	18	-43.22	WAR FRONT
17	30	5	+0.17	ORATORIO
17	47	8	-2.19	SIYOUNI
16	37	6	-4.03	CHOISIR
16	125	20	+4.58	GALILEO
16	38	6	-7.55	VADAMOS
15	41	6	+2.25	MEDICEAN
15	34	5	-21.05	SCAT DADDY
15	59	9	+25.75	TORONADO
14	168	23	+59.92	CANFORD CLIFFS
14	50	7	+28.50	LORD SHANAKILL
14	126	18	+22.99	MEHMAS
14	56	8	-11.50	PRIDE OF DUBAI
13	39	5	-4.29	ART CONNOISSEUR
13	108	14	-21.90	AUSTRALIA
13	166	21	-19.90	BATED BREATH
13	38	5	+17.00	BELARDO
13	76	10	+3.75	DANSILI
13	48	6	-14.00	DUTCH ART
13	56	7	-22.54	SO YOU THINK
12	95	11	-34.47	APPROVE
12	182	22	+21.13	DRAGON PULSE
12	57	7	-3.42	ELNADIM
12	188	23	+73.66	ELZAAM
12	42	5	+65.75	FREE EAGLE
12	78	9	-6.75	HAATEF
12	78	9	-3.33	MAYSON

DUNDALK DRAW AND PACE STATISTICS

5f

Front-Runners	2.6
Prominent Horses	1.0
Hold Up Horses	0.5

STALL	RUNNERS	WINNERS	%W/R
1	59	8	14
2	64	7	11
3	61	6	10
4	63	8	13
5	61	11	18
6	60	6	10
7	57	4	7
8	51	2	4
9	46	3	7
10	35	3	9
11	31	1	3
12	18	1	6
13	18	1	6
14	14	2	14
15	9	2	22
16	5	0	0

6f

Front-Runners	2.4
Prominent Horses	1.3
Hold Up Horses	0.6

STALL	RUNNERS	WINNERS	%W/R
1	96	10	10
2	102	10	10
3	103	13	13
4	101	9	9
5	104	11	11
6	97	9	9
7	95	6	6
8	89	8	9
9	86	1	1
10	80	8	10
11	73	3	4
12	70	7	10
13	58	3	5
14	52	4	8
15	37	3	8
16	29	4	14
17	23	1	4

The bias towards the low numbers over 5f will be no surprise to anyone given the description of the sprint track earlier in the chapter. When combined with early speed, a low stall is a huge advantage over the trip so a glance at a horse's previous running style will be crucial when working out how the race is likely to pan out. A low draw is also an advantage over 6f, if not to quite the same extent, but again early pace is a major advantage.

7f

Front-Runners   1.6
Prominent Horses   1.5
Hold Up Horses   0.7

STALL	RUNNERS	WINNERS	%W/R
1	159	8	5
2	156	10	6
3	166	13	8
4	168	18	11
5	163	16	10
6	163	15	9
7	160	12	8
8	160	21	13
9	148	10	7
10	137	17	12
11	125	13	10
12	118	8	7
13	100	7	7
14	87	5	6
15	82	3	4
16	70	2	3
17	56	6	11

1m

Front-Runners   2.1
Prominent Horses   1.2
Hold Up Horses   0.7

STALL	RUNNERS	WINNERS	%W/R
1	154	11	7
2	151	13	9
3	164	18	11
4	153	11	7
5	160	13	8
6	154	16	10
7	147	9	6

STALL	RUNNERS	WINNERS	%W/R
8	149	9	6
9	144	15	10
10	132	5	4
11	138	12	9
12	126	13	10
13	124	11	9
14	95	6	6
15	88	4	5
16	74	2	3
17	60	8	13

With a long run to the first bend the draw statistics over 7f and 1m have evened out, though those ridden up with the pace still enjoy an advantage.

1m2f 150yds

Front-Runners	1.8
Prominent Horses	1.4
Hold Up Horses	0.7

STALL	RUNNERS	WINNERS	%W/R
1	105	9	9
2	104	5	5
3	100	10	10
4	101	7	7
5	102	10	10
6	105	12	11
7	96	6	6
8	96	9	9
9	101	7	7
10	81	4	5
11	83	8	10
12	87	12	14
13	75	6	8
14	70	3	4
15	66	6	9
16	59	4	7
17	47	1	2

1m4f

Front-Runners	1.1
Prominent Horses	1.2
Hold Up Horses	0.9

STALL	RUNNERS	WINNERS	%W/R
1	90	4	4
2	90	7	8

3	92	9	10
4	85	7	8
5	87	3	3
6	86	6	7
7	89	9	10
8	90	9	10
9	78	7	9
10	73	7	10
11	72	4	6
12	69	5	7
13	72	3	4
14	65	4	6
15	54	5	9
16	50	7	14
17	49	5	10

Despite the 1m2f start being quite close to the first bend, the advantage enjoyed by the low stalls is only marginal, but a very wide stall is clearly an issue.

2m

Front-Runners	2.0
Prominent Horses	1.3
Hold Up Horses	0.7

STALL	RUNNERS	WINNERS	%W/R
1	21	3	14
2	18	3	17
3	21	1	5
4	18	1	6
5	19	2	11
6	20	0	0
7	18	1	6
8	18	2	11
9	19	0	0
10	17	2	12
11	16	0	0
12	16	2	13
13	14	1	7
14	11	2	18
15	8	0	0
16	8	2	25
17	6	0	0

The statistics for two miles show that making the running clearly isn't a disadvantage!

KEMPTON

When the idea was first mooted that Kempton should change its Flat turf track to an All-Weather surface, I had mixed feelings. I had been going there since I was seven or eight years old and so had so many special memories there, especially over jumps such as seeing Pendil win his two King George VI Chases. Even attending Charisma Gold Cup Day in the October of each year was interesting, watching all the hippies turn up for the post-race concert. Who remembers Chilli Willi and the Red Hot Peppers? There were notable memories on the Flat too, such as the first ladies' race won by Scorched Earth under Meriel Tufnell in 1972 and even seeing Fred Winter win a Flat race aboard Never A Lady in June 1978!

I could also see the other side, though. Although most of the action taking place so far from the crowds might work at a course such as Newmarket, it didn't really have the same effect on the old Jubilee Course at Kempton, a dog-leg track where the 1m2f start appeared to be a distant speck on the horizon from the stands. For many of the races that took place on this track, the horses appeared to be running towards you for much of the journey. Races over 5f and 6f took place on a straight track which bisected the round course, so if you wanted to get closer to the action and eliminate the awkward angle of the finishing line from the stands, that meant taking a little stroll.

Although the switch to an All-Weather surface was now on, the jumps track was (rightly) to remain in place, albeit a lot wider than it used to be as it absorbed the old Flat round course. The change was eventually made, and the first All-Weather meeting took place on 25 March 2006, another fixture I had the pleasure of attending. Admittedly the Kempton All-Weather track is a fair way from you, being on the inside of the jumps course, but at least the bulk of the race takes place closer to the enclosures than it used to on the old turf track.

Another tight finish to a race at Kempton (Hoycubed Photography).

Kempton has had floodlights from the very start of staging All-Weather racing so there are plenty of evening meetings all year round, but one thing they did which I believe was important is that they retained all the traditional Flat races which used to be run on the grass track, such as the Group 3 September Stakes (the Derby winner Slip Anchor was beaten in it in 1985) and the Group 3 Sirenia Stakes, plus established handicaps like the Rosebery and Queen's Prize. This link with the past suits everyone. It suits traditionalists like me who feel comfortable with continuity, but also everyone else as it means you get to see some good horses around here.

Had the September Stakes been moved to another track, the Kempton crowds would have been denied the opportunity to see Enable win the race in 2018 and 2020. She isn't alone in being a top-class horse to have run at Kempton either. Indeed, later in the book there is a list of horses who, since 2010, had made their debut on a British or Irish All-Weather track before going on to Group 1 success in Europe. Many of them did so around here, so when you are sizing up that next Kempton novice or maiden with many of those taking part making their racecourse debut, you may just be witnessing the emergence of a top-class talent.

Kempton has a Polytrack surface like Chelmsford, Dundalk and Lingfield, but it's different to all the other All-Weather tracks in the British Isles in two ways. Firstly, it's the only right-handed

Enable wins the 2018 September Stakes from Crystal Ocean (hidden)
(Hoycubed Photography).

track and that will be a fundamental issue throughout this book, as there are many horses who do well around there for that reason. It's certainly a crucial factor when assessing form for a meeting at this venue. Kempton is also unique in that you get two courses for the price of one. The two tracks share most of the circuit but have different home bends.

The reason for this is that had there only been the larger outer circuit, races over 5f and 1m2f would have started too close to a bend, hence the need for a longer period before they encounter one. Races over these trips use the inner home bend which means the runners for a 5f race stay straight for about 1f before hitting the bend, while over a mile and 2f it's about a quarter of a mile until they start to turn.

The outer track is around 10f in circumference with a home straight of just under 3f, while the inner loop is about 1m round with a run-in of just under 2f. The outer track tends to suit the more galloping types, provided they don't have an issue with going right-handed! There is a cutaway where the two courses meet in the home straight (at around the 2f marker on the outer track) and that is a very interesting factor when it comes to races on the round course.

The track widens at this point so it provides options for the jockeys as to where they would like to go. You will see on many occasions that they will make a beeline for the inside rail on reaching the cutaway and from what I have seen, doing this isn't the guaranteed kiss of death that it can be on some of the other tracks. In fact, it can prove to be a race-winning move, but again it's not possible to predict what the jockey will do (or will be forced to do) beforehand.

As is the case elsewhere, it may mean waiting for a couple of races to see if those horses who take this route are favoured or otherwise. If the rail is 'bad' and therefore the area closest to the inside rail is slowing horses down, those who make that manoeuvre will come unstuck no matter how well they are travelling at the time. There can also be a problem with overcrowding, as if several riders have the same intention of diving for the inside rail then they can't all get there, and someone is likely to get squeezed out. This is another area that can be of benefit to in-running punters, though, especially if you have identified a bias towards those taking the inside rail route after the cutaway.

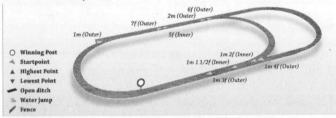

FIVE-SEASON TOP JOCKEY, TRAINER AND SIRE STATISTICS FOR KEMPTON

JOCKEYS

%	RIDES	WNS	P/L (£1)	NAME
23	199	46	-35.77	WILLIAM BUICK
20	185	37	+25.40	ANDREA ATZENI
20	295	60	-3.45	JAMES DOYLE
19	286	54	-57.26	JIM CROWLEY
19	513	96	-80.41	OISIN MURPHY
18	164	29	-10.06	JOE FANNING
16	79	13	+9.58	GERALD MOSSE
16	399	62	-105.02	ROBERT HAVLIN
16	213	34	-79.96	S. DE SOUSA
15	156	23	-27.86	BEN CURTIS
15	158	23	+3.05	EDWARD GREATREX
15	112	17	-37.23	RYAN MOORE

14	588	80	-118.86	HOLLIE DOYLE
14	325	45	-38.53	JACK MITCHELL
14	146	20	-7.15	JAMIE SPENCER
13	524	68	-161.48	ADAM KIRBY
13	231	30	-74.04	DAVID EGAN
13	130	17	+26.98	FRAN BERRY
13	77	10	-17.88	PAT DOBBS
13	204	27	+14.63	P.J. MCDONALD
13	374	49	-94.20	R. KINGSCOTE
12	169	20	-26.22	FRANNY NORTON
12	126	15	-2.76	PAT COSGRAVE
12	435	52	-11.70	ROB HORNBY
12	347	42	-67.28	ROSSA RYAN
12	629	74	-92.41	TOM MARQUAND
11	100	11	-29.25	A. RAWLINSON
11	789	83	-142.74	DAVID PROBERT
11	185	21	-26.67	HARRY BENTLEY
11	148	17	+6.71	MARCO GHIANI
11	146	16	-53.35	MARTIN HARLEY
11	88	10	-7.00	RHYS CLUTTERBUCK
10	162	16	-18.63	CIEREN FALLON
10	362	37	-67.48	DANIEL MUSCUTT
10	319	32	-73.93	JASON WATSON
10	242	25	-41.21	MARTIN DWYER
10	296	29	+1.33	NICOLA CURRIE
10	126	12	-11.50	ROBERT WINSTON
10	130	13	-28.10	RYAN TATE
10	116	12	-21.68	STEFANO CHERCHI

TRAINERS

%	RIDES	WNS	P/L (£1)	NAME
35	139	48	-23.81	CHARLIE APPLEBY
24	326	78	-64.13	J. & T. GOSDEN
22	127	28	+14.18	S. & E. CRISFORD
23	257	59	-7.57	ROGER VARIAN
23	139	32	-19.30	SAEED BIN SUROOR
20	56	11	-8.50	K.P. DE FOY
19	67	13	+4.21	CONRAD ALLEN
18	260	47	-54.46	ARCHIE WATSON
18	173	32	-15.24	HUGO PALMER
18	61	11	-7.75	OWEN BURROWS

18	245	43	-15.71	RALPH BECKETT
18	166	30	-13.68	SIR M. STOUTE
18	186	33	-63.06	WILLIAM HAGGAS
17	72	12	+34.16	JAMES EUSTACE
17	223	39	-8.66	ROGER CHARLTON
16	382	60	+52.75	ANDREW BALDING
16	79	13	-9.33	RAE GUEST
15	130	19	-16.79	JAMES TATE
14	316	44	-22.34	C. & M. JOHNSTON
14	313	43	-29.41	CLIVE COX
14	113	16	+28.00	DAVID ELSWORTH
14	98	14	+30.93	DAVID LOUGHNANE
14	77	11	-50.16	GEORGE BOUGHEY
14	123	17	-16.38	TOM WARD
13	180	23	+45.60	CHARLES HILLS
13	246	33	-81.99	ED WALKER
13	253	33	-114.88	JAMES FANSHAWE
13	264	33	-14.33	STUART WILLIAMS
12	224	26	-67.62	DAVID SIMCOCK
12	152	18	+23.13	GEORGE BAKER
11	171	19	-38.00	AMANDA PERRETT
11	158	18	-62.02	HUGHIE MORRISON
11	358	38	-3.47	MARCO BOTTI
11	275	31	-61.42	MICHAEL APPLEBY
11	106	11	-19.30	P. & O. COLE
11	107	12	-14.67	PHIL MCENTEE
11	90	10	-16.67	SHAUN KEIGHTLEY
10	174	17	-58.97	ALAN KING
10	100	10	+50.50	AMY MURPHY
10	123	12	-41.59	ED DE GILES
10	124	13	-33.89	HENRY CANDY
10	103	10	-45.82	IVAN FURTADO
10	278	27	-56.65	JOHN BUTLER
10	547	55	-177.40	RICHARD HANNON
10	97	10	+37.00	ROGER TEAL
10	223	22	-22.42	WILLIAM KNIGHT

SIRES

%	RNRS	WNS	P/L (£1)	NAME
29	28	8	+27.32	ACLAIM
25	32	8	+17.33	NEW BAY

24	55	13	+12.21	FREE EAGLE
23	40	9	-1.09	CHOISIR
21	48	10	+15.78	AQLAAM
21	42	9	+46.11	SCAT DADDY
20	262	53	-126.20	DUBAWI
20	184	36	+44.81	SHAMARDAL
20	30	6	-2.67	THE FACTOR
19	52	10	+7.25	ELUSIVE QUALITY
19	43	8	+26.13	MAKFI
19	27	5	+3.63	WOOTTON BASSETT
18	56	10	+7.75	BAHAMIAN BOUNTY
18	182	33	+7.65	DANSILI
18	78	14	-4.05	NIGHT OF THUNDER
17	172	30	-68.26	FRANKEL
17	46	8	+76.25	IVAWOOD
17	149	26	-38.40	KINGMAN
17	36	6	+9.00	MORPHEUS
16	38	6	-12.67	AUSSIE RULES
16	55	9	-2.18	ELZAAM
16	51	8	-6.97	FARHH
16	88	14	-9.87	GOLDEN HORN
16	92	15	+20.21	HIGH CHAPARRAL
16	57	9	-13.27	KITTEN'S JOY
16	87	14	-10.77	RAVEN'S PASS
16	137	22	+4.62	SIYOUNI
16	107	17	+18.12	TORONADO
15	201	31	+54.13	DELEGATOR
15	62	9	-23.82	LILBOURNE LAD
15	97	15	+17.75	NO NAY NEVER

There are some big stables at the top of the trainers' table and that's an impressive strike rate of 35 per cent for Charlie Appleby, but as with most of the other top yards the profit and loss column indicates that their horses are often sent off at short odds. The number of winners doesn't compensate.

KEMPTON DRAW AND PACE STATISTICS

5f
Front-Runners   2.9
Prominent Horses   1.3
Hold Up Horses   0.1

STALL	RUNNERS	WINNERS	%W/R
1	19	5	26
2	20	3	15
3	20	2	10
4	19	3	16
5	18	0	0
6	15	1	7
7	14	2	14
8	9	3	33
9	8	1	13
10	5	0	0

6f

Front-Runners	2.1
Prominent Horses	1.0
Hold Up Horses	0.7

STALL	RUNNERS	WINNERS	%W/R
1	197	37	19
2	194	35	18
3	199	24	12
4	196	25	13
5	187	18	10
6	186	16	9
7	182	14	8
8	163	15	9
9	137	13	9
10	111	3	3
11	85	4	5
12	69	2	3

The statistics for the two shortest trips are quite stark. It should be borne in mind that the sample of races over 5f is limited, but you still get the idea. With half of the race being run around a sweeping right-handed bend on the inner loop, a low draw is a big advantage, especially when coupled with early speed, hence the high IV for Front-Runners. There is no doubting what the statistics for 6f are telling us, though, given the much bigger sample.

7f

Front-Runners	2.2
Prominent Horses	1.3
Hold Up Horses	0.6

STALL	RUNNERS	WINNERS	%W/R
1	238	24	10

2	237	36	15
3	230	22	10
4	230	26	11
5	242	24	10
6	237	26	11
7	227	18	8
8	208	16	8
9	206	20	10
10	165	9	5
11	125	9	7
12	105	7	7
13	83	10	12
14	57	2	4

1m

Front-Runners	1.9
Prominent Horses	1.3
Hold Up Horses	0.7

STALL	RUNNERS	WINNERS	%W/R
1	283	30	11
2	276	33	12
3	276	30	11
4	275	27	10
5	271	33	12
6	268	31	12
7	256	25	10
8	235	23	10
9	222	16	7
10	193	9	5
11	168	15	9
12	124	8	6
13	90	5	6
14	70	5	7

The bias towards those drawn low and a prominent racing style continues over 7f and 1m. I was especially interested that that was the case over the longer trip as, with a run of over 3f to the first bend, you would think the runners would have sorted themselves out by then. Not a bit of it according to these statistics, though, and I can only assume that those drawn very wide have a problem tucking in.

1m1f 219yds

Front-Runners	0.6
Prominent Horses	2.4
Hold Up Horses	0.2

STALL	RUNNERS	WINNERS	%W/R
1	10	0	0
2	11	2	18
3	10	1	10
4	11	1	9
5	10	1	10
6	9	4	44
7	7	0	0
8	6	0	0
9	5	0	0
10	5	1	20
11	5	1	20
12	4	0	0

1m2f 219yds

Front-Runners	1.4
Prominent Horses	1.5
Hold Up Horses	0.7

STALL	RUNNERS	WINNERS	%W/R
1	78	7	9
2	83	8	10
3	83	9	11
4	84	10	12
5	78	19	24
6	76	12	16
7	70	3	4
8	64	5	8
9	54	3	6
10	47	4	9
11	41	4	10
12	26	2	8
13	22	2	9
14	17	0	0

Comparisons between the above two distances are misleading, as races over 1m2f use the inner loop, but over the extra furlong they use the outer track. As is the case over 5f, there aren't very many races run over 10f throughout the year so it's hard to draw too many conclusions, but the numbers for 1m3f are quite interesting. The pace bias is starting to level out, but with a run of only 1f to the opening bend it's still generally better to be drawn closer to the rail than out wide.

1m3f 219yds

Front-Runners	1.6

Prominent Horses   1.3
Hold Up Horses   0.7

STALL	RUNNERS	WINNERS	%W/R
1	122	9	7
2	123	15	12
3	121	14	12
4	117	15	13
5	123	14	11
6	119	16	13
7	108	13	12
8	94	9	10
9	87	5	6
10	72	7	10
11	61	4	7
12	42	3	7
13	29	3	10
14	20	1	5

1m7f 218yds

Front-Runners   1.1
Prominent Horses   1.1
Hold Up Horses   0.9

STALL	RUNNERS	WINNERS	%W/R
1	60	12	20
2	61	6	10
3	60	13	22
4	58	7	12
5	61	9	15
6	56	4	7
7	47	5	11
8	36	2	6
9	31	1	3
10	24	2	8
11	18	1	6
12	16	1	6
13	12	0	0
14	11	1	9

Under normal circumstances the statistics for the two longest trips should be levelling out, especially the draw, but again those emerging from lower stalls seem to hold an advantage.

LINGFIELD

Lingfield wasn't a track I visited very often when we went racing as a family in my younger days, mainly because it took an age to get there. These were pre-M25 days so it took almost as long for my dad to drive to the Surrey venue as it did to reach York. Therefore, those few fixtures I did attend, mainly in the early 1970s, tend to have lingered in my mind for one reason or another. One such occurrence was when I wandered around the other side of the old Tote building and came across Ronnie Corbett studying the race card with great concentration. When I returned to the same spot after the following race, he was stood on a wooden box entertaining a small group of racegoers with his stand-up routine!

I shouldn't think many claiming races would find their way into horseracing folklore, but division one of the 1m claimer run at Lingfield at 11am on Monday, 30 October 1989 certainly will. This was the first All-Weather race to be run in Britain and I remember it well, even though I viewed the action from afar (via SIS in my local betting shop). As the 7-2 favourite Niklas Angel (Conrad Allen/ Richard Quinn) passed the winning post in first place ahead of Good For The Roses (Gavin Pritchard-Gordon/Billy Newnes) and Briery Fille (Robert Williams/Darren Biggs), there was no way of telling how things would go now that this new venture was under way.

Niklas Angel ended his career with a record of 8-47 on the Flat, but this proved to be his only All-Weather success in seven attempts. He had taken to the surface well enough to record this history-making success, but an All-Weather specialist he clearly was not.

In those days they also raced over hurdles at the two All-Weather tracks in existence at the time (Lingfield and Southwell) and although the likes of Viking Flagship and Pridwell were both successful in All-Weather jumping contests, the concept never really captured my imagination. There were always safety concerns as

Several are still in with a chance in the closing stages at Lingfield (Hoycubed Photography).

regards the horses and when that issue came to a head at the start of 1994, it wasn't long before All-Weather jumping was discontinued.

Suffice to say not everyone was on board with this new development and it took several years for this form of racing to be seen as nothing more than the turf's poor relation. That remains the case for some even now, but looking at some of the equine names who have been successful on an artificial surface in recent years we must be close to some sort of parity by now.

This opening meeting was staged on Equitrack and that continued until 2001, at which point it became apparent the old surface needed replacing. It was decided that the track should switch to Polytrack, the first course in the country to make such a move, with the first meeting taking place on the new surface on Tuesday, 13 November (it was re-laid again in October 2012). There is no doubt that once 7-1 shot Devolution (James Eustace/Jason Tate) had taken the first division of the 1m handicap, the status of All-Weather racing moved up a notch. The Polytrack was immediately well received, and connections were now more prepared to run a good horse on it.

Lingfield has been responsible for a couple of other major innovations. One was the inception of the Winter Derby in 1998 which that year was won easily by one of the original legends of All-Weather racing in Running Stag (Philip Mitchell/Ray Cochrane). This started to give the winter All-Weather scene the beginning of some sort of structure to it, as it provided an end-of-season climax.

Perhaps not quite the same way as the Cheltenham Festival, but hopefully you get my drift. The race was a Class 2 conditions contest in that first year but was given Listed status in 1999 and promoted to a Group 3 in 2006, which it remains to this day.

All-Weather racing was given another boost with the introduction of the All-Weather Championships in 2014 and this innovation proved significant on several levels. It provided an end-of-season target for horses in several different categories, not just one like the Winter Derby. It also made the rest of season more interesting, as you could qualify for one of the valuable contests on Finals Day provided you had raced enough times on the All-Weather during the winter and were officially rated high enough (thereby increasing the incentive to win races and move up the handicap), or had landed any of the Fast-Track Qualifiers (win it and you're in it) spread throughout the winter months.

The decision to stage the Championships Finals at Lingfield on Good Friday (which had been a blank day before that) was another good idea in my view, as was the decision to run some of the Fast-Track Qualifiers in Ireland and France, thereby increasing the international flavour. That move certainly paid dividends when three of the six races on Finals Day in 2018 were won by French-trained horses.

The finals were moved to Newcastle in 2022 while Lingfield staged a series of valuable handicaps for those horses not rated quite high enough to make the finals themselves. The first running of this All-Weather 'Vase' meeting was very competitive, though, and that is just what we want as punters.

The Lingfield All-Weather track is a triangular-shaped left-handed circuit of just under 1m2f, with a run-in of around 1.5f, and at the time of writing remains the only All-Weather track in the British Isles without floodlights. Although the track is quite long in terms of circumference, the relatively short run-in raises its own issues, especially when combined with the downhill run towards the sweeping home bend. You often get trouble here, with racing room at a premium as those who have been held up attempt to get a clear run, just as the leaders are falling back into their laps. Many Lingfield races are won by those who have been skilfully handled or just plain lucky, rather than the best horse.

So how do you overcome this? Sadly, as punters we are in the lap of the gods to some extent as there is no way of telling how the race will pan out once under way, but that doesn't mean we can't do all the usual homework to find the horse with the best chance of winning provided things go smoothly. You can make a difference if you are a jockey, though, especially if your name is Adam Kirby. Adam has won many a race around at Lingfield by setting his horse alight on the outside of the field on the run to the final bend, utilising a slingshot effect rounding the turn to send his horse into the lead and, with the run-in so short, establishing enough of an advantage to last home. This concept, which became known as the 'Kirby Kick', was a joy to behold (even if you hadn't backed his mount) and I always enjoyed referring to it if I was doing the *Racing Post* analysis for that race.

The home bend is certainly a key area for races at Lingfield, as I believe on many occasions they are either won or lost at this point. For reasons I will come on to, I like to see my selection a few horse-widths off the inside rail when making this turn, but the very nature of the bend means that many horses fail to negotiate the turn at all well, forcing them very wide and with insufficient time in which to make up the lost ground. I don't like to see them tight against the rail, though, unless they are manoeuvred away from it once in line for home. I have believed for some time now that the rail isn't the place to be at Lingfield, whether in front or trying to come from behind. In fact, attempting to put in a sustained run on the inside looks especially difficult and if a horse does manage to achieve it, their performance can certainly be marked up. By the same token horses can be forgiven if they attempt such a move and fail.

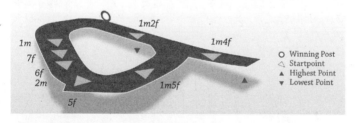

FIVE-SEASON TOP JOCKEY, TRAINER AND SIRE STATISTICS FOR LINGFIELD

JOCKEYS

%	RIDES	WNS	P/L (£1)	NAME
48	25	12	+9.68	FRANKIE DETTORI
29	77	22	+12.76	ANDREA ATZENI
29	123	36	-5.62	RYAN MOORE

22	140	31	-41.04	JAMES DOYLE
21	61	13	+0.25	JAMIE SPENCER
21	141	30	-23.56	JIM CROWLEY
21	104	22	+14.42	MARCO GHIANI
21	116	24	-33.81	WILLIAM BUICK
19	228	44	-61.11	OISIN MURPHY
19	80	15	+33.68	PAT COSGRAVE
18	321	57	-50.78	R. KINGSCOTE
17	433	72	-98.45	ADAM KIRBY
17	231	39	+26.34	SEAN LEVEY
17	162	28	-33.67	S. DE SOUSA
16	64	10	+26.67	GEORGE BASS
16	64	10	-16.97	JASON HART
16	193	31	-27.23	JOE FANNING
16	319	50	-118.62	ROBERT HAVLIN
15	152	23	-35.54	FRANNY NORTON
15	536	81	-122.87	HOLLIE DOYLE
15	92	14	+12.10	JOSHUA BRYAN
15	419	63	-16.42	TOM MARQUAND
14	265	38	-69.67	JACK MITCHELL
14	235	32	-88.49	KIERAN SHOEMARK
14	168	23	-11.94	RHYS CLUTTERBUCK
13	125	16	-41.88	BEN CURTIS
13	221	28	-69.97	DANIEL MUSCUTT
13	257	34	-4.17	DARRAGH KEENAN
13	90	12	-11.29	DAVID EGAN
13	531	69	+16.50	DAVID PROBERT
13	92	12	-3.50	FRAN BERRY
13	207	27	-30.86	JASON WATSON
13	136	17	-45.75	J.F. EGAN
13	76	10	-16.93	ROBERT WINSTON
12	139	16	+27.89	DOUGIE COSTELLO
12	169	21	-18.37	MARTIN HARLEY
11	92	10	+37.63	GEORGE DOWNING
11	152	16	-90.84	HAYLEY TURNER
11	210	23	-27.98	HECTOR CROUCH
11	96	11	-29.63	LAURA PEARSON
10	103	10	-35.25	GEORGE WOOD
10	803	80	-183.08	LUKE MORRIS
10	97	10	-34.25	PADDY BRADLEY
10	253	26	-85.01	ROSSA RYAN

TRAINERS

%	RIDES	WNS	P/L (£1)	NAME
31	68	21	-10.03	CHARLIE APPLEBY
29	59	17	+7.32	SIR M. STOUTE
28	112	31	-3.11	S. & E. CRISFORD
27	212	57	-22.37	J. & T. GOSDEN
25	52	13	+7.73	NICK LITTMODEN
25	112	28	+29.58	ROGER VARIAN
24	63	15	-13.27	SAEED BIN SUROOR
22	136	30	-30.92	WILLIAM HAGGAS
21	310	64	-27.34	ARCHIE WATSON
19	63	12	-11.08	ALICE HAYNES
19	203	38	+22.35	ANDREW BALDING
18	346	63	-33.39	C. & M. JOHNSTON
17	63	11	-7.25	BRIAN MEEHAN
17	139	23	-16.71	CHARLES HILLS
17	102	17	-28.48	JAMES FANSHAWE
17	113	19	-26.19	SIR M. PRESCOTT
17	58	10	-7.20	TOM DASCOMBE
16	105	17	-7.60	GEORGE BOUGHEY
16	114	18	-36.54	HUGO PALMER
16	112	18	+17.50	RICHARD SPENCER
16	80	13	-26.22	ROGER CHARLTON
16	164	26	-8.01	STUART WILLIAMS
15	111	17	-16.29	DAVID LOUGHNANE
15	65	10	-7.92	K.R. BURKE
15	154	23	-22.46	PAT PHELAN
14	200	28	-24.62	DAVID O'MEARA
14	136	19	+39.38	GEORGE BAKER
14	378	54	-71.01	RICHARD HANNON
14	237	34	-65.55	RICHARD HUGHES
13	304	39	-35.08	GARY MOORE
13	104	13	-25.38	J. CHAPPLE-HYAM
13	99	13	-26.17	JOHN RYAN
13	104	13	-52.73	ROBERT COWELL
13	100	13	-22.11	ROGER TEAL
13	129	17	+6.73	WILLIAM KNIGHT
12	120	14	-26.92	AMY MURPHY
12	134	16	-51.83	CLIVE COX
12	273	33	-57.74	DAVID EVANS

12	141	17	-49.17	DAVID SIMCOCK
12	145	18	-63.38	ED WALKER
12	113	14	-16.75	IAN WILLIAMS
12	89	11	-34.30	JAMES TATE
12	128	15	-30.00	MARCO BOTTI
12	92	11	-27.13	TOM CLOVER
11	162	18	-66.46	AMANDA PERRETT
11	134	15	-32.13	BRETT JOHNSON
11	150	16	+23.58	DEAN IVORY
11	168	19	-45.90	JAMIE OSBORNE
11	218	25	-44.04	JOHN BUTLER
11	153	17	-53.71	MICK CHANNON
11	123	13	-60.88	RALPH BECKETT
11	97	11	+0.50	MUIR & GRASSICK
10	104	10	-59.34	CHARLIE FELLOWES
10	125	12	-5.75	JONATHAN PORTMAN
10	230	24	-38.21	MICHAEL APPLEBY
10	137	14	-64.89	PHIL MCENTEE

SIRES

%	RNRS	WNS	P/L (£1)	NAME
30	20	6	+4.58	NEW BAY
27	100	27	+19.56	KINGMAN
25	20	5	+3.68	ACLAIM
24	21	5	-0.13	REDOUTE'S CHOICE
23	113	26	+0.28	PIVOTAL
23	64	15	-5.28	WAR FRONT
22	36	8	-10.54	AWTAAD
22	129	29	-4.38	SHAMARDAL
21	29	6	+15.63	DABIRSIM
21	68	14	+12.91	MAKFI
20	108	22	+27.56	ARCHIPENKO
20	140	28	-4.84	CAPE CROSS
20	141	28	+0.83	DANSILI
19	88	17	-22.50	DAWN APPROACH
19	100	19	-4.25	FRANKEL
19	43	8	-13.53	LE HAVRE
19	74	14	-6.33	MEHMAS
19	42	8	+13.25	THEWAYYOUARE
19	106	20	+10.54	TORONADO
18	33	6	+2.66	FARHH

18	62	11	-10.23	GOLDEN HORN
18	28	5	-3.83	MARKAZ
17	103	17	-12.87	ARCANO
17	77	13	-50.27	AUSTRALIA
17	36	6	-13.25	MAKE BELIEVE
17	46	8	-8.43	SPEIGHTSTOWN
17	29	5	+6.50	VADAMOS
16	43	7	+19.33	BELARDO
16	38	6	+6.33	BOBBY'S KITTEN
16	87	14	-24.41	CHARM SPIRIT
16	353	55	-0.82	DARK ANGEL
16	149	24	-53.32	DUBAWI
16	177	28	+12.18	KYLLACHY
16	160	26	-42.92	LOPE DE VEGA
16	117	19	-30.33	SEA THE STARS
16	167	26	2.34	SEPOY
16	94	15	-2.28	SIYOUNI
15	72	11	-7.46	ADAAY
15	34	5	+30.6	AUTHORIZED
15	39	6	-17.34	FASTNET ROCK

The first thing to note is that rather like with Chelmsford, on the relatively rare occasions Frankie Dettori is booked to ride at Lingfield he means business. They can't all be steering jobs, though, as otherwise he wouldn't show a level-stake profit!

LINGFIELD DRAW AND PACE STATISTICS

5f 6yds

Front-Runners	2.0
Prominent Horses	1.1
Hold Up Horses	0.6

STALL	RUNNERS	WINNERS	%W/R
1	114	12	11
2	116	16	14
3	115	17	15
4	112	16	14
5	113	17	15
6	105	13	12
7	84	9	11
8	73	11	15

9	50	6	12
10	29	2	7

6f 1yd

Front-Runners	2.0
Prominent Horses	1.1
Hold Up Horses	0.7

STALL	RUNNERS	WINNERS	%W/R
1	182	20	11
2	177	29	16
3	178	17	10
4	179	27	15
5	172	27	16
6	158	20	13
7	136	14	10
8	121	16	13
9	96	9	9
10	72	4	6
11	51	2	4
12	33	2	6

It's no great surprise that front-runners are favoured over sprint trips here, given the sharp nature of the track, but while there isn't a significant draw bias over 5f (except against stall ten), the higher draws are certainly up against it over 6f. The first bend comes up quickly and if you are stuck out wide when you reach it and are unable to tuck in, you are going to cover an awful lot more ground than your rivals.

7f 1yd

Front-Runners	1.4
Prominent Horses	1.6
Hold Up Horses	0.6

STALL	RUNNERS	WINNERS	%W/R
1	194	18	9
2	191	23	12
3	186	17	9
4	185	30	16
5	187	20	11
6	176	23	13
7	155	19	12
8	149	13	9
9	123	13	11
10	99	6	6

STALL	RUNNERS	WINNERS	%W/R
11	72	5	7
12	62	6	10
13	39	2	5
14	27	2	7

1m 1yd

Front-Runners	1.2
Prominent Horses	1.2
Hold Up Horses	0.9

STALL	RUNNERS	WINNERS	%W/R
1	193	22	11
2	201	23	11
3	193	21	11
4	198	27	14
5	193	27	14
6	189	21	11
7	171	20	12
8	142	11	8
9	132	12	9
10	116	7	6
11	87	10	11
12	62	6	10

The bias towards front-runners lessens over 7f and a mile, but in general a low draw is still favoured albeit not to the same extent as over 6f.

1m2f

Front-Runners	1.2
Prominent Horses	1.2
Hold Up Horses	0.8

STALL	RUNNERS	WINNERS	%W/R
1	197	24	12
2	194	30	15
3	198	20	10
4	192	15	8
5	191	22	12
6	168	22	13
7	156	23	15
8	137	17	12
9	121	6	5
10	103	9	9
11	80	8	10

12	58	5	9
13	32	4	13
14	17	1	6

1m4f

Front-Runners	1.2
Prominent Horses	1.4
Hold Up Horses	0.8

STALL	RUNNERS	WINNERS	%W/R
1	131	21	16
2	136	13	10
3	136	26	19
4	137	15	11
5	125	22	18
6	118	14	12
7	99	8	8
8	84	6	7
9	73	10	14
10	54	7	13
11	42	1	2
12	29	1	3
13	15	0	0
14	11	0	0
15	8	0	0
16	5	1	20

The slight bias against those drawn very high continues over 1m2f and 1m4f, which is a little surprising given there is a run of over 2f until they reach the first bend over the longer trip. However, as is the case over 6f, I have seen many horses get stuck out wide in big field and unable to get in before starting the turn.

1m5f

Front-Runners	0.5
Prominent Horses	0.8
Hold Up Horses	1.2

STALL	RUNNERS	WINNERS	%W/R
1	15	0	0
2	15	1	7
3	16	2	13
4	15	2	13
5	16	3	19
6	15	1	7
7	15	0	0
8	14	1	7

9	12	4	33
10	9	0	0
11	6	1	17
12	4	1	25
13	3	0	0
14	1	0	0

1m7f 169yds

Front-Runners	1.1
Prominent Horses	1.5
Hold Up Horses	0.8

STALL	RUNNERS	WINNERS	%W/R
1	39	3	8
2	39	3	8
3	40	5	13
4	40	9	23
5	37	3	8
6	35	7	20
7	29	0	0
8	29	4	14
9	22	1	5
10	18	3	17
11	16	0	0
12	13	2	15

The statistics for the two longest trips are of limited significance, given the relatively small samples involved.

NEWCASTLE

I have fond memories of Newcastle from my formative years. Although it's around 250 miles from where I live, we did visit it a few times as a family when I was young, though it wasn't because we specifically wanted to go to Newcastle. For many years our annual holiday was to attend the Ebor Meeting at York (then three days from Tuesday to Thursday). The first year was 1972 when I witnessed the inaugural running of the Benson and Hedges Gold Cup (now the Juddmonte International). The race that year became one of the most famous in racing folklore when Roberto inflicted the one and only defeat on Brigadier Gerard in his career.

Once the three days were over, we then added a couple more days on to the vacation and went on to go racing at Newcastle (my dad must have had a winning York!). We did the same thing in 1975 and the meeting we attended that year would also turn out to be a notable one. On that day Gunner B (Geoff Toft/Brian Connorton) was victorious in the 6f maiden and that turned out to be the start of a long and illustrious career for the colt, the pinnacle being his win in the 1978 Eclipse Stakes as a five-year-old after having been moved to Henry Cecil. As a sire he was responsible for the likes of Royal Gait, Red Marauder and Iris's Gift and was nearly 30 years old when he died. It would be a long time before I visited Newcastle again, but it had nothing to do with me not liking the place – I do love it there and it was just a question of distance. That, however, was all about to change.

It may have taken 27 years since the first meeting on an artificial surface had taken place at Lingfield, but on Tuesday, 17 May 2016 the north of England finally had its own All-Weather track when the first meeting was staged at Newcastle and it was only while on my way up to attend the opening fixture that I realised how northern-

Trueshan gamely wins the 2022 Northumberland Plate (Grossick Racing Photography).

based stables had been missing out for all those years. If they wished to run a horse on the All-Weather before now, the nearest options were either Southwell or Wolverhampton.

For a southerner like me, attending those tracks meant quite a long journey north, but for horses based in northern yards they were facing a similar amount of time on the road, just in the other direction! When passing junction 21A for the A46, which is where I usually turn off for Southwell, I was still only halfway to Newcastle. At least now the opening of the new All-Weather track gave horses trained in the north who appreciated a non-turf surface a lot more options. That first meeting also made history in other ways, as it would stage the first race to be run over a straight 1m on an artificial surface anywhere in the world.

By the time Tap The Honey (Karl Burke/Joey Haynes) had bolted up in the opening 1m2f maiden there was a real sense that All-Weather racing had taken another step forward. It was good to see that northern stables were so successful at that first meeting too, as apart from Karl Burke there were wins for David O'Meara (two), Peter Niven, Brian Ellison, Mark Johnston and David Nicholls, while the closing contest went to an Irish raider.

The decision to replace the Flat turf course with an All-Weather track while continuing with jumps racing (like Kempton) wasn't to everyone's taste and one question on many people's lips was what would happen to the Northumberland Plate. The great staying handicap was first run in 1833 and had been staged at Gosforth Park since 1882, and with tradition being such a large part of horseracing its future was always going to be important. There was a suggestion that in order to continue the tradition of the racing being staged on grass, it could be run on the hurdles track, but from where I'm standing the race has lost none of its lustre for being held on the All-Weather. Indeed, the consistency of an artificial surface compared to turf was probably a key reason why the race produced one of the most notable performances by a horse on the Flat in recent history.

For the second year in a row, in 2022 Trueshan had been forced to miss the Ascot Gold Cup due to fast ground and as had been the case the previous year, Alan King's gelding was rerouted to the Northumberland Plate instead. He could manage only sixth of the 20 runners off an official mark of 118 under 9st 13lb (after his rider's 5lb claim) in 2021, but now here he was racing off a mark of 120 under a fully fledged jockey in Hollie Doyle under 10st 8lb! He proved equal to the task, though, and defied the highest handicap mark of the modern era on the Flat.

The track received another vote of confidence in the autumn of 2019. Following torrential rain, the meeting at Doncaster due to take place on Saturday, 26 October was abandoned, but the fixture had been due to stage the Group 1 Vertem Futurity, one of the premier two-year-old races of the season. Losing a race like this would have been serious, but where could you transfer such an event on a safe surface at that time of year? Step forward Newcastle where, like Doncaster, they had a straight 1m track. So, what seemed a rather surreal situation took place the following Friday evening when the contest was run under the floodlights at Gosforth Park, becoming the first Group 1 race to be run on an All-Weather surface in Britain.

Aidan O'Brien ran five in the race which suggested he had no problem with the change of venue or surface, but it was won by Kameko (Andrew Balding/Oisin Murphy) and the form of the rescheduled race received the ultimate boost when the combination went on to land the 2,000 Guineas at Newmarket the following June.

The latest vote of confidence came on Good Friday 2022, when the All-Weather Championships Finals meeting was held at Newcastle for the first time having been staged at Lingfield ever since its inception. Newcastle had been racing on Good Friday since 2017 with the Burradon Stakes, a Listed race run over 1m, as its feature.

Kameko returns to the winner's enclosure after landing the transferred Vertem Futurity in November 2019 (Grossick Racing Photography).

This race was kept and staged alongside the championship races, therefore boosting the prestige of the fixture even further. Despite the change of venue, the meeting lost none of its quality and there was again another success for France despite their raiders having further to travel.

The Newcastle All-Weather track replaced the previous turf track so follows the same conformation. It's a big circuit, with the round course about 1m6f in circumference and a run from the home turn to the winning post of just under 4f. It's a stiff finish too, so the ability to stay the trip is much more significant than at a sharp track like Lingfield. As previously mentioned, the track is unique among All-Weather venues in that it has a straight track catering for races of between 5f and 1m. In fact, it's only the straight track that is floodlit, which is understandable given how big the round course is. For this reason, between autumn and spring the longer races on the round track are staged at the beginning of the meeting, when they can be run in daylight.

The surface at Newcastle is Tapeta and when it opened in 2016 it joined Wolverhampton, which had switched to that surface two years earlier. Tapeta is like Polytrack in that it comprises silica sand, wax and fibres and it simulates the root structure of turf. It does appear to be a slower surface than Polytrack, albeit not as slow as the old Fibresand at Southwell, but it's another reason why stamina is properly tested here.

FIVE-SEASON TOP JOCKEY, TRAINER AND SIRE STATISTICS FOR NEWCASTLE

JOCKEYS

%	RIDES	WNS	P/L (£1)	NAME
34	53	18	-4.35	JIM CROWLEY
31	32	10	-4.41	JAMES DOYLE
27	124	33	-30.62	ROBERT HAVLIN
24	51	12	-2.42	DAVID PROBERT
23	62	14	+16.43	OISIN MURPHY
20	445	87	+24.27	BEN CURTIS
20	312	63	-10.61	DANIEL TUDHOPE
20	137	28	+0.38	HOLLIE DOYLE
19	193	36	-48.06	JACK MITCHELL
19	70	13	-50.00	JAMIE SPENCER
17	82	14	+9.20	ANDREA ATZENI
17	93	16	+36.70	DANIEL MUSCUTT
17	65	11	-17.68	S. DE SOUSA
17	126	22	-6.08	TOM MARQUAND
15	365	55	-1.63	CALLUM RODRIGUEZ
15	95	14	-23.82	DAVID EGAN
15	287	43	-1.14	KEVIN STOTT
14	147	20	-49.08	FRANNY NORTON
14	384	52	-29.50	JOE FANNING
14	141	20	-22.04	OLIVER STAMMERS
13	186	25	+28.58	HARRY RUSSELL
13	104	13	+89.08	JOANNA MASON
12	543	63	-127.27	P.J. MCDONALD

11	145	16	-10.42	DAVID NOLAN
11	481	52	+1.28	JASON HART
11	468	52	-117.70	PAUL MULRENNAN
10	176	17	-32.53	CONNOR BEASLEY
10	279	27	-127.84	LUKE MORRIS
10	261	27	-74.56	PAUL HANAGAN

TRAINERS

%	RNRS	WNS	P/L (£1)	NAME
36	44	16	+2.71	CHARLIE APPLEBY
34	50	17	-4.99	SIR M. STOUTE
31	153	47	-27.14	J. & T. GOSDEN
29	131	38	-8.43	WILLIAM HAGGAS
27	75	20	+33.12	ANDREW BALDING
26	57	15	+12.33	GEORGE BOUGHEY
25	59	15	-16.68	SAEED BIN SUROOR
24	166	40	-31.12	ROGER VARIAN
24	50	12	+45.95	WILLIAM KNIGHT
23	120	27	-6.32	ARCHIE WATSON
22	79	17	+2.08	CHARLIE FELLOWES
21	92	19	-13.60	JAMES TATE
21	67	14	+42.24	MICHAEL WIGHAM
20	84	17	+33.24	CHARLES HILLS
20	70	14	-50.27	S. & E. CRISFORD
11	380	40	-119.57	C. & M. JOHNSTON
18	61	11	+31.58	HEATHER MAIN
18	95	17	+2.46	HUGO PALMER
18	101	18	+41.88	MARCO BOTTI
17	71	12	-4.54	GILLIAN BOANAS
15	91	14	-27.88	JAMES FANSHAWE
15	66	10	-3.82	SIR M. PRESCOTT
14	88	12	+76.20	ALAN BROWN
13	87	11	-36.13	DAVID SIMCOCK
13	164	22	+24.68	JOHN QUINN
13	87	11	+22.00	LES EYRE
13	254	33	+17.64	MICHAEL APPLEBY
12	299	35	-31.29	BEN HASLAM
12	226	27	-2.90	BRYAN SMART
12	122	15	+14.63	JAMES BETHELL
12	329	38	-52.36	KEITH DALGLEISH
12	202	24	+22.41	M. & D. EASTERBY

12	650	79	-49.82	RICHARD FAHEY
11	188	21	-4.47	GRANT TUER
11	418	48	+70.50	JIM GOLDIE
11	230	25	-57.67	JULIE CAMACHO
11	107	12	-34.67	KAREN MCLINTOCK
11	229	25	-62.48	KEVIN RYAN
11	340	39	+40.80	K.R. BURKE
11	225	24	-72.63	MICHAEL DODS
10	430	43	-84.95	ANTONY BRITTAIN
10	336	32	-52.21	DAVID O'MEARA
10	207	20	-47.38	JEDD O'KEEFFE
10	218	22	-86.48	TRACY WAGGOTT

SIRES

%	RNRS	WNS	P/L (£1)	NAME
32	22	7	+42.88	KUROSHIO
27	30	8	+4.53	KITTEN'S JOY
26	100	26	-3.80	DUBAWI
26	23	6	-4.28	SEA THE MOON
25	20	5	+1.63	ES QUE LOVE
24	89	21	+31.59	SEA THE STARS
23	78	18	-27.50	KINGMAN
22	32	7	-6.88	CHARMING THOUGHT
21	58	12	-9.05	TAMAYUZ
20	89	18	-39.18	FRANKEL
20	25	5	+1.70	LE HAVRE
20	45	9	+31.18	NIGHT OF THUNDER
19	59	11	+19.63	FASTNET ROCK
19	32	6	-7.17	FREE EAGLE
19	27	5	-5.63	LONHRO
19	27	5	+14.60	POUR MOI
18	89	16	+4.98	BRAZEN BEAU
18	38	7	+7.17	DISTORTED HUMOR
18	61	11	-32.21	GOLDEN HORN
18	45	8	+37.25	HIGH CHAPARRAL
17	53	9	+34.25	GARSWOOD
17	29	5	+5.00	LUCKY STORY
17	82	14	+90.28	MUKHADRAM
17	103	18	-29.90	NATHANIEL
17	77	13	-3.77	SIYOUNI
17	42	7	-22.12	WAR FRONT

16	56	9	+14.25	AUSTRALIA
16	62	10	-3.52	HOT STREAK
15	80	12	+32.75	CAPE CROSS
15	41	6	+6.00	DABIRSIM
15	72	11	+2.50	TORONADO

NEWCASTLE DRAW AND PACE STATISTICS

5f

Front-Runners	1.9
Prominent Horses	1.0
Hold Up Horses	0.7

STALL	RUNNERS	WINNERS	%W/R
1	119	12	10
2	125	12	10
3	123	16	13
4	123	13	11
5	120	12	10
6	117	8	7
7	107	20	19
8	91	9	10
9	78	6	8
10	66	7	11
11	52	7	13
12	43	4	9
13	29	1	3
14	24	3	13

6f

Front-Runners	2.0
Prominent Horses	1.0
Hold Up Horses	0.8

STALL	RUNNERS	WINNERS	%W/R
1	183	20	11
2	176	15	9
3	183	19	10
4	183	19	10
5	173	17	10
6	165	16	10
7	165	16	10
8	154	18	12
9	142	10	7
10	130	10	8

11	110	10	9
12	97	10	10
13	66	9	14
14	54	4	7
15	1	0	0

I was surprised when I first saw the draw statistics for the straight course at Newcastle. It always looked to be a fair track and the way I approached races of up to 6f with larger fields was to try and work out on which side the pace was likely to be, or wait and see if one side or the other appeared to be favoured after a couple of races. I still believe this is the percentage call, but these statistics for the shorter trips are difficult to ignore and in general they do suggest that a low-to-middle draw is favoured. The pace statistics at up to 6f are consistent with the other tracks, though, showing that the ability to establish a prominent early position is a big plus.

7f 14yds

Front-Runners	1.9
Prominent Horses	1.1
Hold Up Horses	0.7

STALL	RUNNERS	WINNERS	%W/R
1	194	16	8
2	195	14	7
3	194	26	13
4	193	19	10
5	196	22	11
6	185	23	12
7	180	20	11
8	165	16	10
9	139	13	9
10	122	10	8
11	105	8	8
12	83	11	13
13	54	5	9
14	43	1	2

1m 5yds

Front-Runners	1.2
Prominent Horses	1.1
Hold Up Horses	0.9

STALL	RUNNERS	WINNERS	%W/R
1	199	19	10
2	195	26	13

3	200	37	19
4	194	13	7
5	188	18	10
6	180	23	13
7	166	14	8
8	154	15	10
9	135	10	7
10	115	8	7
11	89	8	9
12	70	6	9
13	49	6	12
14	35	4	11

Over 7f there is still an advantage in being handy and a middle draw appears to be a slight advantage over 7f and 1m, but it's probably more important to look out to see if one side of the track is advantaged over all trips up to a mile on a meeting-to-meeting basis (there is a perfect example of this in the 'Journal' section of this book).

1m2f 42yds

Front-Runners	1.7
Prominent Horses	1.1
Hold Up Horses	0.8

STALL	RUNNERS	WINNERS	%W/R
1	103	12	12
2	107	14	13
3	99	9	9
4	102	17	17
5	103	14	14
6	99	10	10
7	86	7	8
8	75	10	13
9	68	0	0
10	60	3	5
11	49	8	16
12	38	2	5
13	24	1	4
14	16	3	19

1m4f 98yds

Front-Runners	1.1
Prominent Horses	1.2
Hold Up Horses	0.8

STALL	RUNNERS	WINNERS	%W/R
1	70	7	10
2	71	6	8
3	72	14	19
4	71	5	7
5	67	11	16
6	57	11	19
7	50	6	12
8	44	3	7
9	34	2	6
10	27	3	11
11	18	4	22
12	12	1	8
13	9	1	11
14	7	0	0

2m 56yds

Front-Runners	1.2
Prominent Horses	1.2
Hold Up Horses	0.8

STALL	RUNNERS	WINNERS	%W/R
1	41	3	7
2	41	7	17
3	42	2	5
4	42	3	7
5	38	6	16
6	40	6	15
7	36	1	3
8	31	1	3
9	26	6	23
10	20	3	15
11	16	1	6
12	13	2	15
13	11	1	9
14	8	0	0
15	5	0	0
16	5	0	0
17	5	2	40
18	5	0	0
19	5	0	0
20	3	0	0

The statistics for all races on the round track don't provide enough evidence for many hard-and-fast conclusions, though a low draw and handy position seem a slight advantage over a mile and a quarter.

SOUTHWELL

Southwell will always hold a special place in my affections, because as described in the introduction it was the first All-Weather track I ever attended. That love affair with Southwell isn't just down to that profitable first visit back in 1994, though, as I genuinely like the place. There is always such a friendly atmosphere when I do attend and given that it is a relatively minor track the facilities for the racegoers are very good, at least in my opinion. If that wasn't the case, then I wouldn't be prepared to take on the four and a half-hour round trip as often as I do.

There were times when I feared for the track's future, particularly following the floods of 2007 which forced the venue to close for five months. The spectacle of water laying on the ground floor of the grandstand with dead fish floating in it was heartbreaking and I hoped I wouldn't see the like again, but unfortunately a similar thing happened at the end of 2012 with the track closed for more than two months. Happily, reports of Southwell's death proved greatly exaggerated and the venue is still going strong now, albeit in a different format.

I do have to admit that in the old Fibresand days I did do very well there on the punting front. There are a few reasons for this, the first being that once you had sussed what was going on you just knew that you had to focus on previous Fibresand form ahead of everything else, but it was surprising how many people hadn't latched on to this. They still used the old pounds and ounces formula to work out that Horse A was well handicapped on its form on the other All-Weather surfaces (or even on turf), only to see their selection gasping for breath from a long way out while Horse B (often an established Fibresand stalwart) waltzed his or her merry way up the long Southwell straight.

Lord Torranaga wins the last race to be staged on the Southwell Fibresand on 15 August 2021 (Proshot Photography).

Fibresand was certainly an unforgiving surface as once your selection had come off the bridle and there was still some way to go, you knew you'd had it. There was only one direction a horse would go from there and that was backwards. Horses didn't quicken to win races on Fibresand, they just maintained the gallop for longer than their rivals. Some horses used to relish the surface and there was nothing better than trying to unearth one whose recent form at other venues was ordinary to say the least but had flourished on the Fibresand in the past. Quite often they were off a lower handicap mark than when they last encountered the surface due to their modest efforts in the meantime but came back to life when returned to it. This was an example of where in-the-know punters held an advantage, not that this would have been universally applauded (especially by the bookmakers).

However, in December 2020 everything was about to change when Arena Racing Company announced that the Fibresand was due to be replaced with Tapeta, thereby bringing Southwell into line with Newcastle and Wolverhampton. When I first heard the news, I felt a mix of emotions. I can't say I was that surprised, as there had been murmurings about the surface being replaced after the floods of 2007 and there were often complaints about the Fibresand riding too deep and the kickback being unpleasant. However, as with many bad occurrences in your life, even though you're expecting it there is still a bit of a shock when it happens. Most of my initial thoughts

Carausius wins the first race to be run on Tapeta at Southwell on 7 December 2021 (Proshot Photography).

were negative. I felt I was losing an old friend and thought back to all those memorable days at Southwell when an enjoyable race-day experience coincided with making a few quid. I also worried what would happen to all those horses for whom the Fibresand provided the best (and sometimes only) chance of recording a victory.

I then became a bit more pragmatic. Lingfield and Wolverhampton had changed their surfaces and I got used to them, so I realised I would just have to adapt like I had for those two venues. There were other sweeteners too, with the change of surface meaning that some Fast-Track Qualifiers would now be scheduled for Southwell, something that never happened on the Fibresand. Some top stables rarely had runners at the track in the past but were now prepared to send them here, so the quality of the racing might improve. Not that Southwell had a major problem with small field sizes in the Fibresand days.

The first meeting on the new surface was scheduled to take place in the summer of 2021, but due to circumstances beyond the track's control the date was pushed back and instead of staging the first Tapeta meeting the fixture that took place on 15 August was an opportunity to wave goodbye to the Fibresand. Once Lord Torranaga (Philip Kirby/Billy Garritty) had sauntered past the post six lengths clear in the concluding 1m4f handicap there was the realisation that the end of an era had been reached. It was now time to look forward to 7 December and the revised start date for the new surface, another meeting I was determined to attend.

It was a slightly surreal atmosphere when I arrived for that first twilight Tapeta fixture four months later. Because of the time of year, most of the meeting was going to take place under the floodlights so I wasn't quite sure how much of a difference I would notice compared to the old Fibresand, especially as the conformation of the track and the race distances were the same as before. That feeling was even more enhanced when the 12 runners in the opening 1m4f handicap finished spread out over almost 100 lengths! Had they really changed the surface at all?

Of course they had, but the race had a familiar look to it with the leaders going off at a rate of knots and several coming off the bridle a long way out. Such positive tactics may have been fine in the old days, but we had a new surface now and of those who were up with the pace early, only one managed to finish in the first six. The comfortable winner Carausius (Charles Hills/Kieran Shoemark) was given a patient ride and won the race with a wide sweeping move rounding the home bend which took him to the front before forging clear. I didn't take this as a sure sign of how things would be in the future, not after just one race, and the other seven winners on the night were given contrasting rides. The evidence of this first fixture according to my own calculation (the method for which I will explain later) was that the track didn't have a major bias. If anything, it was slightly in favour of hold up horses, but it was still early days and it would take some time and a few meetings before any bias might be detected, if at all.

The next meeting three days later did suggest a bias might exist, with four of the seven races on the round track being won by horses brought wide off the final bend, but an innovation at Southwell may have had something to do with it. Unlike before, the track now had a false rail on the inside as the home bend met the straight, just as at Dundalk. This had the effect of making the field fan out on turning in, while providing the jockeys with a choice of where they wanted to go, namely far side, near side, or up the centre. On this occasion the nearside was proving to be an advantage and those who had latched on to this soon enough had an opportunity to make some money in-running, provided they were quick enough.

Southwell is a left-handed oval circuit of about 10f in circumference with races over 5f run on a straight course, which made it unique on British All-Weather tracks until the opening of

Newcastle in 2016. So, what is the situation as regards the track now? It does seem to me that the very inside isn't the place to be at most meetings, at least in races on the round course where a switch to the inside requires a definite manoeuvre once the false rail ends. Those with longer memories may remember that the inside rail was a huge disadvantage in the older Fibresand days, so if a horse managed to win despite going there the effort could be marked up significantly, while those who were beaten having taken that route could be forgiven. We may not be quite at that stage, but the ideal spot does appear to be centre-to-nearside and, although it isn't that long since the first Tapeta fixture, quite a lot of meetings took place at Southwell within the first few months after the new surface was laid, so we now have something of a picture.

The winner of that first Tapeta race, Carausius, went on to complete a hat-trick over the same course and distance, thereby confirming my long-held view that Southwell form is still of most relevance back at Southwell. It also reaffirms my belief that the venue will again have its fair share of track specialists, just as at the other courses. That's something that hasn't changed even after the switch of surface.

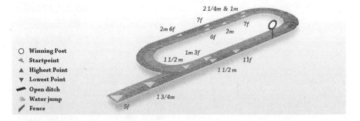

TOP JOCKEY, TRAINER AND SIRE STATISTICS FOR SOUTHWELL

With the Tapeta only coming online in December 2021, there is a smaller sample available for the statistics up to the end of June 2022. Jockeys, trainers, and sires still need to have a strike rate of at least ten per cent, but only need to have had at least three winners.

JOCKEYS

%	RIDES	WNS	P/L (£1)	NAME
27	44	12	+29.50	DANIEL MUSCUTT
24	21	5	+20.83	LAURA PEARSON
20	25	5	+9.82	DANIEL TUDHOPE
19	75	14	+3.84	DAVID PROBERT

18	44	8	-7.73	HOLLIE DOYLE
18	34	6	+1.38	LEWIS EDMUNDS
17	36	6	-6.60	MARCO GHIANI
16	31	5	-10.38	CALLUM SHEPHERD
15	75	11	+29.33	CONNOR BEASLEY
14	71	10	-6.13	LUKE MORRIS
13	30	4	-8.67	JACK MITCHELL
13	55	7	+9.00	JONATHAN FISHER
13	23	3	+2.00	ROB HORNBY
13	23	3	-11.25	TOM EAVES
12	33	4	-18.30	DOUGIE COSTELLO
12	52	6	-27.59	JASON WATSON
11	27	3	-12.25	CLIFFORD LEE
11	66	7	-21.75	KIERAN O'NEILL
11	38	4	-18.50	P.J. MCDONALD
10	88	9	-57.25	CAM HARDIE

TRAINERS

%	RIDES	WNS	P/L (£1)	NAME
32	28	9	+24.63	ROY BOWRING
24	34	8	-12.08	REBECCA MENZIES
23	26	6	+21.08	DAVID LOUGHNANE
21	24	5	+39.00	DAVID THOMPSON
20	25	5	-2.25	ALICE HAYNES
20	25	5	+2.13	DAVID BARRON
20	20	4	+3.83	KEITH DALGLEISH
16	25	4	-10.59	ARCHIE WATSON
16	51	8	-17.18	DEREK SHAW
16	32	5	-4.25	RICHARD FAHEY
14	21	3	-4.75	C. & M. JOHNSTON
14	21	3	0.00	JOHN BUTLER
13	24	3	-3.17	BRYAN SMART
13	23	3	-1.50	CHARLIE WALLIS
13	45	6	-7.25	M HERRINGTON
13	31	4	-18.08	PHILIP KIRBY
10	29	3	-14.25	K.R. BURKE

SIRES

%	RIDES	WNS	P/L (£1)	NAME
21	24	5	+18.50	BELARDO
21	24	5	+8.63	KODI BEAR
20	30	6	+8.75	CABLE BAY

20	20	4	+34.50	DREAM AHEAD
20	20	4	-1.56	SEPOY
18	39	7	+1.50	EXCEED AND EXCEL
17	29	5	-13.63	BATED BREATH
16	37	6	-2.21	HELMET
16	31	5	13.74	SWISS SPIRIT
14	21	3	+83.00	BRAZEN BEAU
14	21	3	+3.50	HARBOUR WATCH
13	48	6	-1.25	MAYSON
13	32	4	+7.00	MEHMAS
12	49	6	-23.63	DANDY MAN
11	44	5	+11.53	SHOWCASING
10	29	3	+58.13	ACCLAMATION
10	40	4	+17.33	HEERAAT

SOUTHWELL TAPETA DRAW AND PACE STATISTICS

These statistics run from 7 December 2021 to 30 June 2022.

4f 214yds

Front-Runners	2.7
Prominent Horses	0.9
Hold Up Horses	0.6

STALL	RUNNERS	WINNERS	%W/R
1	41	5	12
2	40	7	18
3	40	4	10
4	40	4	10
5	39	3	8
6	41	7	17
7	38	4	11
8	36	2	6
9	31	0	0
10	24	4	17
11	17	1	6
12	16	0	0
13	11	0	0
14	10	1	10

6f 16yds

Front-Runners	2.0
Prominent Horses	1.1
Hold Up Horses	0.8

STALL	RUNNERS	WINNERS	%W/R
1	40	4	10
2	40	5	13
3	41	5	12
4	38	4	11
5	41	7	17
6	40	2	5
7	36	1	3
8	34	3	9
9	27	4	15
10	25	3	12
11	20	0	0
12	17	3	18
13	10	0	0
14	11	1	9

The advantage enjoyed by front-runners on the straight track was significant on the Fibresand and these statistics show that still to be the case. Although the IV for 6f isn't quite as high, it's still noteworthy enough, as is the bias towards those drawn low-to-middle over both trips.

7f 14yds

Front-Runners	1.9
Prominent Horses	1.1
Hold Up Horses	0.7

STALL	RUNNERS	WINNERS	%W/R
1	47	6	13
2	48	7	15
3	48	9	19
4	48	5	10
5	47	2	4
6	44	7	16
7	40	5	13
8	40	1	3
9	38	4	11
10	30	2	7
11	21	1	5
12	20	0	0
13	5	0	0
14	4	2	50

1m 13yds

Front-Runners	1.6
Prominent Horses	1.0
Hold Up Horses	0.9

STALL	RUNNERS	WINNERS	%W/R
1	45	9	20
2	44	5	11
3	46	2	4
4	46	6	13
5	43	1	2
6	43	5	12
7	38	0	0
8	35	5	14
9	33	4	12
10	29	3	10
11	27	3	11
12	17	1	6
13	11	2	18
14	7	0	0

A low draw and a prominent early position are still of value over 7f and even over the mile to some extent, though the draw stats for the longer trip are starting to even out.

1m3f 23yds

Front-Runners	1.5
Prominent Horses	0.3
Hold Up Horses	1.2

STALL	RUNNERS	WINNERS	%W/R
1	10	0	0
2	11	2	18
3	11	0	0
4	10	0	0
5	11	0	0
6	10	1	10
7	10	4	40
8	8	2	25
9	7	0	0
10	6	2	33
11	5	0	0
12	4	0	0
13	2	0	0
14	2	0	0

1m4f 14yds

Front-Runners	0.8
Prominent Horses	1.1
Hold Up Horses	1.0

STALL	RUNNERS	WINNERS	%W/R
1	24	2	8
2	25	3	12
3	25	0	0
4	25	3	12
5	24	4	17
6	21	3	14
7	20	3	15
8	18	3	17
9	16	2	13
10	9	0	0
11	9	1	11
12	9	0	0
13	3	1	33
14	3	0	0

The statistics over 1m3f are inconclusive with the distance not used that often, but over 1m4f it does seem an advantage to be drawn in the middle and it also shows that it isn't easy to make all the running over the longer trip.

1m6f 21yds

Front-Runners	0.0
Prominent Horses	1.7
Hold Up Horses	1.0

STALL	RUNNERS	WINNERS	%W/R
1	4	0	0
2	3	0	0
3	4	0	0
4	3	0	0
5	3	0	0
6	5	2	40
7	5	1	20
8	4	0	0
9	4	1	25
10	4	0	0
11	4	0	0
12	3	1	33

2m 102yds

Front-Runners	2.1
Prominent Horses	0.4
Hold Up Horses	1.0

STALL	RUNNERS	WINNERS	%W/R
1	9	0	0
2	8	2	25
3	8	1	13
4	8	1	13
5	7	1	14
6	8	2	25
7	6	0	0
8	5	0	0
9	4	1	25
10	5	1	20
11	3	0	0
12	2	0	0
13	1	0	0

2m 2f 98yds

Front-Runners	0.0
Prominent Horses	1.5
Hold Up Horses	0.8

STALL	RUNNERS	WINNERS	%W/R
1	2	0	0
2	2	0	0
3	2	0	0
4	2	1	50
5	2	0	0
6	2	0	0
7	2	1	50
8	1	0	0

There isn't enough evidence yet to draw firm any conclusions regarding the staying trips.

Just to illustrate what a difference a change in surface can mean, below shows how the pace bias was affected after the Tapeta replaced the Fibresand in December 2021. It shows the last few meetings on the old surface and first few on the new one (round track only).

Date	Surface	Variant/Going	Pace Bias
04APR2021	Fibresand	+20 Very Slow	60
08APR2021	Fibresand	+21 Very Slow	50
20APR2021	Fibresand	+24 Very Slow	67
26APR2021	Fibresand	+23 Very Slow	69
29APR2021	Fibresand	+21 Very Slow	53
15AUG2021	Fibresand	+14 Very Slow	67
07DEC2021	Tapeta	+13 Very Slow	38

10DEC2021	Tapeta	+9 Slow	24
16DEC2021	Tapeta	+11 Very Slow	29
17DEC2021	Tapeta	+13 Very Slow	14
22DEC2021	Tapeta	+9 Slow	33
29DEC2021	Tapeta	+9 Slow	23

As you can see, for the Fibresand meeting on 4 April the track variant was +20, meaning that according to my calculations the surface was slowing down the horses by 20 lengths for every mile they ran, equating to a going description of Very Slow. The Pace Bias on a scale of 0 to 100 was 60, meaning there was a bias towards front-runners, albeit not an overwhelming one. Notice how the Pace Bias reduces dramatically once the Tapeta is in place after 7 December, while that meeting ten days later where the bias has dropped right down to 14 is well worth looking into deeper.

Leaving aside the first race which was run on the straight track, these are the initial parts of the close-up comments for the other seven winners on the night, together with where the early leader eventually finished.

Race	Winner's Close-Up Comment	Early Leader Finished
2	in rear	6th of 9
3	held up in rear	6th of 8
4	close up	6th of 7
5	midfield	11th of 11
6	in rear	6th of 14
7	midfield	10th of 12
8	midfield	7th of 10

This may be a rather extreme example, but despite the new surface having only been down for a handful of meetings it does show there was already money to be made and it had nothing to do with trying to find a winner! By halfway through the card, it seemed clear that attempting to make all the running at this fixture was going to be difficult and if you were sharp enough you could take on the early leader in-running and put yourself in a very nice position.

This bias towards hold up horses lasted until just into 2022, before returning to an average of between 40 and 60 for most meetings, meaning no significant bias either way. I'm always on the lookout for a similar trend to reoccur, though, where there seems to be a bias one way or another after a handful of fixtures, not just at one which may be down to a blip.

WOLVERHAMPTON

Wolverhampton used to stage Flat and jumps racing on turf, and I can recall attending a Flat meeting there with my family in the early 1970s, but I couldn't be sure exactly when. The one thing I do remember is that it took an age to get there and back, but rather like with the M25 and Lingfield the M40 has made the journey to Wolverhampton a lot easier than it was. I do like Wolverhampton, despite having been asked where the ladies' toilets are and if I could order someone a taxi (the press lanyard can make me look like racecourse staff). I try to get there as often as I can and even the near four-hour round trip isn't enough to put me off. The facilities are very good, and I certainly recommend basing yourself in the Horizons Restaurant for one of the Saturday evening fixtures.

The first All-Weather fixture took place at Wolverhampton in December 1993 and it became the first track in Britain to race under floodlights. It wasn't until August 1995 that I paid my first visit to the track with the family, basing ourselves in the restaurant for the evening. As was the case with that very first Southwell fixture the previous year, I hastily put together some speed figures so at least I had something to go on. I hadn't realised how crucial they would be at the time, but in those days Wolverhampton had a Fibresand surface and if speed figures were to quickly prove their worth on any terrain, then it would be this one.

Two races went by, and I had gone close with my bets in both, but as yet no cigar. However, the third race was now approaching, a Class D handicap (which would now be a Class 4) over 6f. My speed figures told me that the one to be on was a horse called Four Of Spades (David Evans/Amanda Sanders), but it looked as though he was going to be a big price. However, I must have still been in holiday mode (I had only returned from attending the Ebor Meeting the previous day) as I stuck £20 on the nose despite his long odds. I decided to back him on the Tote, partly because it was a long way from the top floor of the grandstand to the bookies and this was a family outing, so it would have been rude to just disappear at regular intervals.

Then something rather surreal happened. As I stood in the queue waiting to place my bet, I noticed the gentleman in front of me had quite a lot of hair, both on his head and on his chin. He looked a bit familiar to me and I remember thinking, 'Is it? Isn't it? No, surely it can't be!' But then I realised it was. I was standing behind no less than Roy Wood! I realised that he might be local, but I wasn't expecting to see him here. Soon I had the lyrics of 'Fire Brigade', 'Blackberry Way' and 'See My Baby Jive' echoing through my head. For those below a certain age this may not mean a lot, but I can assure you that every time we reach December in any given year his voice will be echoing around wherever you go. When you next hear 'I Wish It Could Be Christmas Everyday' think of me standing in that Tote queue behind the man himself.

When it came to the race, I still remember it very well as Four Of Spades was delivered with a wide sweeping move down the wide outside and just got up to win by a neck. I was elated, especially when going to collect my winnings as the Tote dividend almost exactly matched the starting price, and it was a very nice to see a big pile of £20 notes mounting up on the counter in front of me, finally reaching its total of £420. I had always enjoyed tinkering around with ratings and the opportunity to calculate my own speed figures and use them for this new (to me) form of racing was a challenge I wanted to take on. This fixture, as much as any, is the reason I have been so passionate about All-Weather racing ever since.

In December of that year Wolverhampton broke new ground when it staged the first Listed All-Weather race to be run in this country, the £50,000 Bass Wulfrun Stakes run over the extended 1m1f. The first running was won by Prince Of Andros (David Loder/Richard Hughes), already a triple Group-race winner on turf. He would return a year later and win the race again (this time under John Reid), narrowly defeating Decorated Hero who three months earlier had been one of Frankie's Magnificent Seven. Unfortunately, the race didn't survive beyond 1998, but a race of Listed status made a welcome return to Wolverhampton when the Lady Wulfruna Stakes was upgraded in 2007.

Wolverhampton is a left-hand circuit of almost exactly 1m in circumference with separate chutes for races over six and 7f. It's a

Lancelot Du Lac wins the big sprint handicap at Wolverhampton in March 2018 (Jonathan Hipkiss Photography).

tight circuit, but the bends are sweeping with a run-in of just under 2f. However, being such a tight track in some of the staying events, it has been known for a jockey to finish a circuit early, including some high-profile ones!

When Fibresand was the surface at Wolverhampton there was a major track bias, rather like the one at Southwell which of course was also Fibresand at the time. The inside of the track was an absolute no-go area, though the penny hadn't dropped with everyone, and it was common to see horses floundering against the inside rail once they came off the bridle. It may have appeared to be the quickest way home, but if your fancy ended up there you could basically tear up your ticket there and then. The theory was that because of the way the bends were cambered the Fibresand was rolling towards the inside rail, thereby making the surface deeper there.

When it was decided that the Fibresand was to be replaced with Polytrack in 2004 I felt a certain sadness (like I felt with Southwell towards the end of 2021), partly because I may not be able to use the track bias to my advantage on the new surface, but also because I had nice memories of the old surface there. In the early days I had proudly displayed a sticker on the back window of my car which said, 'We Do It Under The Lights At Dunstall Park Every Saturday Night'. Clearly, I wasn't bothered about the image that might portray.

The Polytrack continued to be used for the next ten years, or at least I think it was. Towards the end of its life, it wasn't clear just exactly what the surface was composed of, but at least in 2014 we would be in no doubt what it would be, namely Britain's first Tapeta surface. This did mean that, as had been the case with Lingfield in 2001, Southwell in 2021 and Wolverhampton itself in 2004, all my existing statistics had to be reset to zero. It's a bit of a pain but it is necessary and with so many All-Weather meetings in the calendar now, it doesn't take long before enough meaningful statistics for a new surface begin to accumulate.

Does a track bias still exist? The answer is that it's still not easy to put in a sustained effort against the inside rail, though not to the same extent as somewhere such as Lingfield. There can be trouble when things get tight on the bend approaching the home straight and many a horse can get pinched against the inside rail as those ahead of them start to roll to their left. On the other hand, horses can lose their race by being carried too wide off the home bend and the short straight means that they have insufficient time to make up the lost ground. A stalking position, two or three horse-widths off the inside rail, seems to be the ideal position from where to launch a challenge.

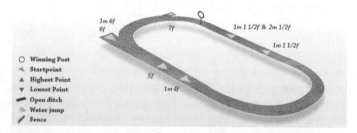

FIVE-SEASON JOCKEY, TRAINER AND SIRE STATISTICS FOR WOLVERHAMPTON

JOCKEYS

%	RIDES	WNS	P/L (£1)	NAME
54	26	14	+19.29	RYAN MOORE
31	54	17	+4.62	JIM CROWLEY
29	160	47	+4.74	JAMES DOYLE
24	239	58	-32.69	OISIN MURPHY
22	58	13	+7.63	DANE O'NEILL
20	281	57	-26.34	ADAM KIRBY
20	404	82	-29.13	JACK MITCHELL

19	70	13	-25.35	WILLIAM BUICK
18	61	11	-21.16	ANDREA ATZENI
18	133	24	+4.81	MARTIN HARLEY
18	233	41	-57.32	ROBERT HAVLIN
18	382	70	+48.00	ROSSA RYAN
17	216	37	-8.08	JASON WATSON
16	128	20	+13.17	CALLUM RODRIGUEZ
16	605	94	-49.37	HOLLIE DOYLE
16	91	15	+93.50	OLIVER STAMMERS
16	116	18	+81.33	PAUL MULRENNAN
16	152	24	-60.16	S. DE SOUSA
15	327	49	-28.92	BEN CURTIS
15	96	14	+3.33	DAVID NOLAN
15	141	21	+6.11	MARCO GHIANI
15	642	94	-179.88	R. KINGSCOTE
15	103	15	-23.83	ROBERT WINSTON
15	138	21	+6.82	SEAN LEVEY
14	185	25	-33.85	CIEREN FALLON
14	377	52	-93.70	JOE FANNING
14	345	47	-77.21	P.J. MCDONALD
14	69	10	+2.03	POPPY BRIDGWATER
14	376	54	-77.18	TOM MARQUAND
13	246	32	+21.45	CLIFFORD LEE
13	328	44	-100.20	DANIEL MUSCUTT
13	166	21	-41.00	EDWARD GREATREX
13	100	13	+96.00	FINLEY MARSH
13	171	22	-29.09	GEORGE ROOKE
13	87	11	-22.18	PAT COSGRAVE
13	123	16	-29.10	SAM JAMES
12	190	22	-40.92	A. RAWLINSON
12	386	48	-123.84	CALLUM SHEPHERD
12	154	19	-40.45	DAVID EGAN
12	752	92	-7.65	DAVID PROBERT
12	148	18	-53.59	HECTOR CROUCH
12	275	32	+30.45	STEVIE DONOHOE
12	137	17	-22.79	THOMAS GREATREX
12	163	19	-45.61	TONY HAMILTON
11	272	30	-41.53	FRANNY NORTON
11	270	31	-13.97	JASON HART
11	112	12	-13.92	LAURA PEARSON
11	128	14	-1.57	RAY DAWSON

11	244	28	+32.46	ROB HORNBY
11	128	14	-40.55	T. HAMMER HANSEN
10	134	13	-59.16	GRACE MCENTEE
10	195	20	-67.86	LEWIS EDMUNDS
10	1004	102	-323.13	LUKE MORRIS
10	132	13	-28.13	SHANE GRAY
10	369	36	-117.11	SHANE KELLY
10	129	13	-1.00	TOM QUEALLY

TRAINERS

%	RNRS	WNS	P/L (£1)	NAME
33	94	31	-14.05	CHARLIE APPLEBY
29	156	45	-21.25	WILLIAM HAGGAS
28	101	28	-3.31	SAEED BIN SUROOR
26	42	11	-8.09	JAMES FERGUSON
26	184	48	-25.10	J. & T. GOSDEN
26	149	38	-11.02	ROGER VARIAN
25	99	25	-50.05	SIR M. STOUTE
24	45	11	+9.10	JOSEPH PARR
23	129	30	+2.74	HUGO PALMER
23	148	34	-28.27	S and E CRISFORD
22	45	10	-8.75	K.P. DE FOY
22	60	13	+21.31	SEAN CURRAN
20	189	37	-30.29	JAMES TATE
19	53	10	-13.38	DAVID BROWN
18	150	27	+8.92	ALAN KING
18	119	21	-6.67	CHARLES HILLS
17	186	32	-35.61	ANDREW BALDING
17	114	19	+5.79	DAVID BARRON
17	185	31	-14.10	DAVID SIMCOCK
17	125	21	-9.98	GEORGE BOUGHEY
17	95	16	-25.51	GRANT TUER
17	66	11	+55.58	MICKY HAMMOND
17	171	29	-43.93	STUART WILLIAMS
17	83	14	-50.67	TOM CLOVER
16	301	47	-102.74	ARCHIE WATSON
16	183	29	-18.32	CLIVE COX
16	111	18	-50.56	JAMES FANSHAWE
16	195	31	-44.90	RICHARD HUGHES
16	109	17	-29.56	ROGER CHARLTON
15	157	24	-44.86	ED WALKER
15	102	15	-25.02	RALPH BECKETT

15	85	13	-9.25	REBECCA MENZIES
15	301	46	83.49	TOM DASCOMBE
14	467	65	-101.36	C. & M. JOHNSTON
14	102	14	-28.41	HUGHIE MORRISON
14	197	28	20.92	KEITH DALGLEISH
14	90	13	26.60	MICHAEL BELL
14	146	21	-43.14	SIR M. PRESCOTT
14	79	11	-28.85	WILLIAM KNIGHT
13	104	14	+52.33	KEVIN RYAN
13	276	36	+5.06	K.R. BURKE
13	101	13	-8.67	PHILIP MCBRIDE
13	335	44	-11.52	RICHARD HANNON
13	136	18	-27.87	ROGER TEAL
12	113	13	-2.33	ADRIAN WINTLE
12	497	61	-12.19	DAVID LOUGHNANE
12	349	41	+6.23	MARCO BOTTI
12	192	23	-30.38	M. HERRINGTON
12	128	15	-11.38	MICK CHANNON
11	105	12	-18.93	CHELSEA BANHAM
11	590	66	-88.38	DAVID EVANS
11	374	41	-63.68	DAVID O'MEARA
11	259	28	-130.10	IVAN FURTADO
11	365	39	-74.76	JOHN BUTLER
11	113	12	+35.75	JONATHAN PORTMAN
11	601	64	-47.41	TONY CARROLL
11	108	11	+7.25	MUIR & GRASSICK
10	500	48	-112.82	ANTONY BRITTAIN
10	143	14	-33.72	BRIAN ELLISON
10	100	10	-31.40	CHARLIE FELLOWES
10	145	14	-38.50	DEAN IVORY
10	140	14	+10.63	GAY KELLEWAY
10	570	59	-111.32	MICHAEL APPLEBY
10	432	42	-94.33	RICHARD FAHEY
10	248	24	-45.54	RONALD HARRIS
10	165	16	-62.92	SYLVESTER KIRK

SIRES

%	RNRS	WNS	P/L (£1)	NAME
28	47	13	+20.03	AWTAAD
27	33	9	+8.74	UNIVERSAL
26	112	29	+14.63	KINGMAN

24	25	6	+38.75	ARABIAN GLEAM
24	37	9	+0.88	GALE FORCE TEN
24	71	17	-12.71	GOLDEN HORN
24	62	15	+32.36	NIGHT OF THUNDER
24	21	5	+8.88	ULYSSES
23	70	16	+75.49	KODI BEAR
23	26	6	+36.21	PLANTEUR
23	66	15	+3.98	SPEIGHTSTOWN
21	58	12	+1.33	THE GURKHA
20	169	34	-73.34	DUBAWI
20	49	10	-6.97	FREE EAGLE
20	25	5	-10.52	NEW BAY
20	30	6	-10.97	REDOUTE'S CHOICE
20	30	6	-0.75	RIO DE LA PLATA
19	113	21	-5.15	CAMELOT
19	27	5	-7.00	DISTORTED HUMOR
19	58	11	-12.05	FARHH
19	48	9	+7.50	RED JAZZ
19	27	5	+11.50	SOVIET STAR
19	81	15	-1.21	WAR FRONT
18	65	12	+59.93	AVONBRIDGE
18	93	17	-27.03	DECLARATION OF WAR
18	101	18	-0.05	MUKHADRAM
18	171	30	-43.63	SHAMARDAL
18	106	19	+54.84	TORONADO
17	47	8	+26.00	CACIQUE
17	122	21	-49.42	FRANKEL
17	86	15	+43.42	INTELLO
17	48	8	+4.37	IVAWOOD
17	52	9	+15.88	MORPHEUS
17	52	9	+91.62	OLYMPIC GLORY
17	125	21	+97.98	POWER
16	195	32	-5.96	CAPE CROSS
16	187	29	-2.07	DANSILI
16	73	12	-10.03	FASTNET ROCK
16	77	12	-0.58	GREGORIAN
16	134	21	-47.20	MEHMAS
16	143	23	-42.19	SEA THE STARS
15	108	16	-9.53	CHARM SPIRIT
15	47	7	-0.42	CHOISIR
15	157	23	-48.67	DRAGON PULSE
15	95	14	+1.05	DUE DILIGENCE

15	41	6	+9.95	ESTIDHKAAR
15	33	5	-2.25	FROZEN POWER
15	299	45	-73.91	INVINCIBLE SPIRIT
15	48	7	-13.06	KENDARGENT
15	285	44	-86.91	LOPE DE VEGA
15	92	14	+12.75	MULTIPLEX

WOLVERHAMPTON DRAW AND PACE STATISTICS

5f 21yds

Front-Runners   1.9
Prominent Horses   1.3
Hold Up Horses   0.6

STALL	RUNNERS	WINNERS	%W/R
1	186	28	15
2	190	30	16
3	180	18	10
4	186	30	16
5	188	15	8
6	174	19	11
7	162	23	14
8	148	8	5
9	122	8	7
10	103	13	13
11	64	4	6

6f 20yds

Front-Runners   1.7
Prominent Horses   1.4
Hold Up Horses   0.6

STALL	RUNNERS	WINNERS	%W/R
1	251	31	12
2	252	25	10
3	245	22	9
4	247	28	11
5	247	32	13
6	240	26	11
7	236	26	11
8	213	26	12
9	190	13	7
10	163	15	9
11	114	8	7
12	74	3	4
13	46	3	7

The above statistics for the sprint trips at Wolverhampton make things quite clear. You don't want to be drawn too wide, and a prominent position is an advantage. This is hardly surprising given that we are taking about a turning left-handed track, but it's still good to have the data to prove it.

7f 36yds

Front-Runners   1.4
Prominent Horses   1.5
Hold Up Horses   0.6

STALL	RUNNERS	WINNERS	%W/R
1	301	29	10
2	297	34	11
3	299	46	15
4	298	36	12
5	293	32	11
6	288	36	13
7	275	31	11
8	258	29	11
9	239	8	3
10	197	15	8
11	150	11	7
12	109	6	6

1m 142yds

Front-Runners   1.0
Prominent Horses   1.6
Hold Up Horses   0.7

STALL	RUNNERS	WINNERS	%W/R
1	237	31	13
2	228	11	5
3	229	26	11
4	235	30	13
5	224	27	12
6	223	28	13
7	203	25	12
8	188	14	7
9	172	16	9
10	149	12	8
11	113	13	12
12	79	6	8
13	57	4	7

The 7f statistics are fascinating, but they will make perfect sense to anyone who has witnessed races over the trip around Wolverhampton. The start may be a on a chute, but the first bend comes up very quickly and if you are stuck out wide you will cover a lot of valuable ground, which will come back to bite you when the contest begins in earnest. Even for races over the extended 1m trip a low-to-middle drawn is preferable, as again the first bend comes up quite quickly.

1m1f 104yds

Front-Runners   1.0
Prominent Horses   1.3
Hold Up Horses   0.9

STALL	RUNNERS	WINNERS	%W/R
1	211	16	8
2	210	21	10
3	212	26	12
4	208	25	12
5	208	25	12
6	201	25	12
7	198	22	11
8	167	23	14
9	153	14	9
10	122	11	9
11	93	4	4
12	65	4	6
13	45	3	7

1m4f 51yds

Front-Runners   0.9
Prominent Horses   1.4
Hold Up Horses   0.8

STALL	RUNNERS	WINNERS	%W/R
1	144	16	11
2	146	17	12
3	141	17	12
4	143	17	12
5	134	19	14
6	122	19	16
7	110	12	11
8	88	10	11
9	73	7	10
10	56	5	9
11	48	7	15
12	33	3	9

The extended 1m1f start is at the entrance to the home straight and the runners cover nearly 2f before encountering the opening bend, so the consensus may be that because of the length of time involved the draw will matter less, but these statistics suggest otherwise as even here it appears that a wide draw is a disadvantage. It's also noticeable that the advantage enjoyed by front-runners generally decreases as the race distance increases.

1m5f 219yds

Front-Runners   0.9
Prominent Horses   1.4
Hold Up Horses   0.8

STALL	RUNNERS	WINNERS	%W/R
1	49	3	6
2	50	4	8
3	52	5	10
4	52	9	17
5	47	7	15
6	43	8	19
7	35	5	14
8	32	7	22
9	25	1	4
10	22	0	0
11	15	3	20
12	10	0	0
13	7	2	29

2m 120yds

Front-Runners   0.3
Prominent Horses   1.3
Hold Up Horses   1.0

STALL	RUNNERS	WINNERS	%W/R
1	38	2	5
2	37	4	11
3	38	8	21
4	36	8	22
5	34	5	15
6	31	2	6
7	24	1	4
8	25	4	16
9	22	1	5
10	17	2	12
11	9	0	0

| 12 | 10 | 0 | 0 |
| 13 | 8 | 1 | 13 |

The draw statistics are inconclusive over the longer distances with only limited data, but even so I'm happy to concede that trying to make all the running over staying trips at Wolverhampton is difficult, as the IVs would suggest.

ASSESSING FORM

Assessing the form for an All-Weather race, or indeed a race of any sort, is a complex business and no one should be in any doubts about that. The problem is just how deep do you go in trying to work out whether Horse A is a contender or whether there is a flaw in the prospects of Horse B? There is no perfect answer to these questions. Of course, you can choose a horse in the most basic of ways such as sticking a pin in the list of runners, backing your favourite number or colour or by following your favourite jockey/trainer blind.

That's not the ideal way to go about it, but neither is over-complicating things and the reality is that there is no limit to the amount of research you can do on any horse, because there are so many factors that could come into play. None of us has a limitless amount of time available (at least I don't know anyone who has) so the next best thing is to prioritise those factors that are likely to be the most important. Things such as the suitability of the trip, what type of surface they are racing on and fitness (among others) are fundamental, and they don't really need books written about them per se. However, concentrating on All-Weather racing as a sole entity does bring several benefits. The most obvious one is that you are basically dealing with a few hundred horses rather than a few thousand, as you would be with Flat turf or National Hunt racing. Of course, you will need to assess horses who are switching to an artificial surface for the first time, or indeed appearing on the racecourse for the first time, but there are methods for dealing with those.

The biggest problem I had to work out when I first started to specialise in All-Weather racing was how much significance I should give turf form when assessing the chance of a horse either appearing on an artificial surface for the first time or returning to it after racing on grass. There is probably no perfect answer, but one of the reasons

I got into All-Weather racing in the first place was to make the whole process more manageable, so I decided to focus on a horse's record on the All-Weather only. I still do that to a large extent and merely use recent turf form as a sign of current wellbeing, though even that isn't an exact science.

In many cases separating turf and All-Weather form can make what first looks a mirky picture a little clearer and the race cards I produce in tabular format on the Sandform website show All-Weather performances only. Here is an example from the summer of 2022 of how effective this method can be. The race in question, a 0-80 handicap run over 1m, took place at Newcastle on 24 June.

Of the 13 runners declared at the 48-hour stage, 12 eventually took part and next to each of the contenders shown below are two columns. The first column shows (reading from left to right) each horse's last six form figures on the Flat, irrespective of whether it was on turf or the All-Weather, while the second column shows their last six runs on the All-Weather only.

Name	Latest Flat Form	Latest All-Weather Form
Dual Identity	452122	3412
Mango Boy	432541	34
Amaysmont	203058	216132
Danielsflyer	984359	542913
Gainsbourg	615354	95
Bashful	323512	331
Holy Endeavour	184317	21843
Clear Angel	142U21	521442
Jewel Maker	324466	732446
Plastic Paddy (N/R)	160233	160233
Chief's Will	28125	
Fiorina	764266	742
Billyb	957416	5

Separating the form out this way serves two main purposes. Firstly, many people won't bother to do so which means they will often only be utilising the individual's wellbeing purely on how they have been performing on grass. Current wellbeing is important of course, but it doesn't guarantee they will be able to show the same level of form on a different surface, in the same way soft-ground horses may not act on fast ground and vice-versa. Remember, these are the people you will be betting against and the more you know compared to them, the better position you will find yourself in.

The other advantage in doing things this way is that it might suggest an imminent return to form for a particular horse, now that he or she is back on an All-Weather surface. Many of the horses lining up for this Newcastle race had been showing a similar level of form on both sand and surf, so the type of horse to look out for is one whose two sets of form figures as shown here are a contrast. For instance, if the left-hand column were to show an impressive set of wins or near-misses but the right-hand column showed a lot of high digits (or duck eggs) then that horse is likely to be better on turf, or at the very least out of form on the last few occasions they tackled an artificial surface. As we are assessing a race on the Tapeta as opposed to turf, we are looking for a horse whose form shown in the right-hand column is rather better than on the left, and one glaring example here is Amaysmont.

Clearly stripping his form down to show how he had been performing on the All-Weather made what had originally looked a horse with an average chance rather more interesting. To find out just how interesting, let's open things up a bit more and put a bit of flesh on the bones for the All-Weather form shown above. Here is the card as it was shown on the Sandform website showing each horse's past All-Weather form.

Key:

Date	Date of the race
Track	Name of the course
Surf	The racing surface – Polytrack, Tapeta, Fibresand or Dirt (some results from abroad, such as Meydan, are included)
Dist	Distance of the race in furlongs
Gng	A description of the going based on race times (VF – very fast; FT – fast; SD – standard; SW – slow; VS – very slow)
Bias	On a scale of 0-100. The higher the figure the more the surface was favouring front-runners
Rtype	Race type. The initial digit is the race class
Pos	Finishing position
Ran	Number of runners that took part
Wght	Weight carried after any allowances have been deducted or overweight added
Dr	Draw the horses started from
Pce	The early position the horse took (Led, Prominent or Held Up)

Hdgr   Any headgear worn (Blinkers, Visor, Cheekpieces, Hood, Tongue-Tie, Eyeshield or Eyecover

Sectnl   The adjusted halfway sectional time for the race

SF   Speed figure

It's worth taking a close look at what is shown for Amaysmont.

5-30 JENNINGSBET HANDICAP (0-80) (4) 3-Y-O+ (Winner 4994.99)
8f Par 105 13 runners Median Time 1m 40.3

1 (11) DUAL IDENTITY (IRE) 4-10-2 WILLIAM KNIGHT - BEN CURTIS

Date	Track	Surf	Dist	Gng	Bias	Rtype	Pos	Ran	Wght	Dr	Pce	Hdgr	Sectnl	SF
04JUN2022	LING	POLY	10	SW	43	4HCP	2	5	9-7	1	P	-	+0.18	99
10MAY2022	NEWC	TPTA	10.2	VS	33	4HCP	1	8	9-5	1	P	-	-1.33	103
20AUG2021	KEMP	POLY	12	SD	54	5HCP	4	8	9-11	8	P	-	-0.51	100
21OCT2020	KEMP	POLY	7	SW	46	5CND	3	10	9-5	2	P	-	-0.51	95

2 (10) MANGO BOY 4-10-0 CHRIS WALL - JACK MITCHELL

Date	Track	Surf	Dist	Gng	Bias	Rtype	Pos	Ran	Wght	Dr	Pce	Hdgr	Sectnl	SF
10MAY2022	NEWC	TPTA	10.2	VS	33	4HCP	4	8	9-6	3	H	-	-1.33	102
04AUG2021	KEMP	POLY	8	SW	56	4CND	3	10	9-2	7	P	-	+0.87	97

3 (7)   AMAYSMONT 5-9-13 RICHARD FAHEY - OISIN MCSWEENEY(5)

Date	Track	Surf	Dist	Gng	Bias	Rtype	Pos	Ran	Wght	Dr	Pce	Hdgr	Sectnl	SF
08FEB2021	WOLV	TPTA	8.6	SW	48	3HCP	2	7	9-1	2	P	-	-1.06	107
22JAN2021	CHEL	POLY	8	SW	60	3HCP	3	7	9-1	4	H	-	-1.22	107
09JAN2021	CHEL	POLY	8	SD	65	3HCP	1	5	8-0	2	P	-	---	110
27DEC2020	WOLV	TPTA	9.5	SD	48	4HCP	6	10	9-4	10	H	-	+0.72	98
07DEC2020	WOLV	TPTA	8.6	SD	31	4HCP	1	6	9-1	4	H	-	-2.66	106
20NOV2020	NEWC	TPTA	8	SD	56	4HCP	2	8	9-7	1	P	-	+0.07	101
06NOV2020	NEWC	TPTA	6	FT	61	4HCP	7	13	9-7	10	P	-	+0.21	99
05JUN2020	LING	POLY	7	SW	57	3HCP	6	11	8-13	5	H	-	---	101

4 (13)   DANIELSFLYER (IRE) 8-9-12(C) MICHAEL DODS - CONNOR BEASLEY

Date	Track	Surf	Dist	Gng	Bias	Rtype	Pos	Ran	Wght	Dr	Pce	Hdgr	Sectnl	SF
03MAR2022	NEWC	TPTA	7.1	VS	67	4HCP	3	7	9-7	3	P	-	-2.72	102
02MAR2021	NEWC	TPTA	7.1	SW	50	4HCP	1	9	9-0	2	H	C	+0.62	107
05FEB2021	NEWC	TPTA	6	FT	75	4HCP	9	10	9-5	6	H	C	+1.28	89
23JAN2021	NEWC	TPTA	7.1	SD	33	4HCP	2	9	9-2	7	H	C	+0.71	103
31DEC2020	NEWC	TPTA	7.1	SW	52	4HCP	4	9	9-2	7	P	C	+1.41	97
07DEC2020	WOLV	TPTA	7.2	SD	31	4HCP	5	12	9-2	3	L	C	-0.09	103
21NOV2020	WOLV	TPTA	7.2	SW	69	4HCP	6	12	9-7	10	P	C	+1.96	97

5 (5)   GAINSBOURG 4-9-10 EDWARD BETHELL - KEVIN STOTT

Date	Track	Surf	Dist	Gng	Bias	Rtype	Pos	Ran	Wght	Dr	Pce	Hdgr	Sectnl	SF
25APR2022	SOUT	TPTA	7.1	FT	52	4HCP	5	8	9-3	4	P	-	-0.14	105
30APR2021	NEWC	TPTA	7.1	SD	38	5MDN	9	14	9-1	1	H	-	+0.44	90

6 (8)   BASHFUL 4-9-10 IAIN JARDINE - ANDREW MULLEN

Date	Track	Surf	Dist	Gng	Bias	Rtype	Pos	Ran	Wght	Dr	Pce	Hdgr	Sectnl	SF
20OCT2021	KEMP	POLY	12	SW	63	5CND	1	5	9-4	1	L	-	-0.60	99
26AUG2021	LING	POLY	12	FT	25	3HCP	3	8	8-0	8	H	-	+0.13	106
20JUL2021	WOLV	TPTA	12.2	VS	69	6CND	3	7	9-3	7	L	-	-1.96	102

7 (1)   HOLY ENDEAVOUR (IRE) 4-9-9 RICHARD FAHEY - P.J. MCDONALD

Date	Track	Surf	Dist	Gng	Bias	Rtype	Pos	Ran	Wght	Dr	Pce	Hdgr	Sectnl	SF
25MAR2022	NEWC	TPTA	8	VS	64	4HCP	3	8	8-13	7	L	-	-0.86	100
14FEB2022	WOLV	TPTA	7.2	SW	58	5HCP	4	6	9-5	5	H	-	-0.87	105
28NOV2020	WOLV	TPTA	8.6	SD	50	4HCP	8	8	9-4	2	P	-	-1.41	85
10NOV2020	NEWC	TPTA	7.1	FT	73	5CND	1	10	8-11	5	L	-	+1.95	98
25SEP2020	NEWC	TPTA	7.1	SD	27	5CND	2	12	8-11	7	P	-	---	90

8 (4)   CLEAR ANGEL 4-9-8(H) SUSAN CORBETT - HARRY RUSSELL(3)

Date	Track	Surf	Dist	Gng	Bias	Rtype	Pos	Ran	Wght	Dr	Pce	Hdgr	Sectnl	SF
24MAY2022	NEWC	TPTA	8	VS	33	6HCP	2	14	9-4	11	L	H	-0.87	99
01MAR2022	NEWC	TPTA	7.1	VS	46	6HCP	2	12	9-1	4	P	H	-0.60	100
24FEB2022	NEWC	TPTA	7.1	VS	39	5HCP	4	9	8-10	7	H	H	---	109
10FEB2022	NEWC	TPTA	6	VS	42	6HCP	1	7	9-1	4	H	H	-2.99	99
27JAN2022	NEWC	TPTA	6	VS	69	6HCP	2	11	9-1	8	P	H	-2.27	106
18JAN2022	SOUT	TPTA	5	SW	78	6HCP	5	8	9-5	4	H	H	-0.42	95
21DEC2021	NEWC	TPTA	6	VS	60	4CND	4	8	9-2	9	P	H	-1.63	102
08NOV2021	NEWC	TPTA	6	SW	43	5CND	8	11	9-5	9	P	-	-0.83	90

9 (9)   JEWEL MAKER (IRE) 7-9-6 TIM EASTERBY - SEAN KIRRANE(3)

Date	Track	Surf	Dist	Gng	Bias	Rtype	Pos	Ran	Wght	Dr	Pce	Hdgr	Sectnl	SF
15FEB2022	NEWC	TPTA	8	VS	42	5HCP	6	9	9-0	8	H	-	-3.67	101
24JAN2022	SOUT	TPTA	8.1	VS	38	5HCP	4	9	9-5	7	H	-	+4.35	85
22DEC2021	WOLV	TPTA	8.6	SW	46	4HCP	4	4	9-2	3	P	-	+4.40	84
08DEC2021	WOLV	TPTA	8.6	SD	50	4HCP	2	10	9-5	10	H	-	-0.67	105
20NOV2021	WOLV	TPTA	8.6	FT	52	5HCP	3	12	9-4	8	H	-	-0.41	102
05NOV2021	NEWC	TPTA	8	SW	15	4HCP	7	9	9-2	2	H	-	-0.75	100
12OCT2021	NEWC	TPTA	8	FT	36	4HCP	11	12	9-8	1	H	-	+2.15	92
09MAR2021	SOUT	FIBR	8.1	VS	63	4HCP	3	7	9-0	1	H	-	-3.22	99
19FEB2021	SOUT	FIBR	8.1	VS	58	5HCP	1	5	9-7	1	L	-	-3.64	103
28JAN2021	NEWC	TPTA	8	SW	56	5HCP	4	12	9-6	2	H	-	+1.43	96
15JAN2021	NEWC	TPTA	8	SD	73	4HCP	4	9	8-13	8	H	-	+0.86	102
28DEC2020	NEWC	TPTA	8	SD	50	5HCP	1	7	9-10	5	H	-	+0.72	95

Date	Track	Surf	Dist	Gng	Bias	Rtype	Pos	Ran	Wght	Dr	Pce	Hdgr	Sectnl	SF
21DEC2020	NEWC	TPTA	8	SD	60	4HCP	3	9	8-7	6	H	-	+4.14	90
15DEC2020	NEWC	TPTA	8	FT	70	4HCP	2	8	9-0	1	L	-	+1.05	103
04DEC2020	NEWC	TPTA	8	FT	48	6HCP	1	14	9-7	12	H	-	+0.34	102
04JUN2020	NEWC	TPTA	5	SD	67	5HCP	9	11	9-3	6	P	-	---	96

10 (2)   PLASTIC PADDY 4-9-6(C) MICHAEL APPLEBY - NON-RUNNER

Date	Track	Surf	Dist	Gng	Bias	Rtype	Pos	Ran	Wght	Dr	Pce	Hdgr	Sectnl	SF
27JAN2022	NEWC	TPTA	8	VS	69	4HCP	3	8	8-4	1	P	C	-1.80	102
11JAN2022	SOUT	TPTA	8.1	SW	55	4HCP	3	9	8-4	7	H	-	+2.41	103
28DEC2021	NEWC	TPTA	8	VS	48	5HCP	2	10	9-0	5	H	-	-1.28	101
20NOV2021	LING	POLY	10	SD	48	5HCP	10	13	9-3	4	H	-	+1.98	90
26OCT2021	NEWC	TPTA	8	SW	63	4HCP	6	7	8-11	8	P	-	-0.78	102
19OCT2021	NEWC	TPTA	8	SW	31	6HCP	1	13	9-7	12	H	-	-2.35	106
07OCT2021	CHEL	POLY	8	SD	33	6HCP	2	12	9-11	8	H	-	-1.21	100
27SEP2021	NEWC	TPTA	8	SD	50	6HCP	1	13	9-0	3	H	-	+0.19	104
15AUG2021	SOUT	FIBR	6.1	VS	67	6HCP	6	10	9-3	2	H	-	-2.42	88
16FEB2021	KEMP	POLY	7	VS	48	6HCP	4	13	9-2	6	H	C	+0.41	92
24JAN2021	LING	POLY	6	SD	58	5CND	6	8	8-12	6	H	-	-0.05	95
06JAN2021	WOLV	TPTA	6.1	SD	38	5MDN	6	8	8-12	7	P	-	+2.37	93
22DEC2020	LING	POLY	7	SD	27	5CND	6	8	9-5	1	P	-	+0.04	90

11 (12) CHIEF'S WILL (IRE) 3-9-5(C) ARCHIE WATSON - TOM MARQUAND
12 (6)   FIORINA 3-9-2 GEORGE BOUGHEY - SAM JAMES

Date	Track	Surf	Dist	Gng	Bias	Rtype	Pos	Ran	Wght	Dr	Pce	Hdgr	Sectnl	SF
18MAY2022	KEMP	POLY	8	SW	52	5HCP	2	8	9-8	1	P	-	-0.05	108
10NOV2021	KEMP	POLY	8	SD	44	5CND	4	12	9-0	6	H	-	+1.01	94
13SEP2021	KEMP	POLY	7	SW	38	5MDN	7	11	9-0	6	H	-	+2.09	86

13 (3)   BILLYB (FR) 3-8-13 ANN DUFFIELD - PAUL HANAGAN

Date	Track	Surf	Dist	Gng	Bias	Rtype	Pos	Ran	Wght	Dr	Pce	Hdgr	Sectnl	SF
19OCT2021	NEWC	TPTA	7.1	SW	31	4CND	5	14	9-3	8	H	-	+1.88	92

The first thing to note is that it was no wonder his exploits on artificial surfaces had been smothered by the sands of time (so to speak). He hadn't run on the All-Weather since the beginning of the previous year, with his last eight runs having been on turf. He was in good form when last in action on sand, though, and a little explanation as to what is being shown in this card will reveal why he made so much appeal.

Those last three speed figures of 110, 107 and another 107 are impressive in the context of this race (more on speed figures and how I calculate them will appear later in the book). Each of them is higher than the class par of 105 for this type of race, which means that if he were able to repeat those efforts at this level, he would enjoy a class edge. I'm always encouraged when a horse can earn a series of good speed figures like this, rather than just one which may be a lot higher than anything else they had recorded. It can also be seen that these speed figures were earned in stronger races than this one – three Class 3 handicaps (3HCP) whereas this was a Class 4.

For those who like to use handicap marks as part of their calculations, because of his lesser form on turf he had dropped 8lb lower than when last seen on an All-Weather surface, and 4lb below his last winning mark. The Tapeta was unlikely to be a problem as he had run well on it at Wolverhampton (including a win) and had also run well to finish second over this course and distance in the autumn of 2020. All seemed set fair for a good run if the return to this surface revived him.

Once the race was under way, Amaysmont raced keenly enough and found himself in front a long way from home but, despite the last 3f appearing to last for an eternity, he dug deep and just managed to hold off the persistent challenge of Billyb to win by a nose at odds of 18-1. I'm sure the reason he was sent off at such a long price was because his price was based on what he had been showing on turf since the previous spring. His All-Weather form in isolation would have entitled him to start at around a quarter of those odds.

Here is another example of where such an approach is both interesting and potentially profitable:

In 2022 Tynecastle Park was a nine-year-old gelding trained by Robert Eddery and no one would claim that he was anything special, as at the time of writing he was officially rated 59 on Flat turf, 69 on the All-Weather and 97 over hurdles. This is his career record under all codes between May 2016 and January 2022:

78886-732222P5-2P374125P-27211221-21062062-452418230284666-97

As you can see, there are a few successes buried away in there with six wins from 55 starts, a strike rate of 11 per cent. However, when you strip out the Flat turf and hurdle performances and just leave his record on the All-Weather, things start to look a bit more promising:

86-725-2341-2721121-21262-452166-97

That's six wins from 29 starts, a strike rate of 21 per cent. What has now become obvious is that he is very much at his best on an All-Weather surface with his record on Flat turf and hurdles combined 0-26.

However, if you start to look even more closely and just include his record between 1m6f and 2m2f on the Southwell Fibresand, it makes for truly fascinating reading. To emphasise the point, this is his record under such circumstances in tabular form:

Date	Dist (f)	Race Type	Pos	Runners	Running Style	SP
28AUG2017	16.5	6HCP	2	11	H	9-1
03JAN2018	16.5	6HCP	2	10	P	5-2
27AUG2018	16.5	6HCP	1	13	P	10-3
03JAN2019	16.5	6HCP	2	10	P	11-4
03FEB2019	14.1	6HCP	2	12	P	7-2
14MAR2019	16.5	6HCP	1	7	P	6-4
30MAR2019	16.5	6HCP	1	12	P	5-4
27NOV2019	14.1	5HCP	2	5	L	3-1
05DEC2019	14.1	6HCP	1	11	L	5-1
07FEB2020	18.4	4HCP	2	5	L	11-8
12FEB2020	16.5	3HCP	1	3	L	4-9
08OCT2020	14.1	5HCP	2	10	P	7-1
18DEC2020	18.4	5HCP	2	7	L	15-2
09FEB2021	16.5	3HCP	2	7	P	17-2
29APR2021	18.4	3HCP	1	7	L	6-1

That's a record of 6-15 (40 per cent) and nine silver medals. It became clear to me quite early that the distance of the race was as important to him as the surface. I wouldn't have touched him over a trip shorter than this, even on Fibresand, but given his optimum conditions he was an each-way steal at the very least, especially looking at those odds near the bottom of the list. Most specialist Fibresand stayers over the years were those who could maintain a consistent gallop on a testing surface for longer than their rivals. They weren't horses that quickened either and you can see with Tynecastle Park that he mainly (L)ed or raced (P)rominently and stuck at it dourly.

Those were ideal credentials when racing on this surface over any distance. In fact, in the old days when I was trying to unearth selections for the 'King Of The Sand' column in the *Racing And Football Outlook* and there was no previous All-Weather form to go on, if the horse I liked for whatever reason had the close-up comment 'stayed on at one pace' and 'kept on at one pace' for its runs on turf, then for me that was a positive!

Tynecastle Park returned to Southwell twice in the winter of 2021/22 after the surface had changed to Tapeta but was beaten 15 lengths and 27 lengths respectively in those contests, taking his All-Weather record away from Fibresand to 0-14. It just wasn't the same for him.

There are many horses like him racing on the All-Weather these days and they are well worth looking out for as their potency under a certain set of conditions may not be obvious to everyone, especially those who limit their research to a horse's last few performances. However, while it's all very well using this sort of information to back horses who you know are racing under conditions in which they thrive, I would be a bit more careful when trying to use it to bet against those who appear to be one-dimensional with regard to surface. At least until there is sufficient evidence to take such a dogmatic view. Here's an example:

The horse in question here is called Mulzim, at the time of writing an eight-year-old gelding trained by Mike Murphy. What follows is his entire record at Southwell, the bottom three lines in bold italics showing his runs on Tapeta after the racing surface was changed.

Date	Dist (f)	Race Type	Pos	Runners	Running Style	SP
01JAN2020	5	5HCP	2	7	P	14-1
13JAN2020	5	5HCP	3	6	P	6-1
28JAN2020	5	5HCP	1	7	P	7-2
05FEB2020	5	5HCP	1	6	P	8-13
11DEC2020	5	4HCP	8	14	H	16-1
20DEC2020	5	4HCP	1	9	P	5-1
01JAN2021	5	5HCP	4	6	P	7-4
26JAN2021	5	4HCP	1	6	H	3-1
02FEB2021	5	4HCP	1	8	P	11-10
24FEB2021	5	2HCP	1	5	P	9-4
01JAN2022	*5*	*3HCP*	*11*	*12*	*P*	*25-1*
24JAN2022	*5*	*2HCP*	*6*	*6*	*H*	*25-1*
24FEB2022	*5*	*4HCP*	*1*	*9*	*H*	*12-1*

His record on Fibresand read 6-10 (60 per cent) and when he returned to have a go on the Tapeta in January 2022, two heavy defeats at odds of 25-1 (beating just one horse in the process) suggested that, like Tynecastle Park, he just wasn't going to take to the new surface and that his days off winning at Southwell were over. However, those who decided they would take him on when he turned up back there the following month would learn an expensive lesson, as they would have laid a 12-1 winner. That was his starting price at least, but he had been supported in the market down to those odds so must have been laid at bigger prices than that.

I'm not saying that it would never have been a good idea to oppose Mulzim on Tapeta, I'm just saying that after just two attempts it was far too early to take him on. There could have been any number of reasons for those two modest efforts in January 2022 (in the first he reportedly hung left under pressure, while in the second he took a keen hold at the back of the field). After a few more defeats on the surface, valid excuses would have been less likely, so that would be the time to utilise such knowledge to our advantage. Incidentally, the stewards enquired into Mulzim's improved form when winning on 24 February compared to his previous outing, but the trainer's representative could offer no explanation. If only horses could speak.

Here is an example of where doing proper in-depth research can result in a positive (and ultimately negative) experience at the same time.

On the evening of 22 November 2011, I was in the process of researching the Kempton meeting due to take place the following evening, and it was while studying the 0-75 handicap over 7f that my interest became particularly aroused. One of those taking part in the race was a horse called Ocean Legend, a six-year-old gelding trained by Tony Carroll. At first glance his chance was far from obvious, as his last six form figures were 506809, including a heavy defeat over the same course and distance three months earlier.

However, on closer inspection I began to be drawn to him, particularly when coming across the sort of speed figures he had earned under similar conditions since the previous year. He had certainly become well handicapped because of his indifferent recent efforts and was now 8lb lower then when dead-heating in a 0-85 handicap at Kempton in February 2011. With my interest now well and truly on the rise, I decided to take an even closer look and discovered that when Ocean Legend had run over this course and distance in the past and been drawn in stall seven or lower, his record read 3211131. He was due to start from stall two this time, so he just had to be backed.

Imagine my delight, therefore, when a glance at Oddschecker the previous evening revealed that he was available at 20-1 with one of the major firms. Now I'm not having a pop at their odds compiler, as the gelding probably deserved to be that price given his recent form, but digging deeper in the way I have just described showed he shouldn't have been anything like those odds if bringing his A-game to the table. As there were valid reasons why he might be able to do so this time I decided right away that I was going to have a decent bet on him (a decent bet for me in those days was £20).

The following morning, I was back in the Raceform office and myself and a few of my work-mates were discussing the day's racing as we usually did. It was at that point that one of my colleagues revealed that he had come to a similar conclusion as myself regarding Ocean Legend. He, like me, had delved deeper into the horse's form and after having done so had also taken the 20-1 available with the same company. What could possibly go wrong?

The answer, fortunately, was that nothing did go wrong. Ocean Legend was soon able to take a handy position from his low draw under 3lb claimer Michael O'Connell and, when asked, the gelding found more than enough to go and win his race, beating a horse called Tislaam by just over a length. It's always very nice when you win a tidy sum of money on a horse and £400 was winging its way into my betting account, but this time I felt an even greater sense of satisfaction because the gains were purely down to me putting in the extra work necessary.

Following this success, Ocean Legend went on to win 11 more races in his career, six of them back at Kempton (making it 11 course wins in total), but some rather less convenient consequences were about to be felt. When I tried to place a bet with the same bookmaker soon afterwards, I found that my account had become restricted and that I could barely get a penny on. My enquiries as to why this had happened were met with a straight bat (in other words no meaningful explanation) and despite repeated requests and giving the same explanation as to why I had backed Ocean Legend as I have done here, they refused to budge.

As I have stated I helped myself to the 20-1 available with this one firm the evening before the race, but Ocean Legend was then backed throughout the following day (not surprisingly if people had read between the lines as I had done) and had shortened right into 7-2 before the off. Unwittingly I had become a small part of a proper gamble and I had considered laying off to make a small profit if Ocean Legend didn't win, but thankfully I decided to grow a pair and stick with it.

I can only assume that the bookmaker concerned must have felt that I had some inside information about the horse which most people didn't have access to. In other words, they must have thought that I had been 'in the know' and taken advantage of the information as a result. Perhaps they knew who I worked for, which also might have suggested some sort of conspiracy theory, as ludicrous as that may be. It certainly did nothing to quell the suspicion than some firms just don't like a winner and, although it's true I did know a bit more than many people about Ocean Legend beforehand, it was only because I had used my eyes and put a bit more work into it which had revealed that the odds they were offering were way out of line with the gelding's true chance.

PERFORMANCE PATTERNS

It was around 30 years ago while reading a book called *Betting For A Living* by Nick Mordin that I was introduced to the concept of performance patterns. The idea is that if you look at a horse's entire form in a tabular arrangement, any patterns will jump out at you such as a horse only seems to win over a certain trip, or only on a certain surface or perhaps only at a certain track. In fact, Ocean Legend was a good example of how to identify a horse's preferences in such a way, which resulted in me latching on to him.

These preferences may seem like common sense but looking at the form in this way can also reveal patterns that aren't so obvious when looking at form in traditional formats, such as a horse might be especially suited by going left-handed or their wins are only gained in small fields, or perhaps they have a particularly good record when returning from an absence. The possibilities are endless and if you can find a pattern that may not have yet been uncovered by most punters (especially one that might even have escaped those who make a point of trying to unearth performance patterns!) this can be a most profitable venture.

Nick used to write each horse's form down manually on what he called 'file cards', which must have been quite a chore (even the thought of using a typewriter makes me shudder these days), but fortunately things have changed a bit since then with the arrival of online sources of form and/or electronic form books. Despite their wide availability, however, people using these tools are still in the minority of punters, so it's still an angle well worth exploring. Racing on the All-Weather is an area in which this approach can be especially useful, such as a horse's preference for a particular surface

(Polytrack/Tapeta) being there for all to see. Even their preference for an individual track can stick out like a sore thumb.

Here are a couple of examples from the past where performance patterns would have been so useful, but although we are going back a few years the concept remains to this day. There was a horse named China Castle, who was trained by Patrick Haslam and was the winner of 26 of his 83 starts, 25 of those on an All-Weather track. He clearly loved an artificial surface, but it was the way he was campaigned that was truly fascinating.

He made his racecourse debut in July 1995 and his two-year-old season would have seemed reasonably non-descript at the time. He did win a 7f seller on the Southwell Fibresand on his third start but failed to make the frame in any of his other six outings that year. However, the venue at which he gained that sole juvenile victory would become extremely significant (or at least the surface on which he achieved it) when looking at his entire career. We didn't have long to wait to find out why.

Following a 50-day absence, China Castle had his first start as a three-year-old in a 7f handicap back at Southwell in January 1996 where, under Jason Weaver, he bolted up by 12 lengths. Further victories at Lingfield (then Equitrack) and Wolverhampton (then Fibresand) soon followed, and following a couple of defeats he added another success in a Southwell claimer over a mile and 3f. He didn't win again in ten further outings that year, but that meant that when he returned to Southwell for his first start as a four-year-old in January 1997, he was officially 1lb lower than for his last success in a handicap.

The year started off the same way as it had done 12 months earlier as he rattled off a quick hat-trick (all at Southwell) before the handicapper exacted harsh revenge, preventing him from any further success during that year. However, when it came to his first start as a five-year-old back at Southwell in January 1998, he was again 1lb lower than for the last of his three wins a year earlier. It was an occasion I remember well as I was present on that day (it was my 36th birthday) and by this stage I had already spotted the pattern. Many others must have done as well as he was sent off the 2-1 favourite, but things didn't turn out quite as well this time as he raced lazily early and, although he eventually finished strongly, he failed by a neck to catch the winner Alsahib. There were some long faces afterwards (not least mine), but he still confirmed how potent he was at this time of year by winning a limited stakes (these days a classified stakes) and a Wolverhampton handicap soon afterwards.

Eight further starts that year yielded no further victories, but by the time 1999 came around we were back in familiar territory. He started the year 4lb below his last winning mark and rattled off yet another quick hat-trick at his beloved Southwell before completing the four-timer with another success at Wolverhampton. He then bucked the trend of previous years by winning twice more back at the latter track in February and added another win at Southwell in March from an official mark of 101. The pattern wasn't repeated in quite the same way in subsequent years, but it certainly wasn't the end of his ability to win races as he went on to win nine more, making a total of 26, of which all bar one had been on an All-Weather surface.

At around the same time the stable had a sprinter named Pageboy and his profile also makes interesting reading. Already the winner of five races on turf, following a 132-day absence the gelding gained his first success on the All-Weather over 6f at Lingfield in January 1995 at odds of 7-4. He failed to win again that year but having been off for 101 days he again made a winning return over the trip at Lingfield in January 1996 at odds of 4-1.

He did manage to win twice more later that year, but by the time he returned to Lingfield in January 1997 he was coming back from a 100-day break and again he did the business at a generous-looking 4-1. He failed to make the frame in eight more starts that year, but clearly this performance pattern had gone beneath the radar of most punters as, when he was sent back to Lingfield for his first start of 1998 following a 93-day absence, he was allowed to go off at 8-1! The result was just the same, though, and those who had latched on to this pattern and lumped on accordingly must have been very happy with themselves. Spotting trends like these early can clearly be profitable, but it can also bring on a real sense of satisfaction if you can latch on to them soon enough.

GOING TO THE TRACK

There is nothing quite like a day at the races, not just because of the spectacle and the atmosphere of the occasion, but also the camaraderie and the chance to meet new people (often fellow racing enthusiasts). True, the weather in the middle of winter can be challenging, but it's all part of the buzz in the same way that some people decide to climb a mountain 'because it's there'.

Admittedly the crowds at some All-Weather meetings, especially on weekdays, can be a little thin, but you then get a sense that this whole piece of theatre has been put on just for you and a few other special guests. You tend to forget about the audience watching the races in betting shops around the world, or on the satellite channels, etc. At most meetings you have more freedom to wander about wherever you like with plenty of room to breathe and be able to do what you want, when you want to do it.

There is another major positive in being at the track, which may seem obvious at first, but it can sometimes be understated – you get to see the horses close up and personal. Being able to view the horses in the pre-parade ring and/or the paddock beforehand can be a huge advantage over those punters who are betting on the same race from a remote location. This is especially true when it comes to inexperienced horses or those returning from an absence.

This isn't confined just to All-Weather racing of course – it's true for Flat turf and National Hunt racing as well. Being able to spot a horse whose appearance catches your eye for some reason (either positively or negatively) can be like gold dust, but it's not a skill most people will be able to master overnight. It comes with time through the experience of being there, but it's well worth the effort.

The quality of All-Weather maidens has improved over the years, so you may well be witnessing the beginning of a high-class horse's career in what might otherwise look a routine contest. The appearance of many of the two-year-olds who race at Kempton from the summer onwards is as good as any you will find at a top turf venue, but a star can me born at any of the All-Weather venues these days. Just look at some of the talented John Gosden-trained horses whose first runs were on an All-Weather surface within the last few years. Enable is the one most people will come up with, but she is far from alone.

Her stablemate Anapurna is the perfect example of how you just don't know what you may be witnessing. How many people who saw her run green and trail in a well-beaten ninth of the 13 runners (earning a *Racing Post* Rating of just 42!) when the filly made her debut at Wolverhampton two days after Christmas in 2018 would have imagined her grinding her way up the Epsom straight to land the following year's Oaks? Not many I would suggest, including the connections of the 100-1 and 80-1 shots who finished seventh and eighth in the Dunstall Park contest.

Another from the stable, Star Catcher, could only manage a midfield finish when sent off odds-on for her Chelmsford debut in December 2018, but although she was too inexperienced to make an impact that day just why she was sent off such a short price for her first start made a lot more sense when she landed a hat-trick of successes at the highest level the following season.

Here is a list of horses who, since 2010 and before August 2022, had made their racecourse debut at a British or Irish All-Weather track before going on to Group 1 success in Europe.

Horse	Debut Date	Track	Pos	European Group 1 Wins
Aclaim	09/12/2015	Kempton	1st	2017 Prix de la Forêt
Ambivalent	17/09/2011	Wolverhampton	1st	2013 Pretty Polly Stakes
Anapurna	27/12/2018	Wolverhampton	9th	2019 English Oaks
				2019 Prix de Royallieu
Audarya	14/11/2018	Kempton	2nd	2020 Prix Jean Romanet
Brown Panther	11/11/2010	Southwell	1st	2014 Irish St Leger
Caravaggio	18/04/2016	Dundalk	1st	2016 Phoenix Stakes
				2017 Commonwealth Cup
Covert Love	21/10/2014	Lingfield	5th	2015 Irish Oaks
				2015 Prix de l'Opéra
Cursory Glance	21/05/2014	Kempton	1st	2014 Moyglare Stud Stakes
Enable	28/11/2016	Newcastle	1st	2017 English Oaks
				2017 Irish Oaks
				2017 King George VI and Queen Elizabeth Stakes
				2017 Yorkshire Oaks
				2017 Prix de l'Arc de Triomphe
				2018 Prix de l'Arc de Triomphe
				2019 Eclipse Stakes
				2019 King George VI and Queen Elizabeth Stakes
				2019 Yorkshire Oaks
				2020 King George VI and Queen Elizabeth Stakes
Harbour Law	18/03/2016	Lingfield	2nd	2016 English St Leger
Homecoming Queen	30/04/2011	Dundalk	6th	2012 English 1000 Guineas
Hunter's Light	17/11/2010	Kempton	2nd	2012 Premio Roma
Jack Hobbs	27/12/2014	Wolverhampton	1st	2015 Irish Derby
Joan Of Arc	06/11/2020	Dundalk	2nd	2021 Prix de Diane
Librisa Breeze	25/02/2015	Kempton	2nd	2017 British Champions Sprint
Lightning Spear	29/08/2013	Kempton	1st	2018 Sussex Stakes
Limato	11/06/2014	Kempton	1st	2016 July Cup
				2016 Prix de la Forêt
Loving Dream	11/11/2020	Kempton	7th	2021 Prix de Royallieu
Marsha	04/09/2015	Kempton	2nd	2016 Prix de l'Abbaye
				2017 Nunthorpe Stakes

Miss Yoda	05/08/2019	Kempton	1st	2020 Preis der Diana
Mustashry	21/10/2015	Kempton	4th	2019 Lockinge Stakes
Nezwaah	06/01/2016	Chelmsford	1st	2017 Pretty Polly Stakes
Perfect Power	25/05/2021	Newcastle	3rd	2021 Prix Morny
				2021 Middle Park Stakes
				2022 Commonwealth Cup
Persuasive	04/11/2015	Kempton	1st	2017 Queen Elizabeth II Stakes
Pinatubo	10/05/2019	Wolverhampton	1st	2019 National Stakes
				2019 Dewhurst Stakes
				2020 Prix Jean Prat
Ribbons	15/11/2012	Kempton	1st	2014 Prix Jean Romanet
Robin Of Navan	24/06/2015	Kempton	6th	2015 Critérium de Saint-Cloud
Simple Verse	24/02/2015	Lingfield	6th	2015 English St Leger
				2015 British Champions Fillies and Mares Stakes
Skitter Scatter	28/03/2018	Dundalk	3rd	2018 Moyglare Stud Stakes
Star Catcher	20/12/2018	Chelmsford	6th	2019 Irish Oaks
				2019 Prix Vermeille
				2019 British Champions Fillies and Mares Stakes
Starman	12/07/2020	Lingfield	1st	2021 July Cup
Teona	30/10/2020	Newcastle	2nd	2021 Prix Vermeille
Thistle Bird	27/04/2011	Kempton	4th	2014 Pretty Polly Stakes
Tiggy Wiggy	29/03/2014	Kempton	1st	2014 Cheveley Park Stakes
Winter Power	02/06/2020	Newcastle	3rd	2021 Nunthorpe Stakes
Without Parole	16/12/2017	Newcastle	1st	2018 St James's Palace Stakes

Finally in this chapter, here is an example of when being at the track for an All-Weather meeting should have been a memorable occasion for all the right reasons but ended up being quite the opposite:

It was a cold February Monday back in 2009 and I had enthusiastically made my way up the M6 to Wolverhampton for an afternoon of sport on what was then a Polytrack surface. The second race on the card was a maiden for three-year-olds and upwards over 6f in which nine of the 13 runners had previous racecourse experience, in many cases plenty of it. My research the previous evening had suggested that a horse called Circle Dance, a four-year-old trained by Derek Shaw, was a major contender as in my opinion he had the best form going into the race. The fact that he had already run 15 times without winning was a bit of a worry, but most of his main rivals were in the same boat so I was prepared to give him the benefit of the doubt. Still, a visit to the paddock beforehand was going to be especially crucial in a race like this and what I saw when I got there was a real eye-opener.

I always make a few notes in my race card when studying the runners in the paddock before a contest such as this, and having looked at the field closely for quite some time and added comments next to each of the 13 runners, I then looked at my card and found that I had written the words 'looks like a racehorse' next to just two horses. This may seem a bit harsh and perhaps a bit cruel, but sentiment sometimes has to go out of the window in these circumstances and to my eyes only these two matched what was written on the tin.

One of the pair was Circle Dance, which was pleasing, as it added to my feeling of confidence about him and if he didn't win it wouldn't be because he didn't look the part. The other one to catch the eye was a horse called Just Timmy Marcus, a three-year-old newcomer trained by Brian Baugh. He certainly did look the part; in fact, he looked fantastic and that alone should have been enough for me to have a few quid on him. The problem was that the statistics showed his trainer just didn't have winning newcomers, so now I was in a bit of a quandary. Should I go along with the stats and leave him alone or should I believe my eyes and have something on him? I decided on the former course of action and just backed Circle Dance at 5-1.

Once the race was under way the outcome had an almost inevitable feel about it as Just Timmy Marcus got up to win by half a length at odds of 66-1 with Circle Dance back in fifth. I felt sick, but I had at least learned a sharp lesson. I had been in a privileged position in being able to see the horses up close beforehand, something most punters I was betting against weren't able to do, but I had wasted the opportunity. I vowed there and then that I would never make the same mistake again and there haven't been many similar occurrences in the meantime, at least nothing nearly as costly.

That is not to say that statistics aren't important – they most certainly are. Just Timmy Marcus was Brian Baugh's only winner from 45 newcomers between April 2006 and November 2019 and only two others were placed. The gelding went on to win a handicap over the same course and distance a month later at odds of 10-3 (I did back him this time, though it was scant compensation), but he failed to win any of his 43 subsequent starts. Circle Dance went on to win a 5f maiden at the same venue nine days later, but only by a head at odds of 5-4. That would prove to be his only success in 28 career outings.

SPEED RATINGS

Already in this book I have mentioned speed ratings on several occasions, so what are they and how do they work? It's not easy to explain them, but I will do my best. The first thing to emphasise is that they are a group of ratings like any other. In other words, they are a way of trying to measure just exactly what Horse A has achieved and how that compared to Horse B in another race. The idea is that if the two met at some stage you would have some sort of idea as to what the outcome might be, thereby giving you that vital edge over other punters whose opinions might be based on instinct or such like.

The thing is that ratings come in all shapes and forms and the ones people prefer to use is very much down to personal taste. I have used many different types over the years and when I had them in my possession at the racecourse, I always felt I knew a bit more than most other people. However, for the past 30 years or so speed figures have been my main point of focus, which is around the same length of time I have been into All-Weather racing in a big way and that is not a coincidence. Part of the reason was I soon realised that although speed figures are of value in any type of racing, they are particularly useful on artificial surfaces where races are often (though not always) more truly run. After all, speed ratings and sectional times are a fundamental tool for punters in the US, a country where non-turf racing is dominant.

It was after reading Nick Mordin's landmark book *Betting For A Living* in 1992 and meeting the legendary Andy Beyer at the 1993 Breeders' Cup that I decided speed figures and All-Weather racing were a combination I wanted to pursue in greater deal. Having attended a few All-Weather fixtures, by 1995 I was calculating speed figures of my own with all the necessary components provided by myself. Initially I did it for all types of racing, but the workload was overwhelming with the tools I had available to me at the time, so I decided to concentrate on the All-Weather only, which I had always intended would be my priority. Apart from being able to specialise in one type of racing, it also reduced the number of horses I would have to keep track of, like I said earlier, from a few thousand to a few hundred.

I had been fortunate that in my previous career I had learned how to write computer programs (very simple computer programs admittedly), but that would still help a great deal in putting together a horse database and do the necessary calculations to produce speed figures without a need to resort to pen, paper and a calculator. The language I learnt, called REXX, is very old and it wouldn't surprise me if they had found a REXX script written on the walls of Tutankhamen's tomb, but fortunately with the availability of virtual machines I can run an old operating system beneath a new one on a laptop and still run my old trusty REXX programs.

The first job to do when venturing into the world of speed figures is to establish a set of standard times against which to compare the winning time of each race. This is how I went about it when I took the plunge a few years back, and indeed the whole process about to be described is how I compile my speed figures. It's not to say that any other method is wrong, it's just that this one works for me, and it should demonstrate how useful these ratings can be.

For every race distance at every All-Weather track, I recorded the winning times of each race going back a year, though for some less-used distances (mainly over staying trips) I had to go back a bit further. Having gathered what I believed to be a sufficient sample for each distance (at least 20 race times), not including those confined to two-year-olds (which by their very nature are run in slower times) I then sorted each list so that the fastest times were at the top and the slowest at the bottom. I then took the middle entry in each list as my standard time, or more accurately my *median* time.

Imagine that, for instance, the list below showed the winning times for races run over 6f at Kempton during the past year using the criteria described above. They have been sorted into ascending order, so that the time of 71.06s at the top was the fastest and the 75.11s at the bottom was the slowest. I have purposely limited the number of items in the list to 21 to make things easier.

71.06
71.32
71.47
71.55
72.11
72.41
72.46
72.60
72.67
72.88
72.95 ***
72.99
73.12
73.16
73.28
73.34
73.34
73.67
73.83
74.28
75.11

The time marked with the three stars is the 11th item in this 21-item list, so that time of 72.95s would be the median for the trip until the next occasion the times were recalculated. How often you update these times is a personal choice, but I do it annually to keep pace with any subtle little changes to the track conditions that may occur.

Having done this for all distances at each of the All-Weather tracks, we now have some sort of benchmark against which to measure all future performances over the same distance, but it's not as easy as that. The condition of the track and other factors such as the wind direction and even how the track has been prepared before racing can affect the winning times, so that it's quite possible for a horse of average ability to run a faster time than one rather more talented, for the simple reason that the track may have been riding slower (or deeper) when the better horse ran.

It's for that reason that I use a set of class pars to help work out how quickly a horse ran compared to how quickly he/she *should* have run on a perfectly fair track for the grade they were running in. In other words, to what extent was the state of the track speeding them up or slowing them down? Before I was able to do this, I needed to do some extensive research which did take quite a long time, but fortunately it's a job I only had to do once! I had to work out how much the winners of each race class compared with the other classes in terms of winning times. It seemed logical to me that the average winner of a Class 2 race should run a significantly quicker time than those at Class 5 level, but by how much?

The way I did it was to take a sheet of paper and write the seven race classes (as they were in those days) across the top. I then went through the results of several meetings and looked at the winning time of each race, comparing it with the median time for the course and distance. If the race was a Class 4 over 5f with a winning time of 60.5s and a median time of 60s exactly, then this race was 0.5s slow. If another race was a Class 5 over a mile and 4f with a winning time of 2m 37.8s and a median time of 2m 36s, then that race would be slow by 1.8s. This isn't quite the end of the process, though, because as the race distance increases so does the potential margin between the winning time and the median. This must be allowed for.

The way I do it is the adjust all races so that it appears they have all been run over 1m. That way it becomes possible to compare performances over different distances more easily. I used this method for the job I'm now describing, and it meant dividing 8f (1m) by the number of furlongs in the race and multiplying the result by the difference between the winning and median times. For the first race in our example the calculation would be (8/5)x5 and for the second it would be (8/12)x1.8. These are the results.

RACE	CLASS	DIST (F)	DIFF TO MEDIAN (SEC)	DIFF TO MEDIAN OVER 1M (SEC)
1	4	5	+0.5	+0.8
2	5	12	+1.8	+1.2

The figures shown on the right are the ones I placed under each race class on my sheet of paper. I didn't have to worry about how far the race was now, as this method took care of that, while I didn't need to concern myself with which track the race was run on either, as the median times had dealt with that. All I needed to do was put the resulting differences shown above in their appropriate class columns and once I had done so for enough races, I had a closer look at the results.

I sorted them into ascending order for each race class (fastest times at the top), just as with the median time calculation shown earlier, but instead of looking for the middle figure in the list I was more interested in those at the top. I wanted to know how much on average the faster winners within each category compared. This would then give me a benchmark for each class, a figure that would be attainable by the better winners in each grade, perhaps suggesting they would be capable of winning in a higher class. I took the top few items in each list and averaged them, and the results were quite an eye-opener. I found that there was a rather nice curve stretching down from the higher classes to the lowest, with the better winners at Class 2 level running around 1.8s per mile faster than the median time. In fact, each class was around 0.4s quicker than the one below it, which is about two lengths for every mile they ran.

I then had to decide what sort of scale I wanted to use for my speed ratings as I wasn't constrained by the sort of scale that performance ratings might use (pounds). My speed ratings would be expressed in terms of lengths per mile, and I thought that perhaps 100 would be a neat starting point (but I could have used any figure). If 100 represented the speed figure a horse would earn if running bang on median time on a perfectly fair track, then we have ascertained that the better Class 2 horses were running 1.8s per mile faster than that, which equates to nine lengths (1.8/2). Hence my par speed figure for Class 2 races is 109. Here are the full set of Class Pars (there was a certain amount of guesswork required with Class 1 races as not many existed when I carried out these calculations, but the evidence since has suggested that I was on the right path).

CLASS	PAR
1 (Group 1)	117
1 (Group 2)	115
1 (Group 3)	113
1 (Listed)	111
2	109
3	107
4	105
5	103
6	101
7	99

Allowances are built in for races confined to younger horses, with the amounts to be deducted depending on the time of year.

MONTH	2-Y-OS ONLY	3-Y-OS ONLY
Jan/Feb	-12	-6
Mar Apr	-11	-5
May/June	-10	-4
Jul/Aug	-9	-3
Sep/Oct	-8	-2
Nov/Dec	-7	-1

On top of that, the allowance for races confined to fillies is -3.

Using the above tables, the par figure for a Class 4 race open to both sexes and all ages in March would be 105, but if that race was confined to three-year-old fillies it would be 97 (105-5-3). Now we have everything we need, here is an example of how the speed figures for a real All-Weather meeting were calculated:

Note: the 'F' shown in the Sex column for race seven means the race was restricted to fillies. Some of those with 'B' (meaning both) in that column may have been for colts only, but that isn't relevant. The point is that they weren't for fillies only, which means that the extra allowance isn't invoked.

RACE DETAILS FOR THE MEETING AT LINGFIELD ON 23 JULY 2022

RACE	WINNER	DIST	TIME	MEDIAN	RTYPE	AGE	RNRS	SEX
1	ARCADIAN FRIEND	12	150.83	152.7	6HCP	3-Y-0+	8	B
2	NEANDRA	12	149.02	152.7	4HCP	3-Y-0	6	B
3	ROCKING ENDS	5	59.75	58.3	5CND	2-Y-0	4	B
4	SANDY PARADISE	8	97.15	97.9	6HCP	3-Y-0	10	B
5	COUNSEL	7	84.18	84.0	5CND	3-Y-0+	10	B
6	SHIGAR	7	84.72	84.0	5CND	3-Y-0+	9	B
7	MELODRAMATICA	7	85.10	84.0	5HCP	3-Y-0	8	F
8	HEALING POWER	7	83.37	84.0	6HCP	3-Y-0+	14	B

The first race over a mile and a half was run in a time 1.87s quicker than the median (152.7–150.83) which is 1.25s per mile fast, that is 1.87x(8/12). That works out at 6.23 lengths per mile (1.25/0.2) but it's best to just dispense with the fractions at this stage and round it down to six lengths per mile. A raw speed figure is allocated to the race winner at this stage, based purely on the winning time and without any adjustments for the state of the track. With the race being six lengths per mile faster than median, once added to the base figure of 100 that would be a raw speed figure of 106. This was a Class 6 contest, so if you compare the raw speed figure of 106 with the class par of 101, this race is said to be five lengths per mile fast. To jump to the last race over 7f and give another example, the winning time was 0.63s faster than the median, which is 0.72s over a mile. That equates to 3.6 lengths, rounded down to three lengths per mile. Added to the base figure of 100, that gives a raw winner's speed figure of 103, so when compared to the class par of 101 this race was two lengths per mile fast. Here are the raw speed figures for each race:

RACE	PAR	WINNER	RAW SPEED RATING	COMP TO PAR
1	101	ARCADIAN FRIEND	106	-5
2	102	NEANDRA	112	-10
3	94	ROCKING ENDS	88	+6
4	98	SANDY PARADISE	103	-5
5	103	COUNSEL	98	+5
6	103	SHIGAR	95	+8
7	97	MELODRAMATICA	93	+4
8	101	HEALING POWER	103	-2

Remember that some of the class pars shown here may include allowances for younger horses and/or fillies, such as the second race which was a Class 4 handicap confined to three-year-olds in July, hence the par of 102 (105-3). Race seven was a Class 5 handicap restricted to three-year-old fillies, so a par of 97 (103-3-3).

These comparisons give an indication of how the track was riding, but with half the races run faster than par and the other half slower, it wouldn't suggest the going was particularly fast or slow. It is at this stage that we can work out a figure that would indicate how the track was riding and use that to modify the 'raw' speed figures shown earlier. The way I do this is to use the middle comparison as the benchmark, in the same way we calculated the median times earlier. That is to sort the comparisons to par into a list (biggest to smallest) and use the middle figures as the benchmark. Here the fastest comparison is race two (-10) and the slowest race six (+8) and with a meeting containing an odd number of races it would be straightforward to demonstrate. However, this meeting had eight races so I take an average of the two middle comparisons to par in the sorted list, which in this case would be races eight (-2) and seven (+4). The average of those two races is +1, which means that by my calculations the track was slowing the horses down by a length for every mile they ran.

This figure, sometimes known as a going allowance or a going correction but I prefer 'track variant', is then used to adjust each winner's speed figure, so that if the track had been riding perfectly then they would have run one length per mile faster than they did. Hence, I would show the following at the end of the meeting:

Track Variant = +1   Standard

The text description of Standard after the track variant is just to clarify the figure itself and is allocated depending on the parameters the figure falls within. A very quick track variant (a large negative figure) would be described as 'Very Fast' and a very slow variant (large positive figure) would be 'Very Slow'. In between you have Fast, Standard and Slow.

Once the raw rating for each winner had been adjusted to allow for the track variant, this is how they looked.

Race	Winner	Final Speed Figure
1	ARCADIAN FRIEND	107
2	NEANDRA	113
3	ROCKING ENDS	89
4	SANDY PARADISE	104
5	COUNSEL	99
6	SHIGAR	96
7	MELODRAMATICA	94
8	HEALING POWER	104

So how do we calculate the speed figures for the beaten horses? It's quite straightforward bearing in mind that, as was the case earlier, the longer the race distance the greater the potential for bigger margins between horses. The way to allow for this is to again adjust the beaten distance so that it would appear all races were run over a mile. For instance, if a horse finishes five lengths behind the winner over 5f and another is beaten 16 lengths behind the winner over 2m, they would both earn a speed figure eight points behind the first past the post (adjusted to 1m).

Here are the speed figures awarded to each horse at this Lingfield meeting:

Race 1

NAME	DATE	TRCK	DIST	TV	TYPE	POS	RAN	WGHT	DR	P	HGR	SR
ARCADIAN FRIEND	23JUL2022	LING	12	SD	6HCP	1	8	9-2	7	P	-	107
QUEEN OF CHANGE	23JUL2022	LING	12	SD	6HCP	2	8	9-6	3	P	-	104
BE FAIR	23JUL2022	LING	12	SD	6HCP	3	8	9-6	8	H	-	104
BIG WING	23JUL2022	LING	12	SD	6HCP	4	8	9-9	2	H	-	102
SHUT UP AND DANCE	23JUL2022	LING	12	SD	6HCP	5	8	9-5	6	L	-	99
PYRRHIC DANCER	23JUL2022	LING	12	SD	6HCP	6	8	8-10	5	H	C	98
WANNABE BETSY	23JUL2022	LING	12	SD	6HCP	7	8	9-8	9	H	-	92
MELEAGANT	23JUL2022	LING	12	SD	6HCP	8	8	9-8	1	H	-	91

Race 2

NAME	DATE	TRCK	DIST	TV	TYPE	POS	RAN	WGHT	DR	P	HGR	SR
NEANDRA	23JUL2022	LING	12	SD	4HCP	1	6	9-7	4	H	-	113
MASHKUUR	23JUL2022	LING	12	SD	4HCP	2	6	8-9	2	L	TB	109
THE GADGET MAN	23JUL2022	LING	12	SD	4HCP	3	6	9-11	6	H	-	107
CAPPOQUIN	23JUL2022	LING	12	SD	4HCP	4	6	9-2	1	H	-	105
DREAM HARDER	23JUL2022	LING	12	SD	4HCP	5	6	9-2	3	H	-	95
MHAJIM	23JUL2022	LING	12	SD	4HCP	6	6	9-7	5	P	-	94

Race 3

NAME	DATE	TRCK	DIST	TV	TYPE	POS	RAN	WGHT	DR	P	HGR	SR
ROCKING ENDS	23JUL2022	LING	5	SD	5CND	1	4	9-11	3	L	-	89
MIA PARADIS	23JUL2022	LING	5	SD	5CND	2	4	8-13	2	P	-	86
GUMAIS	23JUL2022	LING	5	SD	5CND	3	4	9-4	1	H	-	84
SENOR POCKETS	23JUL2022	LING	5	SD	5CND	4	4	9-4	4	H	H	79

Race 4

NAME	DATE	TRCK	DIST	TV	TYPE	POS	RAN	WGHT	DR	P	HGR	SR
SANDY PARADISE	23JUL2022	LING	8	SD	6HCP	1	10	9-4	11	H	-	104
TRANS MONTANA	23JUL2022	LING	8	SD	6HCP	2	10	9-8	7	P	V	103
SICILIAN VITO	23JUL2022	LING	8	SD	6HCP	3	10	9-9	3	L	B	102
BUNGLE BAY	23JUL2022	LING	8	SD	6HCP	4	10	8-13	6	H	-	101
BRYNTEG	23JUL2022	LING	8	SD	6HCP	5	10	9-10	8	H	-	100
DAMASCUS FINISH	23JUL2022	LING	8	SD	6HCP	6	10	9-6	9	H	-	99
THE SPOTLIGHT KID	23JUL2022	LING	8	SD	6HCP	7	10	9-7	5	P	-	99
FAMILLE VERTE	23JUL2022	LING	8	SD	6HCP	8	10	9-6	12	H	C	98
SILVERDALE	23JUL2022	LING	8	SD	6HCP	9	10	9-2	1	P	-	94
ADDIE BOO BOO	23JUL2022	LING	8	SD	6HCP	10	10	9-6	10	H	-	90

Race 5

NAME	DATE	TRCK	DIST	TV	TYPE	POS	RAN	WGHT	DR	P	HGR	SR
COUNSEL	23JUL2022	LING	7	SD	5CND	1	10	9-11	6	L	-	99
FASHION LOVE	23JUL2022	LING	7	SD	5CND	2	10	8-13	1	P	-	92
FLAG OF TRUTH	23JUL2022	LING	7	SD	5CND	3	10	9-4	2	H	-	92
SALCOMBE STORM	23JUL2022	LING	7	SD	5CND	4	10	9-4	5	H	-	91
DULY AMAZED	23JUL2022	LING	7	SD	5CND	5	10	9-4	4	L	H	91
KING OF THE DANCE	23JUL2022	LING	7	SD	5CND	6	10	9-4	7	H	-	87
SARKHA	23JUL2022	LING	7	SD	5CND	7	10	9-4	8	H	-	87
TWILIGHT MISCHIEF	23JUL2022	LING	7	SD	5CND	8	10	8-13	3	H	-	85
FAWN AT PLAY	23JUL2022	LING	7	SD	5CND	9	10	8-13	9	H	-	85
GLEN ETIVE	23JUL2022	LING	7	SD	5CND	10	10	9-4	10	H	-	70

Race 6

NAME	DATE	TRCK	DIST	TV	TYPE	POS	RAN	WGHT	DR	P	HGR	SR
SHIGAR	23JUL2022	LING	7	SD	5CND	1	9	9-5	5	H	-	96
FLYAWAYDREAM	23JUL2022	LING	7	SD	5CND	2	9	9-5	8	H	-	96
FAATTIK	23JUL2022	LING	7	SD	5CND	3	9	9-5	7	H	-	95
GRAND CRU GAGA	23JUL2022	LING	7	SD	5CND	4	9	9-0	10	P	-	93
FEDERAL STREET	23JUL2022	LING	7	SD	5CND	5	9	9-5	6	L	C	93
ZANDORA	23JUL2022	LING	7	SD	5CND	6	9	9-0	2	H	-	87
GLEN COVE	23JUL2022	LING	7	SD	5CND	7	9	9-5	1	H	-	87
MARLEY HEAD	23JUL2022	LING	7	SD	5CND	8	9	9-2	9	H	-	87
PERMATA	23JUL2022	LING	7	SD	5CND	9	9	9-2	4	H	-	81

Race 7

NAME	DATE	TRCK	DIST	TV	TYPE	POS	RAN	WGHT	DR	P	HGR	SR
MELODRAMATICA	23JUL2022	LING	7	SD	5HCP	1	8	9-10	6	P	-	94
PRENUP	23JUL2022	LING	7	SD	5HCP	2	8	9-9	5	H	-	94
PUBLIC OPINION	23JUL2022	LING	7	SD	5HCP	3	8	9-10	9	L	-	93
LOQUACE	23JUL2022	LING	7	SD	5HCP	4	8	9-6	2	H	-	93
BRIDES BAY	23JUL2022	LING	7	SD	5HCP	5	8	9-8	1	H	C	92
LUNA QUEEN	23JUL2022	LING	7	SD	5HCP	6	8	9-1	7	H	B	92
MY BONNIE LASSIE	23JUL2022	LING	7	SD	5HCP	7	8	8-6	4	P	-	91
BREACH	23JUL2022	LING	7	SD	5HCP	8	8	8-12	8	H	-	91

Race 8

NAME	DATE	TRCK	DIST	TV	TYPE	POS	RAN	WGHT	DR	P	HGR	SR
HEALING POWER	23JUL2022	LING	7	SD	6HCP	1	14	9-4	9	P	-	104
CATCH MY BREATH	23JUL2022	LING	7	SD	6HCP	2	14	9-9	5	H	B	101
SPERANZOSO	23JUL2022	LING	7	SD	6HCP	3	14	9-7	14	H	HT	99

CAPPANANTY CON	23JUL2022	LING	7	SD	6HCP	4	14	9-11	6	P	C	98
HECTOR LOZA	23JUL2022	LING	7	SD	6HCP	5	14	9-6	3	L	H	98
SIR SEDRIC	23JUL2022	LING	7	SD	6HCP	6	14	9-10	4	H	T	97
BROXI	23JUL2022	LING	7	SD	6HCP	7	14	9-10	12	H	-	97
PRINCESSE ANIMALE	23JUL2022	LING	7	SD	6HCP	8	14	10-0	11	H	H	96
RUITH LE TU	23JUL2022	LING	7	SD	6HCP	9	14	9-2	2	H	C	91
GOLDSMITH	23JUL2022	LING	7	SD	6HCP	10	14	9-7	10	H	H	90
DARK FLYER	23JUL2022	LING	7	SD	6HCP	11	14	9-2	8	H	C	89
INAAM	23JUL2022	LING	7	SD	6HCP	12	14	10-0	7	H	-	88
SIR PHILIP	23JUL2022	LING	7	SD	6HCP	13	14	9-3	1	H	-	87
MAGNIFIQUE	23JUL2022	LING	7	SD	6HCP	14	14	9-1	13	H	C	85

Once generated, these speed figures are immediately appended to my database so that they can be retrieved when a horse runs again. These figures can be seen in the right-hand column in the full race cards as first shown in the 'Assessing Form' chapter, but I also have a more abbreviated version which proved handy for the journal at the end of this book, otherwise the full versions of each race card would have covered a lot of pages! The format of these abbreviated figures is *nnnttdd* where:

nnn   is the speed figure
tt   is the name of the track
dd   is the race distance in furlongs

So 107Wo12 would mean that the horse earned a speed figure of 107 over 1m4f at Wolverhampton, while 98Li05 means the horse earned a speed figure of 98 over 5f at Lingfield.

I always automatically make a note of any horse (not just the winner) who has recorded a speed figure well ahead of the class par. For me that's any speed figure at least four points quicker than par, as this may indicate a horse who can win in a higher grade and would be especially interesting if able to contest the same (or even a lower) class in the near future. One such example here is the winner of the fourth race, Sandy Paradise. Richard Hannon's colt earned a speed figure of 104 for this success, which is six points better than the class par of 98. Despite that, he was allowed to go off at 7-1 when winning again at Kempton 11 days later.

THE EFFECT OF WEIGHT

This is one of the most controversial subjects when it comes to speed figures and one which I suggest may never be resolved. If anyone wishes to factor weight into their calculations, then that must be a personal choice. Some published speed figures are closely tied in with the official ratings scale, so it makes sense that they should include it. However, for me it just doesn't sit comfortably with what I'm trying to achieve. I can understand that adding a significant amount of weight on to a horse's back may have an effect over a long trip on gruelling ground, but that's not what we are talking about when it comes to All-Weather Flat racing.

If it's a question of physics, or how much should extra weight slow a horse down, then surely you must go the whole hog and include the weight of the horse itself, but we don't know it. Also, there is a danger that if you adjust for weight then you may be masking the true ability of the horse itself. We already know how fast a horse has run with our speed figures, so why not leave it at that? Taking weight off a horse's back won't give them a turn of speed they don't already have, and I found this out for myself when trying the get to the bottom of this whole subject a few years ago.

I took a group of horses and compared the weight they carried from one race to the next and noted any effect it had on their speed figures. I found that adding weight to a horse's back did slow them down by around a length for every extra 2lb they carried, but horses whose weight was reduced also slowed down a bit. The convenient explanation for this was that the reason these horses were slowing down was because they were out of form, but I wasn't comfortable with that reasoning. Either a difference in weight has an effect on all horses or it doesn't. You can't have a situation where it affects one group and not another, so for that reason I don't try and come up with some sort of mathematical formula to allow for weight. I would have been delighted if I had been able to find an acceptable one, but I couldn't and I'm not willing to come up with one merely because the weight factor is so ingrained in British handicapping.

TRACK AND PACE BIAS

Earlier in the book I listed the pace statistics (via Impact Values) for every distance at each of the All-Weather tracks. This is how they are calculated:

The pace statistics are divided into three groups, Front-Runners, Prominent Horses and Hold Up Horses. The Hold Up group covers all those who didn't lead or race prominently early. I could have broken the groups down even further to include mid-division horses and those who raced right out the back, but that would just be splitting hairs. If a horse races in mid-division or out the back of the field, then for me the jockey's intention is the same – not to press the pace. Anyway, the idea is to award some sort of figure to these groups to assess how each distance at each track is favoured towards or against those who race on or close to the pace.

The calculations are done in such a way that an Impact Value is created for each group. The easiest way to think of it is that if you had six races each contested by three horses, one who always leads, one who is always prominent and one who is always held up, then with all things being equal you would expect all three groups to have an Impact Value of 1.0. In other words, two of the races should have been won by the front-runners, two by the prominent horses and the other two by the hold up horses. Of course (and thankfully) things aren't like that. In many cases the IV for Front-Runners and Prominent Horses is above 1.0 and I firmly believe this is down to the nature of All-Weather racing, where early speed and the ability to take a handy position are even more important than on turf, where a turn of foot is a much more potent weapon.

All those who took a certain early position are grouped together as basically one horse. In other words, all those runners who were 'prominent', 'close up', 'chased leaders', 'tracked leaders', 'in touch', etc, go into the Prominent Horse category. If this wasn't done then the success rate of those held up off the pace (not leaders or prominent horses) would be artificially high, as there are usually more of them in one race. The way these calculations are done allows for this and the same method is used for the winners (by noting the early position they took). The two groups (runners and winners) for each distance are then compared to produce the IV.

A good example of how Impact Values can be helpful can be shown for the meeting at Chelmsford on 4 July 2020. Going into the fixture my statistics told me that the IV for Front-Runners over 7f was 2.3. In other words, within the previous year front-runners had won 2.3 times more often as they should have done on pure chance alone. Below is what happened with regard to the running styles of the five winners over that trip on the night, together with their close-up comments.

Winner	SP	First Part Of Close-Up Comment
Final Voyage	9-1	made all
Cesifire	10-1	made all
Afraid Of Nothing	17-2	soon led
Miss Celestial	7-2	made all
Full Intention	3-1	led until headed and chased leaders over 6f out

Looking at the odds of most of these horses suggested they weren't among those most fancied to win their respective contests, strongly suggesting that the track bias helped them. Armed with the impact values described above, even if it had taken a couple of races to twig that the track was riding as the data suggested it should, there was still time to take advantage of this situation. This sort of information would have been especially valuable to in-running players as, provided they felt bold enough, they could see who was in front after half a furlong or so and back them blind!

The following example is where spotting a pace bias early could have proved profitable. The meeting in question took place at Kempton on 8 September 2018 and it was the day Enable gained the first of her two wins in the September Stakes. That race was the first on the card and John Gosden's filly duly made all to beat Crystal Ocean by three and a half lengths in a four-horse race. Admittedly she had already shown that she liked to race handily, and she had made all the running before, but she wasn't an established one-dimensional trailblazer, yet her connections had no qualms about letting her stride on. They must have been confident that positive tactics on this track would suit.

Perhaps those paying attention would have taken more notice when the 9-4 favourite Indian Sounds made all to win the following 7f nursery, as if they concluded that there was indeed a speed bias in operation, they may well have been on War Glory who made all to win the London Mile Final at odds of 20-1!

Eyelool took the following mile nursery at 3-1 (pressed leader), Kessaar won the Group 3 Sirenia Stakes at 9-1 (tracked leaders), Podemos won the 1m3f handicap at 11-2 (led after 1f) and although the 7f handicap was won by 7-1 shot Redgrave (held up well in touch), the horse who attempted to make all the running finished third at 66-1. The Pace Index of 86 I awarded this meeting was very high and with the way I present All-Weather form this fact would be visible for every horse who ran at this meeting when they reappeared back on the All-Weather. In other words, if they had run well having always been handy, then the conclusion would be they were helped by the pace bias, whereas if they had never been able to get into it after being held up, they had a valid excuse.

Here is an example of how spotting a bias early should have had profitable consequences. The meeting took place at Chelmsford on 23 October 2021 and it started off with a three-runner novice over 7f. The race was won by the 2-1 second-favourite Windseeker, who started from stall one (nothing particularly significant in that) while handicap blot Ringo Starlight easily took the following 6f nursery with the horse drawn in stall one back in second. However, things then started to get interesting.

The third race, a 5f handicap, was won by the 9-4 favourite Shanghai Rock from stall two, followed by the horses drawn in stall three (22-1) and four (5-2). It was also noticeable that the first three winners had all raced close to the pace, so a handy early position and a low draw were beginning to look an advantage. Those who had latched on to this trend early enough would soon be in seventh heaven as the fourth race, a handicap over 1m, went to 28-1 shot El Camino who made all the running from stall one.

Araifjan then made all the running to win the following 6f handicap at 100-30 having started from stall three, while 2-1 favourite Love Poems took the 1m6f handicap, again from stall one. The 10-11 favourite Emblem Empire (stall one) then bolted up in the 1m2f novice, and although the lowest stall didn't win the final race (the horse starting from that stall was 50-1) it did go to a low-drawn contender in the shape of Wimpole Hall, who was successful from stall two. As I have indicated, in a 12-runner event over this trip at Chelmsford you could narrow it down to those drawn in the bottom half of the field, especially with the way things had already panned out at this meeting. With that in mind Wimpole Hall should never have been a 9-1 shot.

Spotting a significant draw bias before most punters do can be worth its weight in gold, but timing is everything. Firstly, you must be sure that any bias isn't just a temporary blip and that it will last long enough to be of value, while accepting that as time goes on and the bias persists it will become common knowledge and those horses apparently favoured by any bias will be over-bet. We have already seen evidence of this on turf (especially in sprint handicaps) with so many people combining horses drawn on the so-called favoured side being combined in exotics (exactas, tricasts, etc) that it drove the dividends down.

One personal experience I have of spotting a draw bias in time occurred in the mid-2000s. I noticed that horses drawn in stall one over the straight 5f on the Southwell Fibresand seemed to be winning with much greater regularity than average. In fact, horses drawn low were doing well in general, but it was those berthed closest to the far rail who really piqued my interest.

I happened to be keeping my own draw statistics at the time, so could see that it wasn't just my imagination, and the evidence became so noticeable that I ended up backing those horses drawn in stall one blind. Now I'm not one who normally finds following any system 'blind' particularly appealing, which just goes to show how strong this trend must have appeared to be at the time. I did make quite a bit of money for a couple of years until the trend started to disappear, but it was good while it lasted and looking back now, I can now see exactly how things panned out.

Below are the records of those horses drawn in stall one over 5f at Southwell between 2006 and 2008:

Year	Runners	Winners	% w/r	Profit/Loss (£1 level stake)
2006	50	11	22	+£27.75
2007	41	5	12	-£17.38
2008	65	10	15	+41.08
Totals	156	26	17	+£51.45

After 2008 the trend became much more sporadic and although there were occasions during the following years where a profit could

The draw can often be a crucial factor in how a race will turn out on the All-Weather (RP Photos).

have been made, it wasn't to the same degree as in 2006 and 2008. The only real question is how you could have avoided suffering the pain of that losing year in 2007. Probably the best solution would be to see what happens at the very start of the year and then make a judgment.

In January 2006 there were three winners from 11 runners drawn in stall one, being sent off at odds of 14-1, 13-2 and 7-2, while in 2008 there was a 25-1 winner on New Year's Day! As a result, it would have been perfectly acceptable to follow the trend for the rest of the calendar year. However, in January 2007 their record was 0-7 with none of the septet even being placed, which ought to have sounded the alarm bells. The advice then would have been to draw stumps and keep monitoring the situation until there was evidence that the bias was making a comeback, which the following year it most certainly did.

An area where this approach can be most profitable is when a new All-Weather track comes online or an existing one changes its racing surface. I have come across this situation many times over the years and usually you may have to wait several weeks or even months before there is enough data available on which to base meaningful statistics. Fortunately, Southwell staged quite a few fixtures in the early months after the surface change was changed to Tapeta in 2021. In fact, between the opening meeting on 7 December and before the end of the following March no fewer than 28 meetings were staged, so having reset my statistics after the old surface had disappeared it wasn't long before some patterns started to emerge and somewhat coincidentally the low draw bias over the straight 5f soon made a welcome return. I had to be sure it wasn't just a blip in these early fixtures and when it became clear that it was a genuine bias, I then began to exploit it. Below are the results of the first 11 races run over the straight 5f, showing how the runners drawn in the two lowest stalls (closest to the far rail) fared.

Date	Name	Draw	Position	SP
07/12/2021	Rose Hip	1	4	8-1
	Astro Jakk	2	3	28-1
10/12/2021	Giogiobbo	1	1	15-2
	Airshow	2	2	14-1
16/12/2021	Brandy Station	1	6	17-2
	Not Now Zeb	2	10	14-1
16/12/2021	Dusky Prince	1	6	15-2
	Lucky Man	2	3	9-4
16/12/2021	Papas Girl	1	1	22-1
	Cometh The Man	2	8	9-2
16/12/2021	Naughty Ana	1	5	11-1
	Khulu	2	1	4-1
17/12/2021	Charming Kid	1	5	4-1
	Phoenix Star	2	2	13-2
22/12/2021	Birkenhead	1	11	11-1
	Amasova	2	5	12-1
29/12/2021	Good To Go	1	4	11-1
	Share The Profits	2	1	14-1
29/12/2021	Bridgetown	1	2	4-7
	Bernard Spierpoint	2	1	9-2

29/12/2021	Giogiobbo	1	4	14-1
	Show Me A Sunset	2	2	3-1

As you can see, five of these races were won by horses drawn in either stall one or two and if you had put £10 to win on all 22 horses you would have made a profit of £350 based on starting price. It would have been even better than that if you had decided to be a little more adventurous, as on two occasions the two lowest-drawn horses finished first and second. The Giogiobbo/Airshow exacta paid £1,184 to a £10 stake, while the Bernard Spierpoint/Bridgetown exacta paid £96. It does take a little bit of effort to keep an eye out for occurrences like these, but it can be time well spent.

THE GOING

When it comes to turf racing, we all understand what terms such as 'the going' or 'the ground' mean, but what about on All-Weather tracks? Do we treat a slow surface on sand the same way we treat soft ground on turf? Does a fast surface on the All-Weather suit front-runners while a slow surface makes it more difficult for them?

They aren't the easiest questions to answer, especially when attempting to assess how a surface will ride before the meeting gets under way. On turf it's usually obvious when the ground is likely to be testing. Having twice fallen flat on my face while trying to cross the course at Newbury in the winter of 2021/22 (causing my glasses to shift on my nose with the result that I looked like Eric Morecambe), I can concur that the going was testing. The muddy state of my clothing would bear witness to the fact, and I didn't need any other evidence that this was the case. However, on the All-Weather tracks things are rather less clear.

We rely on any information we may get beforehand regarding the preparation of the track, such as if it has been deep-harrowed. The BHA website is a good place to view such information, but where does it get us? Occasionally you may see that the official going description for a certain track is something different from the usual 'Standard', perhaps 'Standard to Slow', and if this is the case then I place extra emphasis on a horse's stamina, just as you would on soft turf. It's not an exact science, though, and I'm of the opinion that an assessment of the going is of more relevance once the meeting is over.

We will be using the race times to calculate the speed figures as explained in the previous chapter, so we have a pretty good idea of how the track was riding, something the clerk of the course doesn't necessarily have before the meetings starts. We calculate the track variant as part of the procedure to calculate the speed figures, so what we now need is a way of telling what impact this bias had on the results, especially in terms of running styles.

The way I do it is to use some of the information I have already collected to help with this procedure. After all, I have made a note of the early position that each horse took (Led, Prominent or Held Up) so that it can be included in the race card (as shown in the 'Assessing Form' chapter) for when the horse reappears. I use this to produce a 'Pace' figure for an individual meeting and I award points like this.

200 points: if a horse has led early and won
100 points: if a horse has led early and finished second or third, or if a horse raced prominently early and won
50 points: if a horse raced prominently early and finished second or third

The task is quite manageable as it's only the first three horses home I will be monitoring in each contest. I then add all the points together and divide that by the number of horses in the sample, so for a seven-race meeting that will be 21 horses. The result is a Pace Index (shown under 'Bias' in the horse's form in the full race cards), or at least that is what I call it, and it's an easy way for me to keep a record of how a track was riding when I look back at a horse's form. This Pace Index is on a scale of 0 to 100 (though in exceptional circumstances it is possible to get one higher than that, these are the parameters I use:

Pace Index	Description
0-20	The track was making it hard for those ridden prominently, therefore suiting hold up horses
21-40	A small bias towards those ridden from off the pace, though it was possible for prominently ridden horses to win
41-60	No significant bias either way
61-80	A small bias towards those who raced prominently, though it was possible for those ridden from off the pace to win
81+	A significant bias towards those who raced on or close to the pace, while those who tried to come from further back were disadvantaged

As usual the best way to demonstrate this method is with a real example. This meeting took place at Chelmsford on 10 May 2018. The first three home are shown in each race together with the early position they took.

Race	First Three	Close-Up Comment	Speed Points
1	Mr Marrakech	tracked leaders	100
	Tadbir	led	100
	Glendavon	tracked leader	50
2	Lucymai	made all	200
	Take The Helm	chased winner	50
	Eljaddaaf	held up in touch	50
3	Mesquite	soon pressing leader	100
	Fountain Of Time	soon led	100
	Talaaqy	soon tracking leaders	50
4	Poet's Prince	soon led	200
	Desert Wind	led early	100
	Zaaki	held up in rear	0
5	Weekender	soon led	200
	Higher Power	chased winner	50
	Ocean Of Love	led briefly	100
6	Elgin	tracked leaders	100
	Its'afreebee	held up in last pair	0
	The Otmoor Poet	chased leader	50
7	Zamjar	chased leaders	100
	Something Lucky	held up in touch	50
	Excellent George	chased leader	50
	Total		**1800**

The total number of horses in the sample is 21, so 1,800 divided by 21 results in a Pace Index of 86.

The reason I selected this fixture is that on a scale of 0-100 a Pace Index of 86 is very high indeed, which means that on the night Chelmsford was a speed-favouring track. That is hardly a surprise looking at the close-up comments for the principals. What is interesting is that the track variant for this meeting was -12. In other words, the track was speeding the horses up by 12 lengths for every mile they ran, so there was very likely a correlation between the quickness of the track and the ability of horses to maintain a prominent position right to the end.

Here is another meeting for the same track on 13 January 2022:

Race	First Three	Close-Up Comment	Speed Points
1	Cinzento	held up in behind leaders	0
	Hannalite	held up in rear	0
	Miss Pollyanna	held up in midfield	0
2	Oasis Irlandes	held up in behind leaders	0
	Shin Saw Gyi	in rear and ran green	0
	Debit Card	led	100
3	Cerulean	led after 1f	200
	Eltham Palace	disputed lead	100
	Typewritten	midfield	0
4	Morlaix	held up in rear	0
	Alhammaam	tracked leaders	50
	Athmad	led	100
5	Dubai Emperor	held up in behind leaders	0
	Diamonds At Dusk	chased leader	50
	Copake	held up in last	0
6	Whittle Le Woods	held up in midfield	0
	Legende D'Art	held up in rear	0
	Full Intention	chased leaders	50
7	Trevie Fountain	in rear	0
	The Game Of Life	in rear	0
	Million Reasons	midfield	0
		Total	**650**

With seven races taking place on the card the total number of horses in the sample is again 21, so 650 divided by 21 results in a Pace Index of 31.

As you can see this Pace Index suggested a bias towards those held up, but not an overwhelming one. In the third race those who raced handily were favoured, but in the other six contests it was harder work for those who raced up with the pace. This sort of information is useful as it means you can decide if a horse's performance flatters them, as they may have been aided by a track bias, and equally it's possible to forgive a seemingly below-par effort if the bias was against them.

Interestingly, the going allowance for this meeting was +20, which means the track was slowing the horses down by 20 lengths for every mile they ran. That could well explain why those who expended a bit more energy early failed to last home.

SECTIONAL TIMES

It has taken a while for sectional times to become part of everyday handicapping in this country, but there is certainly a lot more information in the public domain now than there used to be, which is just as well as I don't fancy having to sit down and time every race furlong per furlong, even if I'm restricting myself to the All-Weather. I just don't have the time (literally), though I have done it on occasions where the data isn't widely available and there is something I wish to check for my own satisfaction.

I wasn't originally sure of the best way to use sectional times. I knew it was important, so I wanted to incorporate some sort of sectional time data into my existing All-Weather race cards even though I didn't have a huge amount of space available, so a complete pace chart was unrealistic. I have managed to include something, which I will describe in more detail later.

When I focussed on the winner's final time only, say 1m 36.8s for a one-mile race, that was the time it had taken that horse to cover the journey from the stalls to the winning post, but it can have been achieved in many ways. For instance, if you had two consecutive races over that trip and the winning time was the same for both, were the winner's achievements the same? Their respective speed figures would suggest they were, but a glance at the sectional times may suggest otherwise.

Let's imagine that the leaders in Race 1 reached the halfway point (after 4f) in 50s (much slower than the average split time for the trip, which for the sake of argument in this example is 48.5s), while in Race 2 they took 47s (much faster), then clearly the last half a mile of the second contest took longer. That is significant when you consider the respective winners' running styles. To demonstrate how this information can be used let's put a bit more detail on these two races.

Sectional Times are an important tool in working out the distribution of effort during a race and how that may affect the outcome (Proshot Photography).

RACE	WINNING TIME (SEC)	HALFWAY SPLIT (4F)	WINNER'S CLOSE-UP COMMENT
1	96.8	50.0	held up in last, headway over 2f out, switched right and ridden over 1f out, ran on strongly inside final furlong, led towards finish
2	96.8	47.0	led, pushed along over 2f out, ridden inside final furlong, kept on strongly, just prevailed

In these circumstances both winners would get credit from me, especially if it turned out their performances had resulted in a good speed figure. The winner of the first race had managed to come from last in a steadily run race, which is never an easy thing to do, while the winner of the second race had set a strong pace and managed to maintain it to the line despite being pressurised late. The narrow winning margin didn't matter, this horse had shown that he/she could keep up a searching gallop and in my mind that demonstrates a touch of class.

However, let's now turn things on their head.

RACE	WINNING TIME (SEC)	HALFWAY SPLIT (4F)	WINNER'S CLOSE-UP COMMENT
1	96.8	47.0	held up in last, headway over 2f out, switched right and ridden over 1f out, ran on strongly inside final furlong, led towards finish
2	96.8	50.0	led, pushed along over 2f out, ridden inside final furlong, kept on strongly, just prevailed

Now the first race is the one in which the pace was very strong until halfway. The final speed figures will be the same, but I would see the respective winners' performances in a slightly different light. The first winner is likely to have benefitted from the leaders going off too quick and had conserved their energy for the business end (often called a place collapse) and so they may be flattered.

With the second winner it's likely they benefitted from being able to set a steady pace without being pressurised and, as has been stated before in this book, any horse who is allowed to establish an uncontested lead is a dangerous opponent. Again, I would consider them to have been potentially flattered and you often find that horses like this cannot reproduce this sort of performance if taken on for the lead from some way out.

Here is an example of a race where the leaders went off far too quick and the winner enjoyed the perfect trip as a result. The contest took place over 6f at Lingfield on 31 March 2022.

POS	NAME	6f-5f	5f-4f	4f-3f	3f-2f	2f-1f	1f-fin	FINAL TIME
1	Lilkian	10.44	10.80	11.51	11.69	12.04	12.57	1m 12.04
2	Cappananty Con	11.26	10.72	11.39	11.44	11.99	12.26	1m 12.06
3	Glamorous Force	10.76	10.76	11.65	11.31	11.89	12.94	1m 12.31
4	Knockout Blow	11.19	10.75	11.25	11.37	12.11	12.78	1m 12.45
5	Intervention	11.85	10.63	11.10	11.26	12.10	12.84	1m 12.78
6	Otago	11.43	10.74	11.41	11.66	12.28	12.66	1m 13.19
7	Pablo Del Pueblo	10.21	10.51	11.63	11.88	12.61	13.48	1m 13.32
8	May Remain	11.11	10.77	11.35	11.39	12.25	13.48	1m 13.34
9	Cool Spirit	10.28	10.53	11.60	11.92	12.53	13.58	1m 13.44
10	Champagne Supanova	10.97	10.80	11.49	11.56	12.40	13.50	1m 13.71

Note: the first furlong takes approximately three seconds longer to run than the others due to the standing start. The first-furlong splits have been reduced by that amount to give a more meaningful comparison with the rest of the race.

The key to how this race was run are the splits for the second furlong, where the entire field dipped under 11 seconds, and it was at this stage the damage was done. Not only did the two leaders, Pablo Del Pueblo and Cool Spirit, go off much too fast, they also took each other on which was never going to do either of them much good. The chart above confirmed what had appeared to be the case to the naked eye, but it doesn't always follow that what appears to be a strong pace really is. You ideally need the data in this format to confirm it.

The early position a horse takes can be a crucial factor if a certain running style is favoured (Proshot Photography).

The winner, Lilkian, was given a peach of a ride, despite his jockey being a 7lb claimer. Liam Wright must have figured that the front pair were doing too much, so instead of mixing it with them he took the gelding back after 1f or so and sat about three lengths off them. Not only did that give him something to aim at, but it also meant he would be in the ideal position when the pace collapsed, as would Glamorous Force who was one place behind him at that stage. Inevitably the pace did collapse as the field turned for home and Lilkian and Glamorous Force took over, with the former going on to win by a diminishing margin. The two tearaway leaders dropped away to finish seventh and ninth.

Looking at those figures on the chart is quite revealing, especially how slow the runners were going over that last furlong. It was almost a slow-motion finish with Lilkian being the victor due to decelerating the least! As a matter of interest, Cappananty Con came from a long way back to grab second (failing by just a head to catch the winner) and on the face of it he looked an eye-catcher, but he is a renowned hold up horse who likes to pick up the pieces following a pace collapse and that is exactly what happened here. Anyone who expected him to fare better soon was going to be disappointed, while those who looked at the way this race was run would have realised that it was perfect for him, but he still hadn't quite been able to take advantage. At the time of writing his losing run was up to 27.

I mentioned that I wanted to include something in my full race cards that would give an indication of how a race was run. The way I do this is to measure how long it has taken for the field to reach the halfway stage of any race. It's not as detailed as the chart shown earlier, but it will show which half of the contest was run at the stronger pace and the result could be displayed in a single column on the card.

I went about establishing a set of standard split times for the halfway stage of all race distances at each All-Weather track, using the same method as for finding the median times (the middle entry in the list). With those in the tool bag, this is how I came up with the sectional time figures for the same Lingfield meeting I used to demonstrate how I calculate my speed figures.

The first race on the card was over 1m4f, for which the standard split time is 78.03s. The field reached the halfway stage (after 6f) in 75.46s, meaning it was 2.57s quicker than the standard split. We now come across a familiar situation, in that as the race distance increases the scope for bigger margins between the split time and the standard split time becomes greater, so we again adjust the difference between these two times to make it seem as though all races had been run over the trip of a mile. That means that instead of 2.57s being recorded as the sectional figure for this race, it will be 1.71s, or 2.57x(8/12). The same adjustment is made for the other differences between the split time and standard split on the card. These are the results.

RACE	WINNER	SPEED RATING	DIFF PER MILE (SEC)
1	ARCADIAN FRIEND	107	-1.71
2	NEANDRA	113	-2.39
3	ROCKING ENDS	89	+4.34
4	SANDY PARADISE	104	-0.79
5	COUNSEL	99	+1.27
6	SHIGAR	96	+1.86
7	MELODRAMATICA	94	+2.07
8	HEALING POWER	104	-1.97

There is one final adjustment to be made, though, as if the track was slowing the horses up significantly then the sectional figures would all be slow and if the track was riding quick then the sectional figures would be fast. We needed some sort of modifier to allow for the speed of the track, but we already have it. As part of calculating the speed figures we also came up with a track variant which for this meeting was +1 (or +0.2s per mile). We now need to adjust the sectional figures by that amount to show that the track was responsible for the runners reaching the halfway point one length per mile slower than they would have on a perfectly standard track. You now get this:

Race	Winner	Speed Rating	Diff (sec)	Diff (adjusted)
1	ARCADIAN FRIEND	107	-1.71	-1.91
2	NEANDRA	113	-2.39	-2.59
3	ROCKING ENDS	89	+4.34	+4.14
4	SANDY PARADISE	104	-0.79	-0.99
5	COUNSEL	99	+1.27	+1.07
6	SHIGAR	96	+1.86	+1.66
7	MELODRAMATICA	94	+2.07	+1.87
8	HEALING POWER	104	-1.97	-2.17

It is those figures in the column on the far right which make their way into the full race cards. Here is another example of how they are shown with the sectional figure column in bold.

1-00   CAZOO HANDICAP (DIV I) (0-55) (6) 3-Y-O+ (Winner 3726.00)
7.2f   Par 101   12 runners   Median Time 1m 28.7
1 (4)   FAR FROM A RUBY 5-9-11 KATIE SCOTT - SAM JAMES

Sire FARHH	Runners	60	Wins	11	(18%)P/L -14.05
Trainer	Runners	20	Wins	2	(10%) P/L -11.00
Jockey	Rides	123	Wins	16	(13%) P/L -29.10

AW Form

DATE	TRACK	SURF	DIST	GNG	BIAS	RTYPE	POS	RAN	WGHT	DR	PCE	HDGR	SECTNL	SF
01MAR2022	NEWC	TPTA	7.1	VS	46	6HCP	9	12	9-7	5	L	H	-0.60	94
21FEB2022	NEWC	TPTA	8	VS	50	6HCP	10	10	9-0	4	H	-	+0.44	91
26JAN2022	KEMP	POLY	7	SW	48	5HCP	8	9	9-0	1	P	-	+0.06	95
10JAN2022	WOLV	TPTA	8.6	SD	52	5HCP	4	10	9-7	9	P	-	-1.22	101
30SEP2021	LING	POLY	8	SD	35	5HCP	4	12	9-2	2	P	-	-0.58	102
18SEP2021	WOLV	TPTA	7.2	SD	63	5HCP	3	8	9-0	8	P	-	+2.76	93
04SEP2021	WOLV	TPTA	8.6	SW	40	6HCP	1	9	9-5	1	H	-	-0.29	99
07JUL2021	KEMP	POLY	8	SD	44	6HCP	1	14	9-0	2	L	-	-0.25	103
21JUN2021	WOLV	TPTA	7.2	SD	69	6HCP	5	11	9-6	1	H	-	+0.14	96
28APR2021	WOLV	TPTA	7.2	SW	46	5HCP	4	7	8-8	5	P	-	-1.72	105
24APR2021	WOLV	TPTA	7.2	SD	69	6HCP	3	11	9-5	4	H	-	-1.98	104
27MAR2021	WOLV	TPTA	7.2	SD	46	6HCP	2	12	8-12	1	H	-	-0.39	104
12MAR2021	LING	POLY	7	SD	43	6HCP	2	12	9-2	2	H	-	-1.56	102

Incidentally, the halfway sectional figure for that Lingfield race won by Lilkian was a whopping -3.57s, which equates to about 18 lengths! Now that's what I call optimism.

SHAPE OF THE RACE

What do we mean by the shape of the race? It may mean different things to different people, but for me it just means working out what position I think each horse will take in the early stages of the race. Will they be at or near the front, will they be tucked away in midfield, or will they be held up near the back to be produced with a late run? Also, will how one horse is ridden in the race affect the chances of another? That can be a crucial question, especially when it comes to front-runners as some can resent being taken on early. They can sulk, or they can expend too much energy in trying to take on the other pacesetter which often, though not always, scuppers each of their prospects. The term often used is 'cutting each other's throats', though I'm not a keen fan of that phrase.

The prospective shape of the race can often be linked to the running styles of the horses taking part, and fortunately the 'Pace' column in the full race cards shown in this book gives an insight into how a horse may be ridden, based on how they have been in the past. The most obvious advantage of being able to do so would be if you saw the 'L' (led) symbol several times against one horse in a race, but it didn't appear much among the opposition. In that case you could be looking at a horse that could be left alone in front and therefore be able to dominate. If so, then their pure ability becomes less significant than it normally would, as any front-runner able to establish an uncontested lead is always a dangerous opponent. Of course, if they were already a serious contender based on several other factors and this discovery merely enhances their prospects in your eyes, then open the wallet and have more on!

Another interesting situation is where more than one horse clearly likes to go forward according to the data we have, as then we could be looking at a contested lead and that could put me off a horse who appeared to have a strong chance otherwise. As I said earlier, if a confirmed front-runner must fight for the early lead, then they are not going to have as much in reserve for when things get tougher later on. They can have all the right credentials to be able to win the type of race they are taking part in, but if the shape of the race goes against them it doesn't matter how much ability they have or how much they appear to have in hand.

There are occasions when the 'L' symbol is conspicuous by its absence among all the runners, and this is another situation that should set the alarm bells ringing. Some horses just need a strong pace to aim at, so rely on established trailblazers to set things up for them. If indeed no one wishes to go on and you end up with a falsely run race, then anything can happen, and proven ability goes out of the window. There is nothing more frustrating than seeing a horse you think has strong claims ruin their chance by pulling like mad (expending valuable energy in the process) or even more galling, finding themselves in a terrible position when the pace eventually lifts.

Although we do have the ability to predict how a race might pan out judged by how horses have been ridden in the past, there is no guarantee things will work out the way we think they will. After all, if you are the rider of a confirmed front-runner and you know there are two or three of your opponents who usually adopt the same tactics, it's highly unlikely they will all still go ahead and try to lead early. One or two may decide to drop in, but though doing so may help the horse's prospects on the day because it means they won't blow themselves out before the race has really begun in earnest, the change of running style may not suit them, as they are being asked to adopt a position that is not their most favoured. Either way, their goose may be well and truly cooked.

It's not all bad news, though, because we now can back horses in-running, so if we have selected one who likes to front-run but is up against similar types, once the contest has got under way, we may find that our selection is going to enjoy the run of the race after all. In other words, it's never too late. There will still be many races where things pan out just as we predicted they would, though, and if that has been a big factor in us finding a winner, the satisfaction is merely enhanced.

Here is a race which wasn't quite run in the way that might have been expected based on previous running styles, but it is a good example of where the shape of the race was crucial, especially when placed alongside a developing track bias. It should have produced a positive outcome for me. I say 'should', because I was too slow to react and rued the missed opportunity at my leisure. This example is also more a case of where those who bet in-running would have capitalised the most, had they been paying attention, while those (like me) who try to predict how a race might pan out based on established running styles wouldn't have necessarily done so.

The meeting took place at Wolverhampton on 29 July 2022 and the race below was the sixth contest on the card.

4-30   DOWNLOAD THE AT THE RACES APP HANDICAP (0-60) (6) 3-Y-O (Winner 3726.00)
5.1f   Par 98   8 runners   Median Time 1m 1.2

1 (3)   FAIR AND SQUARE 3-9-11(B) RONALD HARRIS – CONNOR BEASLEY

Sire KODIAC	Runners	720	Wins	61	(8%) P/L -244.65
Trainer	Runners	248	Wins	24	(10%) P/L -45.54
Jockey	Rides	106	Wins	10	(9%) P/L -52.13

AW Form

DATE	TRACK	SURF	DIST	GNG	BIAS	RTYPE	POS	RAN	WGHT	DR	PCE	HDGR	SECTNL	SF
13JUN2022	LING	POLY	5	SD	35	5HCP	3	7	9-4	1	L	EB	+0.29	96
03MAY2022	LING	POLY	5	SD	62	5HCP	4	8	9-7	4	P	HC	+0.86	88
28FEB2022	WOLV	TPTA	5.1	SD	46	5HCP	3	8	8-11	3	L	HC	+0.67	100
04FEB2022	LING	POLY	5	SD	64	6HCP	2	8	9-6	1	L	V	-0.22	101
28JAN2022	LING	POLY	5	SD	48	5HCP	2	9	8-12	9	P	B	-0.91	105
14JAN2022	WOLV	TPTA	5.1	SD	56	6HCP	2	8	9-3	4	L	B	-0.51	100
16DEC2021	SOUT	TPTA	5	SW	38	5HCP	7	12	8-9	5	P	B	+0.24	93
30NOV2021	LING	POLY	5	SD	19	6HCP	3	10	9-3	8	L	B	+0.31	97
02NOV2021	LING	POLY	5	SD	58	5HCP	3	9	8-9	2	P	B	+0.10	92
21OCT2021	WOLV	TPTA	5.1	SD	48	5HCP	3	11	9-0	4	P	B	+0.47	96
17AUG2021	WOLV	TPTA	6.1	SD	38	5HCP	7	9	9-8	9	H	-	+0.57	82

2(7)   MY JOKER (IRE) 3-9-9 MICHAEL ATTWATER – RHYS CLUTTERBUCK(3)

Sire FREE EAGLE	Runners	51	Wins	10	(20%) P/L -8.97
Trainer	Runners	88	Wins	6	(7%) P/L -38.20
Jockey	Rides	57	Wins	9	(16%) P/L -16.84

AW Form

DATE	TRACK	SURF	DIST	GNG	BIAS	RTYPE	POS	RAN	WGHT	DR	PCE	HDGR	SECTNL	SF
05JUL2022	WOLV	TPTA	5.1	SW	60	6HCP	4	11	9-7	1	P	-	+0.48	96

DATE	TRACK	SURF	DIST	GNG	BIAS	RTYPE	POS	RAN	WGHT	DR	PCE	HDGR	SECTNL	SF
17MAY2022	WOLV	TPTA	5.1	SD	60	6HCP	3	10	9-9	6	P	-	+0.84	93
26FEB2022	LING	POLY	5	SD	42	5MDN	3	9	8-11	1	H	-	+1.61	96
04FEB2022	LING	POLY	5	SD	64	6HCP	3	8	9-4	6	H	-	-0.22	101
26JAN2022	LING	POLY	5	SW	45	5MDN	7	10	9-5	5	P	-	-0.17	95
27DEC2021	WOLV	TPTA	6.1	SD	44	5CND	6	13	9-5	7	P	-	+0.41	88
20NOV2021	LING	POLY	6	SD	48	5MDN	5	10	9-5	6	L	-	+1.75	87

3 (5)   HOTTER IN TIME 3-9-7 DAVID O'MEARA – MARK WINN(7)

Sire HOT STREAK	Runners	86	Wins	6	(7%) P/L +27.00
Trainer	Runners	375	Wins	41	(11%) P/L -64.68
Jockey	Rides	9	Wins	1	(11%) P/L -1.50

No AW Form

4 (8)   MISS BELLADONNA 3-9-3 DEREK SHAW – TOM EAVES

Sire BRAZEN BEAU	Runners	135	Wins	18	(13%) P/L -27.58
Trainer	Runners	270	Wins	21	(8%) P/L -97.37
Jockey	Rides	243	Wins	14	(6%) P/L -132.04

AW Form

DATE	TRACK	SURF	DIST	GNG	BIAS	RTYPE	POS	RAN	WGHT	DR	PCE	HDGR	SECTNL	SF
20JUN2022	WOLV	TPTA	5.1	VS	62	5HCP	2	6	8-4	2	P	-	-1.10	102
28MAY2022	CHEL	POLY	5	SD	43	6HCP	1	10	8-9	11	H	-	-0.22	97
17MAY2022	WOLV	TPTA	5.1	SD	60	6HCP	2	10	8-4	9	H	-	+0.84	94
06MAY2022	WOLV	TPTA	5.1	SD	62	6HCP	4	8	8-9	7	H	-	+0.84	93
12MAR2022	WOLV	TPTA	5.1	SD	40	6HCP	3	7	8-8	8	H	-	+1.21	96
04NOV2021	CHEL	POLY	6	SD	44	6HCP	10	12	8-6	5	H	-	-0.46	80
23OCT2021	CHEL	POLY	6	SD	56	6HCP	7	12	9-2	6	H	-	+0.18	83
21AUG2021	CHEL	POLY	6	FT	55	5CND	5	10	8-12	3	H	-	+1.77	85
09AUG2021	WOLV	TPTA	6.1	SW	56	5CND	7	7	9-0	3	H	-	+0.95	76

5 (4)   PRIMO 3-9-2 ROGER FELL – LIAM KENIRY

Sire ACCLAMATION	Runners	399	Wins	39	(10%) P/L -64.73
Trainer	Runners	103	Wins	7	(7%) P/L +3.75
Jockey	Rides	304	Wins	19	(6%) P/L -152.31

AW Form

DATE	TRACK	SURF	DIST	GNG	BIAS	RTYPE	POS	RAN	WGHT	DR	PCE	HDGR	SECTNL	SF
25APR2022	SOUT	TPTA	7.1	FT	52	6HCP	9	9	9-5	5	H	T	+0.86	79
20JUL2021	CHEL	POLY	6	SD	67	4CND	7	8	9-2	9	H	-	+1.29	78
21JUN2021	WOLV	TPTA	5.1	SD	69	4CND	5	10	8-13	6	H	-	-0.07	80

6 (2)   PEARL OF KUWAIT (IRE) 3-8-9(V) MARK USHER - CHARLIE BENNETT

Sire PEARL SECRET	Runners	22	Wins	1	(5%) P/L -17.00
Trainer	Runners	196	Wins	16	(8%) P/L -70.32
Jockey	Rides	194	Wins	13	(7%) P/L -69.15

AW Form

DATE	TRACK	SURF	DIST	GNG	BIAS	RTYPE	POS	RAN	WGHT	DR	PCE	HDGR	SECTNL	SF
23MAY2022	WOLV	TPTA	7.2	SD	40	5HCP	11	11	8-6	11	H	-	-0.99	90
14JAN2022	WOLV	TPTA	5.1	SD	56	6HCP	8	8	9-2	5	H	-	-0.51	81
13DEC2021	CHEL	POLY	6	SD	45	4CND	10	12	9-0	5	H	-	+1.03	79
26JUL2021	WOLV	TPTA	5.1	SW	50	5CND	2	5	9-0	4	P	-	+1.33	89

7 (6)   NEXT SECOND 3-8-9 RUTH CARR - JOSEPHINE GORDON

Sire HOT STREAK	Runners	86	Wins	6	(7%) P/L +27.00
Trainer	Runners	241	Wins	18	(7%) P/L -54.75
Jockey	Rides	248	Wins	16	(6%) P/L -187.14

AW Form

DATE	TRACK	SURF	DIST	GNG	BIAS	RTYPE	POS	RAN	WGHT	DR	PCE	HDGR	SECTNL	SF
17MAY2022	WOLV	TPTA	5.1	SD	60	6HCP	7	10	8-12	4	H	B	+0.84	89
04OCT2021	WOLV	TPTA	5.1	SD	33	6HCP	3	11	9-5	1	H	-	+1.25	93

8 (1)   ARKID 3-8-9(T) LES EYRE - SAM JAMES

Sire ARDAD	Runners	24	Wins	1	(4%) P/L -18.50
Trainer	Runners	29	Wins	0	(0%) P/L -29.00
Jockey	Rides	123	Wins	16	(13%) P/L -29.10

AW Form

DATE	TRACK	SURF	DIST	GNG	BIAS	RTYPE	POS	RAN	WGHT	DR	PCE	HDGR	SECTNL	SF
13FEB2022	SOUT	TPTA	5	SW	75	6HCP	8	8	9-7	9	H	T	-0.06	83
21JAN2022	SOUT	TPTA	6.1	VS	31	6HCP	8	12	9-3	1	P	T	-0.11	84
08JAN2022	LING	POLY	5	SD	40	6HCP	2	8	9-3	4	P	T	+0.04	97
29DEC2021	SOUT	TPTA	5	SD	56	6HCP	3	14	8-12	4	P	T	+0.76	92
22OCT2021	NEWC	TPTA	5	FT	64	6HCP	9	11	8-6	2	H	-	+2.07	84

Running Style Impact Values And Draw Statistics Over 5.1f In Past Year

Front-Runners	2.0
Prominent Horses	1.4
Hold Up Horses	0.5

Stall	Runners	Winners	w/r(%)
1	71	12	17
2	74	16	22
3	75	11	15
4	76	11	14
5	75	7	9
6	67	6	9
7	63	8	13
8	58	3	5
9	46	1	2
10	34	2	6
11	24	1	4

When researching the race beforehand, I expected Fair And Square might lead as he had done so often in the past and that would set the race up perfectly for my fancy Miss Belladonna, who needed a strong pace to run at, but as the preceding races on the card went by I began to worry. Below are details of the six races which preceded our contest, showing the early position taken by each winner.

Race	Distance	Winner	Early Position (close-up comment)
1	7f	Contactless	prominent
2	7f	Bold Territories	in touch with leaders
3	1m	Dew You Believe	made all
4	1m	Bora Bora	made all
5	1m4f	Haskoy	midfield
6	5f	Grace Angel	made all

Up to this point five of the six races were won by horses that had either been on, or close to, the early pace. In fact, most of the placed horses were also handy, so it was clear that a significant pace bias was in operation. The question was how would this affect my assessment of the upcoming 5f race?

It became clear that my original selection Miss Belladonna was going to have a problem, being an established 'closer', but did this mean that Fair And Square was now a good thing? At first glance it might seem so, especially as he had lots of placings in his form figures, but now comes the value of delving a little deeper and being able to see as many races as you can. Despite having been placed 12 times in his career, he was still a 21-race maiden and if you had seen him often enough you would probably have concluded, like me, that he was a short-runner. That is a horse who barely stays 5f, even on a sharp track like Lingfield.

The Wolverhampton track was certainly suiting horses with early speed such as him, but his record just made it impossible to support him, so how on earth he was allowed to go off the 11-10 favourite is beyond me. Even though I don't like laying horses at odds against, I was a little tempted given how close he was getting towards Evens, but in the end I just decided to just watch the race out of interest.

As it turned out Fair And Square didn't (or couldn't) lead and had to be content with a stalking position. The early leader was 25-1 shot Next Second and, you guessed it, she was never going to be caught and became the fourth horse to make all on the afternoon. I had decided to keep my powder dry, and it was a good job I didn't support Miss Belladonna, who endured a wide trip and never got involved, but perhaps I had missed a trick. With what I had seen so far, I was right in feeling that the early leader also had a good chance of being the winner, but I should have waited to see who that was and if it wasn't Fair And Square, I should have backed them in-running as soon as I could. I had the evidence right there in front of me, so why hadn't I used it to my advantage?

Fair And Square did what he usually does and faded towards the end, eventually finishing fifth. However, despite this being another example of him not getting the trip, he was sent off 5-2 favourite at Windsor just ten days later, but after making the early running he yet again faded to finish third of the seven runners. Sometimes you just want to weep.

As a conclusion to this chapter, I would like to take us back to where I had shown the running styles for each of the earlier winners on the Wolverhampton card. The fifth race had been won by a horse named Haskoy who had managed to win from a midfield position, and it's worth taking a closer look at this contest as it perfectly demonstrates the value of taking a broad look at what was going on. We have concluded without any doubt there was a big pace bias at this fixture, so if a horse manages to win against a bias, then they must be noted.

Haskoy was making her racecourse debut in this 1m4f novice (a race won by star stayer Trueshan three years earlier), but not only that Ralph Beckett's three-year-old was also the only filly in the field. However, despite one or two signs of greenness she ran out a most impressive seven-length winner from a couple of rivals who had already shown fair ability. Her performance was impressive enough even as it stood, but we also knew that she had managed to win in such taking style despite coming from off the pace on a day when the track was favouring those ridden prominently.

I stated at the time (I did the *Racing Post* analysis for this contest) that she was one to look forward to and she duly confirmed that view by winning the Listed Galtres Stakes at the York Ebor Meeting the following month at odds of 13-2.

COMBINING THE TOOLS

There is quite a lot to take in here, but there is nothing like a real example to clarify how several factors can be put together and used to maximum effect. This race was a 0-60 handicap run over 5f at Chelmsford on 5 May 2022 and at first glance it looked a competitive handicap, so was there anything obvious that could help me narrow it down?

Note: To keep things compact only each horse's 2022 All-Weather form is shown.

7-00   LADIES DAY WITH SOPHIE ELLIS-BEXTOR HANDICAP (0-60) (6) 4-Y-O+
(Winner 3618.00)
5f   Par 101   10 runners   Median Time 59.2

1 (10)   SCALE FORCE 6-9-11(B) GAY KELLEWAY – SAFFIE OSBORNE(3)

DATE	TRACK	SURF	DIST	GNG	BIAS	RTYPE	POS	RAN	WGHT	DR	PCE	HDGR	SECTNL	SF
12APR2021	WOLV	TPTA	5.1	SD	55	5HCP	5	9	8-13	2	P	V	+0.39	98
15MAR2022	SOUT	TPTA	5	FT	83	6HCP	4	12	8-13	1	H	V	+0.86	90
28FEB2021	WOLV	TPTA	5.1	SD	46	5HCP	7	10	8-12	11	H	B	-0.40	98
22FEB2022	SOUT	TPTA	5	FT	83	5SEL	2	3	10-0	2	P	B	+2.30	99
08FEB2022	SOUT	TPTA	5	SD	67	5HCP	6	11	9-3	5	P	B	+0.03	91
01FEB2021	WOLV	TPTA	5.1	FT	50	6HCP	3	9	9-8	7	H	B	-0.32	103
18JAN2022	SOUT	TPTA	5	SW	78	5HCP	4	9	8-9	8	H	B	-1.50	103
13JAN2022	NEWC	TPTA	5	VS	63	5HCP	9	9	9-7	1	P	B	-3.34	86

2 (1)   SIR GREGORY (FR) 4-9-11 MICHAEL APPLEBY – GEORGE ROOKE(3)

DATE	TRACK	SURF	DIST	GNG	BIAS	RTYPE	POS	RAN	WGHT	DR	PCE	HDGR	SECTNL	SF
28APR2022	CHEL	POLY	6	SD	50	6HCP	1	8	8-12	2	P	-	-0.28	100

DATE	TRACK	SURF	DIST	GNG	BIAS	RTYPE	POS	RAN	WGHT	DR	PCE	HDGR	SECTNL	SF
08APR2022	KEMP	POLY	6	SW	33	6HCP	10	11	8-11	11	P	-	+0.52	95
02MAR2022	KEMP	POLY	6	SW	48	6HCP	4	12	9-2	2	H	-	-1.26	101
23FEB2022	KEMP	POLY	6	SW	62	5HCP	2	11	8-1	4	H	-	+1.64	101
03FEB2022	SOUT	TPTA	6.1	VS	54	6HCP	3	10	9-6	5	H	-	-1.72	101
24JAN2022	KEMP	POLY	6	SW	45	6HCP	1	11	9-1	1	H	-	-1.36	101
05JAN2021	WOLV	TPTA	6.1	SD	54	6HCP	7	13	8-11	13	H	-	+0.58	94

3 (7)   HEY HO LET'S GO 6-9-10 MARK HOAD – AIDAN KEELEY(7)

DATE	TRACK	SURF	DIST	GNG	BIAS	RTYPE	POS	RAN	WGHT	DR	PCE	HDGR	SECTNL	SF
05MAY2022	CHEL	POLY	5	SD	52	6HCP	6	10	9-3	7	H	-	-2.17	97
20APR2022	LING	POLY	5	SW	52	6HCP	1	5	8-9	5	P	-	-0.54	101
06APR2022	LING	POLY	5	SD	62	6HCP	1	10	9-0	8	L	-	+0.97	101
12MAR2022	KEMP	POLY	5	SD	54	6HCP	4	7	8-9	6	H	-	-1.22	97
02MAR2022	LING	POLY	5	SW	44	6HCP	6	9	8-11	8	P	-	-0.16	93
12FEB2022	LING	POLY	6	SD	44	5HCP	10	11	8-2	7	L	-	-0.93	104
29JAN2022	LING	POLY	6	SD	60	5HCP	3	9	8-7	1	L	-	-0.33	105
12JAN2022	LING	POLY	5	SD	50	5HCP	6	6	8-13	5	P	-	+0.49	84
03JAN2022	LING	POLY	5	SW	40	6HCP	8	9	9-3	9	P	-	-1.06	94

4 (8)   WINGS OF A DOVE (IRE) 4-9-10(B) RICHARD SPENCER – HARRY DAVIES(7)

DATE	TRACK	SURF	DIST	GNG	BIAS	RTYPE	POS	RAN	WGHT	DR	PCE	HDGR	SECTNL	SF
28APR2022	LING	POLY	5	SD	52	6HCP	1	10	9-3	7	H	B	+0.09	98
28JAN2022	LING	POLY	5	SD	48	5HCP	5	10	8-9	8	H	B	+0.02	101
03JAN2022	LING	POLY	5	SW	40	6HCP	3	9	9-1	1	L	B	-1.06	105

5 (4)   IESHA 4-9-8(C) CHARLIE WALLIS – CONNOR BEASLEY

DATE	TRACK	SURF	DIST	GNG	BIAS	RTYPE	POS	RAN	WGHT	DR	PCE	HDGR	SECTNL	SF
01APR2022	SOUT	TPTA	5	VF	50	6HCP	9	14	9-7	13	H	V	+1.37	91
15MAR2022	SOUT	TPTA	5	FT	83	6HCP	3	12	9-2	4	H	C	+0.86	91
11FEB2022	SOUT	TPTA	5	SD	36	6HCP	2	9	9-6	1	H	C	-0.14	99
18JAN2022	SOUT	TPTA	5	SW	78	6HCP	1	8	9-7	2	P	C	-0.42	101
05JAN2021	WOLV	TPTA	6.1	SD	54	6HCP	10	12	9-3	11	L	C	-1.00	94

6 (9)   TOPLIGHT 4-9-7(B) CHELSEA BANHAM – JOEY HAYNES

DATE	TRACK	SURF	DIST	GNG	BIAS	RTYPE	POS	RAN	WGHT	DR	PCE	HDGR	SECTNL	SF
02MAR2022	LING	POLY	5	SW	44	6HCP	8	9	9-1	9	H	B	-0.16	88
28JAN2022	LING	POLY	5	SD	48	5HCP	7	10	8-11	9	H	B	+0.02	101

7 (3)   GREEN DOOR (IRE) 11-9-7(V) ROBERT COWELL – HOLLIE DOYLE
No AW Form in 2022

8 (6)   BERNARD SPIERPOINT 5-9-7(V) CHARLIE WALLIS – DAVID EGAN

DATE	TRACK	SURF	DIST	GNG	BIAS	RTYPE	POS	RAN	WGHT	DR	PCE	HDGR	SECTNL	SF
10FEB2022	NEWC	TPTA	5	VS	42	6HCP	4	10	9-7	10	L	V	-2.73	98
27JAN2022	SOUT	TPTA	5	VF	100	6HCP	2	12	9-11	6	P	V	+1.38	95
18JAN2022	SOUT	TPTA	5	SW	78	6HCP	1	9	9-7	10	L	V	+0.01	100
07JAN2021	WOLV	TPTA	5.1	SD	43	6CLF	1	10	9-7	10	H	V	+0.15	98

9 (2)   YOU'RE COOL 10-9-2(TV) DEREK SHAW – ROSE DAWES(7)

DATE	TRACK	SURF	DIST	GNG	BIAS	RTYPE	POS	RAN	WGHT	DR	PCE	HDGR	SECTNL	SF
15APR2022	CHEL	POLY	5	SW	38	6HCP	5	8	8-8	3	H	TV	-1.99	100
11MAR2021	WOLV	TPTA	6.1	SD	52	6HCP	9	11	9-4	4	P	T	-0.03	93
14FEB2021	WOLV	TPTA	5.1	SW	58	6HCP	4	11	9-4	8	P	T	-0.57	102
28JAN2021	WOLV	TPTA	5.1	SD	29	6HCP	1	8	8-12	1	H	T	+0.51	100
18JAN2022	SOUT	TPTA	5	SW	78	6HCP	6	9	9-0	9	H	T	+0.01	89
11JAN2022	SOUT	TPTA	5	SD	67	6HCP	3	14	9-1	14	P	T	-0.12	97

10 (5)   ASCOT JUNGLE (IRE) 5-8-10 CLARE HOBSON – RHYS CLUTTERBUCK(3)

DATE	TRACK	SURF	DIST	GNG	BIAS	RTYPE	POS	RAN	WGHT	DR	PCE	HDGR	SECTNL	SF
28APR2022	LING	POLY	5	SD	52	6HCP	6	10	8-10	6	H	-	+0.09	91
14JAN2021	WOLV	TPTA	5.1	SD	56	6CLF	8	9	8-11	2	H	HT	+0.31	89

Running Style Impact Values and Draw Statistics over 5f in past year

Front-Runners   1.9
Prominent Horses   1.6
Hold Up Horses   0.5

STALL	RUNNERS	WINNERS	W/R(%)
1	35	4	11
2	36	9	25
3	35	7	20
4	34	4	12
5	32	8	25
6	31	0	0
7	28	1	4
8	21	0	0
9	18	1	6
10	14	1	7

There was clearly a draw bias over this trip at Chelmsford and, looking at it another way, it soon became quite stark. The bottom five draws had a combined record of 32-172, while stalls six to ten were 3-112. That meant that in a ten-runner contest like this I could basically dismiss half the field. I now just had to assess the chances of the five remaining contenders a bit more closely. These were the conclusions I reached.

Stall 1, Sir Gregory: good and consistent speed figures, especially when compared to the race par. Track no problem having won here seven days earlier for which he carried a 5lb penalty, but that was over 6f, and this was his first try at 5f.

Conclusion: A contender if able to keep tabs on the leaders over this shorter trip.

Stall 2, You're Cool: winner of 13 races on the All-Weather, five of them over this course and distance. Just 1lb above last winning mark and best speed figures would give him every chance in this company when compared to the race par.

Conclusion: Strong chance with the conditions clearly no problem.

Stall 3, Green Door: formerly a smart sprinter, but below form for some time now despite a plummeting mark and recent career has included some lengthy absences. Returns from another seven months off with plenty to prove.

Conclusion: Little to recommend him these days and easily passed over.

Stall 4, Iesha: Has a bit to find on speed figures and 5lb above last winning mark but has winning course form over 6f.

Conclusion: Each-way claims.

Stall 5, Ascot Jungle: Maiden after 23 starts and even her best speed figures leave her with plenty to find.

Conclusion: Comfortably dismissed.

It may be obvious, but I really liked You're Cool. Yes, he was a ten-year-old having his 98th start, but that sort of thing matters less at this level and the key was that the conditions were ideal for him.

Also, he was feasibly handicapped and had a great draw. He just had to be backed.

Fortunately, once the race got under way everything went as smoothly as it possibly could have done. Jockey Rose Dawes quickly had the gelding in a nice position just behind the leaders and I soon became very hopeful, especially when she allowed him to stride on soon after turning for home. It was also encouraging that she took him out into the centre of the track in the home straight, as having done so looked to be a positive throughout the meeting. While his two nearest pursuers stuck closer to the inside rail, he kept on strongly and never looked like getting caught. His starting price was 10-1, but he had been available at 20-1 the previous evening and that was just too good to miss. Sir Gregory (11-8) finished second, with the drop in trip appearing to be against him, while Iesha (11-1) was back in third having attempted to make all the running. The exacta paid £28.50 to a £1 stake and the trifecta £259.

At the time of writing, You're Cool had racked up 100 career appearances. His record on the All-Weather read 15 wins from 75 starts, while on turf it was no win from 25 starts. No prizes for guessing what type of surface he prefers!

Here is another example of how delving that little bit deeper can prove to be of benefit. This is another race which took place at Chelmsford, this time on 20 August 2022. Below is the list of runners as they would have appeared in most publications, but this time in each horse's form figures any All-Weather runs are shown in bold.

ECO-DEC SOLUTIONS FILLIES' HANDICAP (CLASS 5) 3-Y-O+ (0-70) 6F

1 (4)	5615-77	Libertine Belle	4-10-1 (t)	Stuart Williams	Luke Catton (5)
2 (5)	0032313	Miss Bella Brand	4-9-13	Ilke Gansera-Leveque	George Wood
3 (3)	5056444	Lucia Joy	3-9-6	George Boughey	Connor Planas (7)
4 (2)	8-35543	Noteable	4-9-6	Craig Lidster	Paddy Mathers
5 (1)	3254153	Bondi Girl	3-9-3	Michael Appleby	Frederick Larson (5)
6 (6)	3614282	Liv Lucky	3-9-1	Charlie & Mark Johnston	Oliver Stammers (3)
7 (7)	9446513	Company Minx	5-8-12	J.R. Jenkins	Marco Ghiani

The majority of the seven fillies were coming into the race in fair form, but once stripping away the turf performances and looking at the field via our full All-Weather race cards things became a lot clearer.

7-05 ECO-DEC SOLUTIONS FILLIES' HANDICAP (0-70) (5) 3-Y-O+
(Winner 5076.00)
6f   Par 100   7 runners   Median Time 1m 11.7

1 (4) LIBERTINE BELLE 4-10-1(T) STUART WILLIAMS – LUKE CATTON(5)

Sire HELMET	Runners	156	Wins	13	(8%) P/L -84.25
Trainer	Runners	394	Wins	52	(13%) P/L -147.16
Jockey	Rides	23	Wins	3	(13%) P/L -3.88

AW Form

DATE	TRACK	SURF	DIST	GNG	BIAS	RTYPE	POS	RAN	WGHT	DR	PCE	HDGR	SECTNL	SF
07OCT2021	CHEL	POLY	6	SD	33	5HCP	5	11	9-8	5	H	T	-0.56	102
30MAR2021	WOLV	TPTA	6.1	SD	55	5HCP	3	11	9-0	2	P	-	-0.05	104
18NOV2020	KEMP	POLY	6	SW	57	5HCP	2	12	9-7	3	H	-	-0.91	101
05NOV2020	CHEL	POLY	6	SD	57	5HCP	4	9	9-2	7	H	-	-0.48	93
28OCT2020	KEMP	POLY	6	SW	39	5HCP	3	10	9-7	3	H	-	+0.44	93
14SEP2020	WOLV	TPTA	6.1	SD	59	5MDN	1	10	8-13	8	H	-	---	95

2 (5) MISS BELLA BRAND 4-9-13 MRS ILKA GANSERA-LEVEQUE –
GEORGE WOOD

Sire POET'S VOICE	Runners	186	Wins	19	(10%) P/L -25.28
Trainer	Runners	21	Wins	1	(5%) P/L -16.00
Jockey	Rides	152	Wins	13	(9%) P/L -17.23

AW Form

DATE	TRACK	SURF	DIST	GNG	BIAS	RTYPE	POS	RAN	WGHT	DR	PCE	HDGR	SECTNL	SF
16AUG2022	CHEL	POLY	6	FT	42	5HCP	3	6	9-8	2	H	-	+0.12	99
12JUL2022	CHEL	POLY	6	SD	62	6HCP	1	9	9-8	4	H	-	+0.61	101
22JUN2022	KEMP	POLY	7	SD	50	5HCP	2	12	9-9	11	H	-	-0.03	99
15APR2022	LING	POLY	7	SD	48	4HCP	11	12	7-13	7	H	-	+0.02	95
30MAR2022	LING	POLY	7	SD	58	5HCP	1	8	9-0	2	H	-	-1.25	102
26FEB2021	WOLV	TPTA	6.1	SD	48	6HCP	5	11	9-2	8	H	-	-0.07	101
17FEB2022	CHEL	POLY	6	VS	38	5HCP	3	12	9-0	7	P	-	-0.96	100
09SEP2021	CHEL	POLY	7	SD	48	6HCP	2	11	9-2	6	H	-	-0.42	102
28APR2021	WOLV	TPTA	6.1	SW	46	5HCP	10	11	8-13	10	H	-	-1.33	97
14MAR2021	LING	POLY	5	SW	60	5CND	3	6	8-10	4	P	-	-0.98	104
27FEB2021	LING	POLY	5	SW	63	5MDN	2	8	8-9	2	H	-	-0.45	96
16FEB2021	KEMP	POLY	5	VS	48	5CND	2	9	8-9	1	P	-	+2.36	93
11JAN2021	WOLV	TPTA	6.1	SD	45	5CND	9	9	8-6	6	P	-	+1.76	61
26DEC2020	WOLV	TPTA	5.1	SD	48	5CND	2	11	8-6	1	H	-	+0.55	95

3 (3)   LUCIA JOY 3-9-6 GEORGE BOUGHEY – CONNOR PLANAS(7)

Sire ULYSSES	Runners	13	Wins	1	(8%) P/L -11.17
Trainer	Runners	71	Wins	5	(7%) P/L -45.27
Jockey	Rides	6	Wins	1	(17%) P/L -3.25

AW Form

DATE	TRACK	SURF	DIST	GNG	BIAS	RTYPE	POS	RAN	WGHT	DR	PCE	HDGR	SECTNL	SF
08AUG2021	WOLV	TPTA	6.1	VS	67	6CLM	4	9	9-2	9	H	-	-1.99	96
24JUL2022	CHEL	POLY	7	SW	38	5HCP	4	8	9-4	6	L	-	+1.02	98
09APR2021	WOLV	TPTA	7.2	SD	52	5CND	2	12	8-11	5	P	-	+0.60	96
02APR2021	WOLV	TPTA	8.6	FT	36	5CND	3	6	9-0	5	H	-	+3.33	84
18MAR2022	NEWC	TPTA	8	SW	43	5MDN	2	7	8-11	1	H	-	+2.66	92

4 (2)   NOTEABLE (IRE) 3-9-6 CRAIG LIDSTER – PADDY MATHERS

Sire PROFITABLE	Runners	31	Wins	5	(16%) P/L -10.55
Trainer	Runners	0	Wins	0	(0%) P/L 0.00
Jockey	Rides	130	Wins	13	(10%) P/L -43.38

No AW Form

5 (1)   BONDI GIRL (IRE) 3-9-3 MICHAEL APPLEBY – FREDERICK LARSON(5)

Sire IVAWOOD	Runners	30	Wins	2	(7%) P/L -4.13
Trainer	Runners	576	Wins	70	(12%) P/L -99.91
Jockey	Rides	30	Wins	2	(7%) P/L -1.50

AW Form

DATE	TRACK	SURF	DIST	GNG	BIAS	RTYPE	POS	RAN	WGHT	DR	PCE	HDGR	SECTNL	SF
16AUG2021	WOLV	TPTA	6.1	SW	67	6HCP	3	6	9-6	1	H	V	-0.38	102
12MAR2022	LING	POLY	7	SD	42	5HCP	5	8	8-7	1	H	-	+2.73	85
13DEC2021	CHEL	POLY	7	SD	45	5MDN	5	14	9-0	9	P	-	+0.27	92
22NOV2021	CHEL	POLY	7	SW	36	5CND	3	14	8-12	3	L	-	-1.53	99
22OCT2021	NEWC	TPTA	5	FT	64	6HCP	10	11	9-7	4	H	-	+2.07	83

6 (6)   LIV LUCKY (IRE) 3-9-1 CHARLIE & MARK JOHNSTON – OLIVER STAMMERS(3)

Sire PROFITABLE	Runners	31	Wins	5	(16%) P/L -10.55
Trainer	Runners	34	Wins	7	(21%) P/L -9.75
Jockey	Rides	25	Wins	0	(0%) P/L -25.00

AW Form

DATE	TRACK	SURF	DIST	GNG	BIAS	RTYPE	POS	RAN	WGHT	DR	PCE	HDGR	SECTNL	SF
27APR2021	WOLV	TPTA	6.1	SD	50	5HCP	2	6	8-2	6	P	-	+1.55	94
30MAR2022	KEMP	POLY	7	SW	69	6HCP	7	9	8-12	6	L	-	-2.45	87
22FEB2022	SOUT	TPTA	7.1	SD	46	6HCP	4	8	9-3	10	H	-	+0.98	92
01FEB2021	WOLV	TPTA	7.2	FT	50	6HCP	2	12	9-7	5	P	-	+1.17	94
16JAN2022	SOUT	TPTA	7.1	VS	44	6HCP	5	11	9-8	3	P	-	+1.54	93
30DEC2021	WOLV	TPTA	6.1	SW	40	6HCP	10	12	9-3	12	L	-	-0.57	81
25NOV2021	CHEL	POLY	6	SD	56	6HCP	9	9	9-9	1	L	-	+1.23	89
27OCT2021	KEMP	POLY	6	VS	65	5HCP	6	11	9-2	5	H	-	-0.05	86
11OCT2021	WOLV	TPTA	6.1	SD	44	5CND	4	10	9-0	4	L	-	+2.08	89
02APR2021	NEWC	TPTA	5	SW	60	4CND	4	7	9-0	2	P	-	+0.33	92

7 (7)   COMPANY MINX (IRE) 5-8-12 J R JENKINS - MARCO GHIANI

Sire FAST COMPANY	Runners	92	Wins	7	(8%) P/L -50.42
Trainer	Runners	161	Wins	12	(7%) P/L -71.75
Jockey	Rides	175	Wins	23	(13%) P/L -45.34

AW Form

DATE	TRACK	SURF	DIST	GNG	BIAS	RTYPE	POS	RAN	WGHT	DR	PCE	HDGR	SECTNL	SF
09AUG2022	CHEL	POLY	6	SW	33	6CLF	3	10	9-4	7	H	-	-0.47	96
02AUG2022	CHEL	POLY	6	SD	75	6CLF	1	11	9-4	1	P	-	-0.87	98
20JUL2022	SOUT	TPTA	6.1	VS	45	6HCP	5	13	9-3	3	H	-	-1.96	101
01APR2022	SOUT	TPTA	6.1	SD	69	6HCP	9	13	9-5	1	P	-	-0.73	98
29NOV2021	KEMP	POLY	6	SW	54	6HCP	7	10	9-4	8	P	-	-0.77	90
18MAR2021	CHEL	POLY	6	SW	48	5HCP	6	6	9-4	6	L	-	-1.47	97
27FEB2021	CHEL	POLY	6	SW	38	4HCP	7	8	9-11	7	H	-	-0.64	94
07OCT2020	KEMP	POLY	7	SW	33	4HCP	14	14	9-4	11	H	-	-2.84	68

Running Style Impact Values and Draw Statistics over 6f in past year

Front-Runners	2.1
Prominent Horses	1.5
Hold Up Horses	0.5

STALL	RUNNERS	WINNERS	W/R(%)
1	65	10	15
2	68	13	19
3	70	10	14
4	67	9	13
5	68	2	3
6	64	8	13

7	54	6	11
8	46	4	9
9	41	4	10
10	32	2	6
11	26	1	4
12	22	2	9
13	8	0	0
14	9	0	0

Using speed figures as the first way to narrow down the contenders left me with just three, namely Libertine Belle, Miss Bella Brand and Bondi Girl, but I decided to eliminate the last-named as her recent good speed figure was achieved on Tapeta and she needed to improve on her previous performances on Polytrack, which had all been over 7f. Miss Bella Brand was solid and there were no issues over the conditions having won over course and distance the previous month, but I really liked Libertine Belle.

There were many reasons for this, namely:

- Her last three speed figures on the All-Weather (including over today's course and distance) all exceeded the class par for the type of race
- She was back off the same handicap mark as for her latest win
- She was successful the last time she contested a race at 0-70 level
- She had a good draw
- She hadn't been seen for 78 days but had won after a similar absence

All of these positive factors may have become clouded by those two modest efforts on turf after returning in May, but if anyone had bothered to look more closely they would have seen that they were both 0-90 contests and with the best will in the world that sort of company was well out of her league.

This was the betting forecast for the race the night before and I felt it was just about right based on the assessment of the race we have just been through:

3-1 Miss Bella Brand; 4-1 Libertine Belle; 9-2 Bondi Girl; 5-1 Liv Lucky; 6-1 Noteable; 8-1 Lucia Joy; 10-1 Company Minx

I fully expected Libertine Belle to have shortened in the lead-up to the contest, so imagine my amazement when I had a look to see how the market was shaping. In fact, these are the starting prices for the seven runners:

5-4 Miss Bella Brand; 2-1 Bondi Girl; 11-1 Company Minx; 12-1 Libertine Belle, Lucia Joy; 14-1 Liv Lucky, Noteable

I did say that the front pair in the market had been among those I had narrowed it down to earlier, but why was the betting so lopsided and why was Libertine Belle such a huge price given all she had going for her? I could find no clear reason for it, so I backed her accordingly and settled down to watch her battle on gamely and beat the All-Weather newcomer Noteable by half a length, with Miss Bella Brand back in third and Bondi Girl fourth.

This really was a Christmas come early situation, but it's not an isolated incident and it's just another example of doing that little bit of extra research and unearthing these gems when they do occur.

JOURNAL

THURSDAY, 3 FEBRUARY: SOUTHWELL

So now was the time to leave all the theories in the classroom and take them out into the field to put them into practice. I'm not suggesting for one moment that you must always attend the racecourse in order to make money at this game. After all, with live pictures now readily accessible via so many different channels you get at least as good a view as those at the track (often a better one) even with big screens now so prevalent on-course. At many fixtures you can also see the sectional times on the live pictures as they occur, meaning you can make an immediate assessment. However, for a traditionalist like me being able to see the horses in the flesh beforehand, both in the pre-parade ring and the paddock, is of vital importance. Of course, when you get down to basics you just can't beat a day at the races!

My plan was to attend a series of All-Weather fixtures for the period of the diary, beginning with this meeting. For consistency I would stick to my average stake of £50 per race, either win only or £25 each way on a few occasions if the price was big enough.

It was good to start with Southwell, as despite being one of the furthest All-Weather tracks from where I live (about 110 miles and a round trip of around five hours) it has never been a chore travelling there. As I mentioned earlier, it was the first All-Weather track I ever visited so holds many special memories for me, so as I always go there full of enthusiasm the journey time passes by very quickly. I have now even forgiven them for changing the racing surface!

It was important for me to get off to a good start punting-wise for this journal, though I wasn't expecting that much from the first race on the card, a 0-75 apprentice handicap over 7f.

1-00   MANSIONBET PROUD PARTNERS OF THE AWC APPRENTICE HANDICAP (0-75) (5) 4-Y-O+
7.1f   Par = 103   6 runners

AW Form	Name	Highest	Last Six Ratings
666-32	JUAN LES PINS	110Ke06	83Ch07 96Ke06 95Ch07 97Ke07 99Li07 103Li07
7214-9	FOLLOW YOUR HEART	108Li08	101Wo05 97Ke07 103Ch06 103Ke07 102Li07 108Li08
45-7-6	BATTERED	114Ne07	114Ne07 102Ch08 104Ke08 100So08
334-39	GYPSY WHISPER	109So07	103Li08 109So07 106So07 99So08 100So08 99So08
9655-9	SPRING ROMANCE	111Wo07	100Ke07 88Ke07 92Wo08 99Ch07 94Ke06 95Li08
2337-2	LOVE YOUR WORK	112So08	95So08 109So07 99So07 104So07 102So08 105So08

One interesting aspect about this race was the likely prospects of Spring Romance. As I have said before, statistics can be of great value, especially those you update and keep yourself. I do maintain statistics for sires, trainers, and jockeys for each of the All-Weather tracks going back five seasons. However, when it comes to Southwell, I had to reset the clock at the start of December 2021 so that my stats only cover the period from when they started to race on Tapeta.

A horse's individual performances on Fibresand would still be shown both on the full cards and in the private handicaps shown in this chapter, but the jockey/trainer and sire statistics are for Tapeta only. What they showed was that trainer Mick Appleby was 1-54 on the new surface and there could be any number of reasons for that, but as a punter such a stark statistic could not be ignored if it persisted, especially if one of his horses was likely to be prominent in the market. However, all of this became academic when Spring Romance was announced as a non-runner.

I had originally decided that this would be a no-bet race for me, but then I had another look. Love Your Work did have plenty going for him, as despite being an established Fibresand performer with four wins that latest run (the 105So08) was on Tapeta where he had been beaten a neck after a 215-day absence. A glance at the remaining five horses' running styles also suggested that the gelding would probably enjoy an uncontested lead should jockey Oliver Stammers so wish it, as the 'Pace' column in the full card had shown that he often liked to lead. Although odds of 5-4 were shorter than I would normally take, I did decide to play.

The race went exactly as I thought it might, as Love Your Work was sent straight to the front and at no stage was the result in much doubt. Only a small profit, but still a good start.

The second race was a 7f maiden and this was a race where paddock inspection was especially useful.

1-30   MANSIONBET BEATEN BY A HEAD MEDIAN AUCTION MAIDEN STAKES (GBB RACE) (5) 3-Y-O+

7.1f   Par = 103   12 runners

AW Form	Name	Highest	Last Six Ratings
8	GORDONONTHEORGAN	45Ch07	45Ch07
05	ROGAN'S FANCY	88So08	81So12 88So08
602-	GRIFFIN PARK	103Li08	88Ke08 84Ke07 103Li08
52-5	JADE COUNTRY	95Li07	90Ke08 95Ke07 95Li07
	MY OPINION		
0-	SHOT TO THE HEART	65Wo06	65Wo06
5-8	VOLOS	94Ke08	94Ke08 93Ch07
6-3	DARK ENCHANTMENT	97So07	93Ke08 97So07
	MY LOVELY SYLV		
8-	SECRET STRIPPER	87Wo06	87Wo06
5	SOI DAO	94Li07	94Li07
4	THEWAYTOTHESTARS	95So07	95So07

It wasn't hard to see why Griffin Park was a major contender in my book. He had finished a clear second behind a nice filly from the Roger Varian stable at Lingfield last time and the speed rating he earned for that was bang on par for a race of its type. The only slight doubt was whether dropping back a furlong would inconvenience him, but with Southwell a more galloping track than Lingfield I concluded that it wouldn't be an issue.

The other likely contender for me was Dark Enchantment, not only because she had run so well over course and distance the previous month, but because she looked magnificent beforehand. I decided to back them both when I saw that they were much bigger prices than I expected them to be (Griffin Park at 3-1 and Dark Enchantment at 5-1). This was mainly due to Jade Country (85-40) and Volos (3-1) also being very much to the fore of the betting market, but they had something to prove as far as I was concerned.

Dark Enchantment made a bold bid to make every yard of the running, but she was eventually worn down by Griffin Park who did indeed need every yard of the trip to get on top. I should have been content with the profit on the race given that the winner was returned at what I believed to be generous odds, but I was kicking myself for not playing the Exacta as well, as I was convinced that only two horses counted. It paid £16 to a £1 stake and I knew that I had missed an opportunity.

The third race on the card was the first division of a 0-55 handicap over 6f, which isn't the sort of race to risk your hard-earned on in most cases.

2-00   READ KATIE WALSH ON BETWAY INSIDER HANDICAP (DIV I)
(0-55) (6) 4-Y-O+
6.1f   Par = 101   10 runners

AW Form	Name	Highest	Last Six Ratings
570-71	SIR GREGORY	101Ke06	80Wo07 94Ke06 93Ch06 75Ke06 94Wo06 101Ke06
97208-	DELAGATE THE LADY	102Li06	100Ch06 93Ke07 89Wo06 96Ch06 84Ch06 95Li06
07-111	ATRAFAN	104Ne06	94Ne06 93Ne07 99So07 104Ne06 96Ne06 101So07
748-73	WON LOVE	96Ke06	89Ke08 87Ke07 96Ke06 88Ke06 92Li06 96Ke06
293-41	BRAZEN ARROW	102Wo06	92Ch06 100Ch06 89Li06 95Ch06 99Ch06 102Wo06
966-62	TWENTYSHARESOFGREY	103Wo07	103Wo07 49Wo07 66Wo06 92Ch06 96Ch07 99So07
6860-5	WICKLOW WARRIOR	103Ne06	99Ne06 95Ne06 93Ne07 98Ne06 94So06 92Ne06
0700-6	EDESSANN	104Ne05	89Ch06 82Ne05 94Ke06 84Ne06 87So05 96Ch07
3990-8	SPIRIT OF HEAVEN	93Wo05	93Ne05 93Wo05 82Wo05 88Wo05 81Wo06 84So05
5642-0	OUTOFTHEGLOOM	96So06	90So06 92So06 93So07 93So06 96So06 91So08

However, the 7-4 favourite was Sir Gregory, trained by (yes, you've guessed it) Mick Appleby. That begged the question – was this an opportunity to make some money by laying him on the exchanges? The problem is that I do not like backing horses at odds-on and laying horses at odds-against is the same thing. I could have laid him for a place for a much bigger profit, but although there were a couple of horses in the race capable of beating him the way I saw it, I wasn't so sure there were enough to knock him out of the first three. I decided to focus on finding a horse who could win the race and settled on Brazen Arrow, who had been given an aggressive ride to get off the mark at the 14th attempt at Wolverhampton the previous month. I backed him at 5-1.

Brazen Arrow again attempted to make all and held a clear lead at one point, but despite never giving up he was outstayed by Twentysharesofgrey with Sir Gregory back in third. I was pleased I had decided not to lay the favourite for a place and at least my trainer statistics remained unblemished, but I was still lighter by £50.

I couldn't find a bet in the second division nor in the 0-90 handicap for three-year-olds which followed, but the 0-60 three-year-old handicap over 6f did look interesting.

3-30   PLAY CORAL RACING-SUPER-SERIES FOR FREE HANDICAP (0-60) (6) 3-Y-O
6.1f   Par = 95   10 runners

AW Form	Name	Highest	Last Six Ratings
33	SWEET AROMA	99Ne06	93Wo06 99Ne06
07-22	MARSH BENHAM	96Ke06	84Ke07 84Wo07 95Ke06 96Ke06
8453-5	BETWEEN THE SHEETS	93Ch06	87Wo06 88Wo06 92Ne07 92Ke07 93Ch06 90Ke07
004-1	SALTA RESTA	97So06	75Ke07 75Ke06 91Wo06 97So06
7254-9	DALGLISH	97Ne05	92Ne05 92Ne05 97Ne05 94Wo05 89Ne06 86So07
9-44	WAVERLEY STAR	92So06	91Ne05 76Ne07 92So06
53-4	BANG ON THE BELL	93So06	88Ch06 92So06 93So06
66-2	BERRA GO	95So06	88Ne05 88Ne06 95So06
0685-4	AL TILAL	89Wo05	82Ke06 85Wo06 88Ch05 89Ne05 88So05 89Wo05
47-7	ANOTHER BERTIE	90Ne06	90Ne06 86Ne06 85So06

I liked the look of Sweet Aroma, who had shown ability in maiden and novice company and didn't appear to be over-faced now making her handicap debut. She was an obvious candidate on the ratings and represented a major yard, Richard Fahey, so I was amazed that she was such a big price. I had already backed one winner on the card who was bigger odds than I had expected so was more than happy to back her at 10-1, though she continued to drift and ended up 11-1.

Whatever the reason for her weakness in the market it was proved right as she ran a stinker, finishing eighth of the ten runners (the jockey reported that she ran too free). The only thing I could console myself with was that I couldn't have backed the winner Another Bertie in a million years! Unplaced in all seven previous starts and officially rated 44, it was hardly a surprise that he was sent off at 80-1. Having said that the gentleman standing just to the left of me while watching the race in front of the stands had clearly spotted something about him that I had missed, judging by the loud screams of celebration as the runners crossed the line. A little later I heard the same man tell an acquaintance that he had backed the winner at 110-1 on the exchanges, so perhaps he was entitled to express his joy in such a fashion!

The penultimate race on the card was the first division of another 0-55 handicap, this time over a mile and a half.

4-00   BETWAY HANDICAP (DIV I) (0-55) (6) 4-Y-O+
12.1f   Par = 101   9 runners

AW Form	Name	Highest	Last Six Ratings
877-11	CAPRICORN PRINCE	106Li12	68Ke16 83Wo14 90Ke12 100Li15 102Li12 93Ke12
-73-35	MR SHADY	112Li13	92De09 96De09 94Li10 112Li13 94Ne12 92So16
4043-4	RAINBOW'S GIFT	103Ne08	85Ne07 103Ne08 82Wo08 95Ne16 79So14 99Ne12
964-31	DONYA	102Ch10	97Ch08 70Ke07 91Wo09 102Ch10 99So12 101Li12
79-5	CODEBOOK	98Li10	97Wo09 91Wo09 98Li10
5435-4	HAMMY END	104Li12	94Wo14 94Li12 85Ke12 98Wo12 84Ke12 99So12
79-6	INDURO DE FONTAINE	98Ch10	93So11 92Wo09 98Ch10
7-40-7	REGIMENTO	103Ne10	82Ne07 103Ne10 87Ne08 86So11
09-843	RANGER BOB	99Ne10	90Du08 94Du08 95Du07 89Ne08 96So08 99Ne10

Two horses dominated the market and would eventually go off as joint-favourites, namely Capricorn Prince and Donya, but here was another opportunity for me to take a view.

Capricorn Prince was coming into this race in fine form and was bidding for a hat-trick following a couple of recent wins on Polytrack, but all five of his All-Weather successes had come on that surface and on the one occasion he had encountered Tapeta (at Wolverhampton) he had been beaten over 23 lengths. That made Donya the more attractive of the pair as although she had got off the mark at Lingfield the previous month, she had run well when third in a 13-runner event over today's course and distance the time before, so I was more than happy to take 3-1 about her.

Hammy End had only finished a short head behind Donya in that race here which would normally have brought him right into the equation, but his record of 1-35 was hard to ignore and he was drifting like a barge in the betting, so surely he couldn't win.

Donya tried to make all and stuck on gamely despite hanging about through the closing stages and only one rival was able to get past her, but that horse was Hammy End. The irony wasn't lost on me and clearly his new headgear combination had done the trick. Capricorn Prince finished back in fourth.

The final race was the second division of this low-grade handicap in which again two horses dominated the market, both bidding for a course hat-trick.

4-30   BETWAY HANDICAP (DIV II) (0-55) (6) 4-Y-O+
12.1f   Par =101   9 runners

AW Form	Name	Highest	Last Six Ratings
3161-1	MAHARASHTRA	102Ch10	88Wo07 92Ch08 101Ch10 102Ch10 90So11 100So11
04/	DINSDALE	101Ke12	87Li10 101Ke12
5966-5	ROMULAN PRINCE	99Wo08	97Ch07 99Wo08 93Ne16 91Wo08 92So12 94So12
03238-	BUG BOY	101Li08	93Wo09 94Ke08 95Ke12 100So11 85Ke12 90So12
6221-1	BATOCCHI	101So12	91Ne08 94Ne08 100Ne12 101Ne12 93So12 101So12
56-	ONLY DEBRIS	95Wo09	89Ne10 95Wo09
-70-63	SO MACHO	107Ne10	96Wo07 95Ne08 107Ne10 84Ne08 90Ne10 97So11
-549-7	ARCHIVE	102Ne12	94Wo14 96Ne12 95Ne12 90Ne12 93Ne12 94So12
60-	MISTER SWIFT	78Ch10	68Ke12 78Ch10

When the betting first opened on this contest the market had Maharashtra favourite ahead of Batocchi, but in the lead-up to the race the pair had flip-flopped and now the latter was shorter in the betting. It may have been partly due to trainer Rebecca Menzies having already struck with Love Your Work earlier on the card and people had combined the pair in doubles, but I had always preferred Batocchi in any case as his two wins had come over this trip, whereas Maharashtra had gained his two victories over a furlong shorter.

It might be that Maharashtra would appreciate the longer trip, but no such guesswork was necessary with Batocchi while Donya and Hammy End, who had finished third and fourth respectively behind him here last time, had hardly let the form down in the previous contest. He was now short enough in the betting, but while he stayed at odds-against I was prepared to keep the faith as he was my nap of the day, so I backed him at 5-4.

Everything seemed to be going well for much of the race, but then I thought I had done my money when Maharashtra seemed to be getting the better of the argument 1f out, at which point Batocchi's rider Cam Hardie dropped a rein. However, despite that slight inconvenience the gelding fought back gamely to win by half a length, and I told myself that it was his proven stamina that had made the difference.

A fair start to the diary, but a feeling that I could have done even better.

SUNDAY, 6 FEBRUARY: KEMPTON

Because of work commitments I don't get to attend many meetings on a Sunday, but I especially enjoy them when I do get the opportunity. There was a good crowd for this one with many families in attendance, many of whom gave the impression they hadn't been racing very often, if at all. There were only six races on the card, but a couple of them did look interesting for a variety of reasons, so I was hoping for a profitable day.

The first race was a 6f maiden which never really appealed as a betting opportunity with two horses appearing to be well ahead of the others. It became even less attractive when one of the pair was taken out, so it was a race I was more than happy to swerve.

The second contest on the card, a handicap over 6f, was a completely different proposition.

2-15   UNIBET HANDICAP (0-75) (5) 4-Y-O+
6f   Par = 103   8 runners

AW Form	Name	Highest		Last Six Ratings
7161-7	EQUITATION	108Ke07	108Ke07 105Ke07 103Ke06 98Ke07 103Ke06 95So06	
3481-	MELLYS FLYER	104Ke06	95So07 94Wo06 88Wo06 104Ke06	
556-22	TYGER BAY	106Ke06	103Ke06 92Ke06 98Ch06 100Ke06 99Ke06 99So06	
9-18-3	HELVETIAN	106Wo05	100Ke06 97Ch05 90Ke05 103Ch06 99Wo06 99Li06	
3278-1	THE BLUE BOWER	109Ke06	102Ke06 99Ke06 97Ke06 90Ke06 90Wo07 109Ke06	
8658-8	SEAS OF ELZAAM	106Ne07	104Wo07 94Ch06 93Wo06 97Wo06 92Ch07 99Wo06	
201-9	PERFECT SIGN	93Ne06	93Ne06 86Ne06 92So06 87Ke06	
4-0-53	DEWEY ROAD	100Li06	100Ke06 91Wo07 99Ke06 100Wo06 100Li06 98Ke07	

This race provided a conundrum and it's one that will reoccur time and time again. The horse in question was The Blue Bower, who as you can see had earned an impressive speed figure of 109 when winning over today's course and distance 11 days earlier. The problem was that it was so big, certainly a lot more than anything she had produced before, so what to do?

My rule of thumb for this situation is to be cautious with experienced horses (the five-year-old mare was having her 31st outing) as it's unlikely she was improving generally at her time of life, but with lightly raced types it's worth giving them the benefit of the doubt, as they are entitled to still be progressing. With that in mind I decided to rule out The Blue Bower, even though she was hovering around a backable price at 6-1.

The one I decided to focus on was Equitation, who although shorter in the betting appeared to have plenty going for him. He had a consistent range of good speed figures (including over today's course and distance) and the stable was in red-hot form. I was more than happy to forgive his effort on Tapeta last time and decided to back him at 7-2.

The favourite was Mellys Flyer, who had earned a speed figure higher than par when making all over course and distance in his most recent start. The problem was that he had been absent for 110 days since and there was nothing in his profile to suggest he could go well fresh. Under the circumstances his odds of around 2-1 looked skinny enough, but you could also argue that his price suggested he was thought ready enough for this return to action.

My decision not to back The Blue Bower was soon vindicated, though only because the mare walked out of the stalls and barely travelled a yard. Equitation was always in a good position just behind the leaders, holding every chance but never quite doing enough, ending up third of the eight runners. The race went to Mellys Flyer who successfully adopted the same positive tactics that had worked so well in his previous start, never looking likely to be caught. This was a race where the market got it spot-on.

The next contest was a novice over 7f.

2-50   UNIBET EXTRA PLACE OFFERS EVERY DAY NOVICE STAKES (GBB RACE) (5) 3-Y-O+

7f   Par = 103   13 runners

AW Form	Name	Highest	Last Six Ratings
0	WALTONS GROVE	82Wo09	82Wo09
88-	TRIDEVI	80Ke06	80Ke06 77Ke06
1	TRANQUIL NIGHT	106Ke07	106Ke07
48	BY YOUR SIDE	99Ke08	96Li08 99Ke08
	CARPE FORTUNA		
9-6	CIRCLE TIME	94Ke07	81Ke08 94Ke07
3-	TEUMESSIAS FOX	98So07	98So07
7	THE PRINCE	94Ke07	94Ke07
	EXCEEDINGLY SONIC		
9-	SWEET SUMMER	80Ke07	80Ke07
5	THOUGHTFUL GIFT	88Wo09	88Wo09
	TIARE		
78	VIVE LA REINE	90So07	82Wo07 90So07

This race portrays perfectly how to view a big speed figure in a different way to the previous contest. The Blue Bower had earned hers on her 31st start, whereas Tranquil Night had done so on only his second, so I was more than happy to believe his impressive number. The bonus was that he had earned it when winning over this course and distance the previous month, but surely with so much going for him he was going to be far too short in the betting to be able to back.

Another interesting aspect to this race was that Tranquil Night was due to be partnered by 17-year-old Harry Davies, a dual pony racing champion who only had his first ride under rules the previous month but had already ridden three winners. This was clearly a big vote of confidence by Godolphin to allow him to partner a fancied horse like this on only his 13th ride.

This was a race I was prepared just to watch rather than bet in, but that was about to change as the original second-favourite Teumessias Fox was backed right into 5-4. He had finished third on his debut at the opening Tapeta fixture at Southwell in December, but I didn't feel at the time the form was anything special and although his speed figure for that performance was creditable, it wasn't in the same parish as Tranquil Night's.

As a result of all the support for Andrew Balding's colt Tranquil Night was now on the drift. As I have already explained, I'm not one for backing any horse at odds-on, but Charlie Appleby's gelding was now widely available at even-money which is bit more of a grey area. It may be a bit of a cliché, but under circumstances like these I treat each situation on an individual basis. In this case there was one horse who I was convinced was going to be too short to back, not just odds-on but *long* odds-on. I had seen the debut effort of the apparent main danger at first hand and hadn't been blown away, so I stuck my chest out and had an even £50 on the favourite.

I never had a moment's worry as Harry Davies always had the gelding in an ideal position and when asked for more, he strode clear for a tidy two-length success with Teumessias Fox back in third. I hadn't expected to be investing in this race at all, so it was something of a bonus.

The next contest, a good handicap over a mile and 3f, was another race I had taken a view on.

3-25   TRY OUR NEW PRICE BOOSTS AT UNIBET HANDICAP
(0-90) (3) 4-Y-O+
11f   Par = 107   7 runners

AW Form	Name	Highest	Last Six Ratings
3-81-9	ANYTHINGTODAY	106Li12	106Ch10 102Ne10 105Ne12 94Ne10 105Li10 106Li12
15-3-3	CLAP YOUR HANDS	108Wo12	108Wo12 101Wo14 95Wo16 105Ch14 97Wo09 102Wo16
5-33-1	PRINCE OF HARTS	111Ke16	103Wo08 95Ch08 111Ke16 87Li15 104Ke11

533-11	OLD PORT	**108Wo09**	95Ch07 94Ke06 96So07 106Wo08 108Wo09
1/	AFFWONN	**103Wo08**	103Wo08
0-0-	ALTERNATIVE FACT	**98Ne10**	84Ke11 98Ne10
-013-8	PRECISELY	**109Li10**	97Wo07 90Li10 109Wo09 91Wo08 109Li10

The favourite was Old Port, who was bidding for a hat-trick after a couple of recent wins at Wolverhampton, and I had no issue with his speed figures, which had a nice progressive look to them. His latest one looked good in the context of this race, but he was now stepping up in trip on a different surface and was climbing two classes having been raised 9lb for this latest success. He had been odds-on when betting opened on the race the previous night, so he looked to be one to take on.

The question I was now asking myself was whether just to lay him on the exchanges or back something else at more generous odds, or both? In the end I decided to back Precisely as the form of the race in which she had finished eighth of 14 (albeit not beaten far) at Lingfield last time was working out well and this was a drop in grade. I gladly parted with my £50 and backed her at 6-1.

She ran creditably to finish fourth of the seven runners, but never really looked like winning. Old Port did manage to land the hat-trick even though it was hard work, but he was sent off 6-4 in the end (there was some 13-8 about) which in hindsight was a fair price given his upward profile.

The penultimate race of the afternoon was the feature event, a Class 2 handicap over 1m.

4-00   UNIBET 3 UNIBOOSTS A DAY HANDICAP
(LONDON MILE SERIES QUALIFIER) (0-105) (2) 4-Y-O+
8f   Par = 109   10 runners

AW Form	Name	Highest	Last Six Ratings
-3421-	MISTY GREY	**113Wo07**	108Wo06 109Wo07 109Li06 108Li06 109Ke08 113Wo07
3-990-	OH THIS IS US	**114Li08**	108Ch07 100Li07 107Li08 100Wo08 105Li07 85Ne06
2-11-1	LA TIHATY	**119Ke08**	97Li07 104Li07 76Ch07 119Ke08
-1332-	KARIBANA	**109Ch07**	109Wo06 99Ke07 108Ch07 108Ch07 109Ch07 104Ke08
2188-2	REVOLUTIONISE	**115Wo07**	106Ch07 106Li07 115Wo07 107Ne07 106Li07 113Wo07
7-8	SEVENTH KINGDOM	**87Ch08**	87Ch08 80Wo09
3-126-	BUGLE MAJOR	**107Li12**	103De09 107De09 107Li12 95Ke11
27-6	ON A SESSION	**104Wo08**	104Wo08 96Wo08 98So07
-350-6	SOAR ABOVE	**112Ke07**	102Ke07 112Ke07 103Ke06 102Ke07 90Ke06 105So06
66-2	HANDEL	**93Wo07**	86Wo09 88So07 93Wo07

A glance at the speed figures these horses had been earning shows just what a classy handicap this was, but as it turned out it would also be a race in which I would experience a sense of déjà vu.

You just couldn't get away from the massive speed figure earned by La Tihaty when winning over course and distance the previous month and, as was the case with Tranquil Night, I was happy to believe it given the colt's unexposed profile. His latest win had come after almost a year away from the track and although now a four-year-old, this was only his fifth career start. Not for the first time at this meeting, I did believe that he would be unbackable at the likely odds so prepared myself not to have a bet and just watch the race. However, that feeling of déjà vu then began to materialise when there was a late plunge on Karibana, who was backed right in to 11-4. As I stood on the grass in front of the stands, I looked over my right shoulder and saw that a few of the bookmakers were offering 5-4 against La Tihaty, so with a fleet of foot that would have made Usain Bolt sit up and take notice I rushed over and invested £50 at that price.

Again, as was the case with Tranquil Night, I never had a moment's worry as Roger Varian's colt quickened up smartly under Jack Mitchell and eventually won going away. I had now backed two winners because of other horses being backed against them, otherwise I wouldn't have touched either. I had been fortunate in a way, but these events had demonstrated the value of the speed figures if nothing else.

The last race on the card was another 1m handicap, not as classy as the previous contest but still competitive enough.

4-30   UNIBET SUPPORT SAFE GAMBLING HANDICAP
(LONDON MILE SERIES QUALIFIER) (0-85) (4) 4-Y-O+
8f   Par = 105   10 runners

AW Form	Name	Highest	Last Six Ratings
1-1	DINGLE	101Ke08	101Ke08 97Li10
574-31	SANAADH	116Ke07	103Ke07 105Ke07 103Ne07 103Ne07 91Ne07 101So08
132-46	UZINCSO	113Ke08	112Ke08 98Ke08 102Ke08 86Ke08 113Ke08 95Li10
6-6-	LARADO	108Li08	93Du07 108Li08
3-13-	YEAR OF THE DRAGON	101Ke07	99Ke07 101Ke07 97Li08
332-11	LAMMAS	106So08	100Ke07 97Li08 101Ke07 105Wo08 103So08 106So08
351-5-	MOSTAWAA	114Ne08	102Li08 103Ne08 92Ne10 100Ch10 107Ke08 105Ke08
6450-6	PINNATA	116Ne07	99Wo08 108Ch07 96Ch08 99Ke07 87Ch08 109Ke08
1-53	HOMER STOKES	111So07	111So07 102Ne07 86So08
44-1	DANCE AT NIGHT	103Ke07	94Ke06 90Ne06 103Ke07

One who was clearly a contender purely on speed figures was Sanaadh, but he was a quirky customer who needed the race to unfold perfectly ahead of him and had needed to be dropped into claimer to end a losing run of 13 at Southwell 12 days earlier. I had thrown enough money at him in that barren spell and was not prepared to fall for him again.

The one who stood out for me was Uzincso whose record over this course and distance coming into the race read 631111411324. He had finished sixth behind Dingle over 1m2f at Lingfield in his previous start, but I was hopeful that he could turn that form around back under his optimum conditions and his odds of 11-1 made him an attractive each-way proposition in a ten-runner field.

He held a good stalking position for most of the contest and had his chance, but he was unable to quicken enough once off the bridle and came home in fifth. To rub salt into the wound my old friend Sanaadh was on a going day and came from the back of the field to run down Dingle and win by half a length. He was returned at a generous 14-1 and I must admit to a slight feeling of nausea.

WEDNESDAY, 9 FEBRUARY: KEMPTON

This meeting wasn't originally on my radar, but I found out a day earlier that an owner with a runner at the fixture wasn't able to attend, so I offered to go along and represent them.

Fortunately, I had already done all my homework for this meeting, as I always do on the All-Weather, especially as I had to find selections for the Sandform website. I must admit that the first race on the six-race card, a 7f maiden, wasn't one I had been particularly excited about.

4-55   UNIBET HORSERACE BETTING OPERATOR OF THE YEAR MAIDEN STAKES (GBB RACE) (5) 3-Y-O+
5f   Par = 103   7 runners

AW Form	Name	Highest	Last Six Ratings
82-547	HIGHEST AMBITION	100So05	98Wo05 94Wo05 100So05 96So05 97So05 87Ch05
563-26	MISS SEAFIRE	100So05	88Ne05 93Ch06 94So05 98So06 100So05 89So05
8-	ANK MARVIN	69Wo05	69Wo05
5695-	ALYA'S GOLD AWARD	96Li05	88Wo05 91Ke06 82Ch06 96Li05
	FLAMING DAWN		
7	MARY OF MODENA	94Li05	94Li05
55	T MAXIE	99Li05	89Ch07 99Li05

However, that was about to change. It wouldn't be a surprise to anyone that in my view this wasn't a great race (maidens on All-Weather tracks at this time of year usually aren't) and it was possible to raise doubts over all those with previous experience. None of them had achieved a speed rating in line with the class par and one who had come closest to it, Miss Seafire, had done so at Southwell. There was a big difference between the straight 5f on the Tapeta there and the turning track on the Polytrack here, while I also felt that it would be disappointing if a four-year-old (and ten-race maiden) was able to win even as modest a race as this (the other four-year-old Highest Ambition was a non-runner).

T Maxie was a possibility, but she had made her debut over 7f and seemed to find this trip too sharp at Lingfield in her latest outing, so I felt that she might again get outpaced on this sharp circuit (races over 5f here are run on the inner track, so for a large part of the race the runners are on the turn). That just left James Tate's newcomer Flaming Dawn and had I not attended this fixture and been unable to see her up close I would have left this race well and truly alone, but now I was here and having viewed her in the paddock I was more than happy with what I saw.

She was also a half-sister to seven winners, a couple of them smart including on the All-Weather, so if she possessed any ability at all then surely she would be too good for this field, so the only real question was her price. A glance at the betting showed that she was available at 7-4, which was something of a double-edged sword. Yes, the odds were short enough, but you could also say it was a sign that there was plenty of confidence behind her. In other words, the market suggested that she was felt to be ready for this debut run, so after having come to the conclusion that the opposition was very beatable, I had £50 on her at that price.

Despite a tardy start, Flaming Dawn travelled well behind the leaders and picked up nicely when asked by Jack Mitchell, coming home comfortably clear of T Maxie and Miss Seafire. This win was something of a bonus for me, but it did show that while it is important to find reasons why a horse can win a race, it's just as profitable if you can find reasons why the opposition can't.

The second race was a 0-65 handicap for three-year-olds over 7f.

5-30   UNIBET SUPPORT'S SAFE GAMBLING HANDICAP (0-65) (6) 3-Y-O
7f   Par = 95   10 runners

AW Form	Name	Highest	Last Six Ratings
427-5	DEACS DELIGHT	100Ch07	89Wo06 95Ke07 95Ke08 100Ch07
8-4	GREYART	93Wo07	93Wo07 80Ke07
82-82	UMMSUQUAIM	94Li08	81Ne06 89Ke07 94Li08 83Ke07
613-73	BURABACK	97Li07	83Ke07 85Ke06 97Li07 94Ke08 82Li07 91Li07
4854-2	ALMODOVAR DEL RIO	97Wo07	94Wo06 85Wo07 90Ke07 94Li07 94Ch07 97Wo07
16-211	EXCELING	97Ke06	86Ch06 94Ke06 92Ch06 94Li06 97Ke06 96Ke06
	FAT GLADIATOR		
35-644	JUDY'S PARK	97Ch06	97Ne06 93Ke06 94Wo07 88Ke07 97Ch06 91Ke06
57-9	GREEK PHILOSOPHER	89Ke06	84Li05 83Li06 89Ke06
8594-4	GIDWA	96Wo07	82Wo06 86Ch05 91Li07 96Wo07 93So07

The one I was against was Exceling, as although she had won three
times over 6f around here including her last two, she had been beaten
a long way in her one previous attempt at this trip. Almodovar Del
Rio was a contender, but he was short enough in the market, so I
sided with Deacs Delight, who had come closest to winning when
second of 13 over this course and distance the previous November.
He hadn't run at all badly in a Chelmsford maiden last time, so he
made some appeal at the available odds in what I considered to be a
very winnable handicap.

I toyed with the idea of backing him each-way, but eventually
decided to go win-only at 10-1. However, it made no difference as
the gelding was on the retreat a long way out, so I soon knew my fate.
The race went to Gidwa, who ran out a comfortable winner while
Exceling ran with some credit to finish fourth.

The next contest was a three-year-old novice over a mile, and
this was another race I took a view on.

6-00   UNIBET NOVICE STAKES (GBB RACE) (5) 3-Y-O
8f   Par = 97   14 runners

AW Form	Name	Highest	Last Six Ratings
	PARLANDO		
6-	ANCIENT CAPITAL	83Ke07	
	83Ke07		
6-8	ANGLESEY ABBEY	98Wo08	98Wo08 82So11
	ARABIAN TALE		
	COMBAT STYLE		
	DOUBLE DARE YOU		

	HELLAVAHEART		
	LANDERMERE		
	MOONIS		
	PAOLO PANINI		
6-3	SICILIAN VITO	93Li10	91Ch07 93Li10
8	SOUS SURVEILLANCE	86Wo09	86Wo09
4	SPIRIT OF CIMARRON	90Wo07	90Wo07
	LUNA LIGHT		

Those at the head of the market looked vulnerable in my opinion. The warm favourite, Parlando, had been off for 120 days since making a successful turf debut, while the newcomers Moonis and Arabian Tale (a stablemate of Parlando) were both drawn high, which my statistics told me was a disadvantage over this trip. One I was very much against, although to be fair he was a big price, was another newcomer Landermere who looked massive in the paddock (he wouldn't have been out of place in the King George VI Chase back here at Christmas). He also had the widest draw in stall 14.

I decided that at the available odds Sicilian Vito might be a good each-way shout, as the colt had shown ability in both of his previous starts and had shaped as though the return to this trip would suit in his latest outing. He was available at 14-1, so was more than happy to have £25 each-way at that price.

As things turned out I couldn't have been more wrong about Landermere, who clearly knew his job and overcame his wide draw to just outstay Parlando and win by a neck with more than five lengths back to the others. Fortunately, they were led home by Sicilian Vito who stayed on to just get the better of Moonis for third, while Arabian Tale proved clueless and was tailed-off throughout.

The next race on the card was the feature, a 0-85 fillies' handicap over the same trip, and a race I felt pretty confident about.

6-30   TRY OUR NEW PRICE BOOSTS AT UNIBET FILLIES' HANDICAP (0-85) (4) 4-Y-O+

8f   Par = 102 5 runners

AW Form	Name	Highest	Last Six Ratings
2713-5	AMBER ISLAND	109Li07	105Ch07 109Li07 102Ch07 95Li07 103Li07 93Li08
225-40	UNIQUE CUT	108Wo07	108Wo07 95Li07 91Li07 90So07 104Li10
-600-7	ARENAS DEL TIEMPO	109Li10	89Ke07 87Ke08 90Ke08 80Li10 109Li10
-59-54	GLOBAL ACCLAIM	105Ke07	101Ke06 94Ke07 102Ke08 85So08 105Ke07
-11-99	UNIVERSAL EFFECT	101Wo08	100Wo08 99Wo08 99Wo08 100Wo08 89Wo08 97Ke08

The favourite was Arenas Del Tiempo who admittedly had some good form to her name, but the best of it had all been over 10f and it had been almost a year since she had tackled a trip this short. Global Acclaim was a contender, even more so when I saw that her trainer Clive Cox was in attendance, but I was particularly keen on the chances of Amber Island. She had failed to beat a rival in her previous outing, but that race had been much classier than this one. Not only was she now back off her last winning mark, on the last two occasions she had tackled 0-85 company she had won, while her latest success was in slightly higher grade.

There was a slight question mark over the trip as she had seemed best over 7f, but the way I saw it there was no guaranteed pacemaker in this field so I felt that this might be steadily run (another reason to take on the favourite) and that Amber Island would be able to do them for toe late on. I thought that 4-1 was a good price under the circumstances so I happily backed her, such was my confidence.

However, this contest proved to be a perfect example of how you can dissect a race as much as you like, but when it comes down to it the jockeys have the power to scupper any pre-conceived ideas you may have. It's something I'm very used to when previewing a race either for myself or when freelancing, especially when trying to predict what the pace will be like. You may have two or more established trailblazers in the field and feel that the contest will develop into a burn-up as a result, but it doesn't always happen. They can't all lead, so what is the rider to do? If they are on one of the front-runners, do they stick with that running style and compromise their chance as a result, or do they drop in which may lead to a similar outcome?

It's a difficult one to solve and in this case a race which I thought would be steadily run turned out to be anything but. Amber Island broke well but was understandably soon settled, but firstly Arenas Del Tiempo went past her and then Unique Cut went past both, the pair soon tearing off clear of the other trio. It soon dawned on me that this was now going to develop into a true test of stamina and, sure enough, despite looming up out wide to possibly hit the front for a couple of strides passing the furlong pole, Amber Island's effort then flattened out. Global Acclaim, who had been ridden cold at the back of the field, came through to just get the better of Arenas Del Tiempo whose stamina enabled her to hang in there for as long as she did.

To illustrate just how strong the early pace was, the field reached the halfway point in a time 5.31s (or around 26 lengths) quicker than in the preceding novice. No wonder Amber Island got tired late on, but her ability as a 7f performer remained undiminished and thankfully that view was confirmed when the mare reappeared at Wolverhampton 16 days later (though I wasn't there in person). Not only was she back over her optimum trip there (she already had winning form over the course and distance), she had been dropped another 2lb since Kempton which also meant she was that much below her latest winning mark. She had a nice draw in stall four, so what was there not to like? However, despite all the positives she was available at a most generous price of 4-1, probably due to a couple of her rivals being backed rather than any negatives on her part.

I just had to have a good bet on her in the hope that she enjoyed a smooth trip and that the race would pan out her way. Happily everything went perfectly – she was able to establish a good early stalking position from her low draw and travelled very smoothly. She did have to be angled quite wide to launch her effort after turning in, but Rossa Ryan still had plenty of horse under him and she was always doing more than enough once hitting the front. A nice result all round.

Back at Kempton the fifth race on the card was another fillies' handicap, though at a slightly lower level and this one was over 7f.

7-00   UNIBET 3 UNIBOOSTS A DAY FILLIES' HANDICAP (0-75) (5) 4-Y-O+
7f   Par = 100 6 runners

AW Form	Name	Highest	Last Six Ratings
-7-311	KHATWAH	104Wo06	96Wo07 96So05 104Wo06 103Wo07 101Ke07
3-62	EXUDING	105Ke06	103So06 95Wo06 105Ke06
67293-	EPONINA	107Wo08	95Wo07 92Ke07 92Wo08 106Ne07 102Li08 101Ch07
355-98	PORTERINTHEJUNGLE	101Du07	99Du07 101Du08 101Du07 96So06 87Li07 89Ke06
128-62	EYES	107Ne07	107Ne07 102Ne07 95Ne08 94So08 95So07 99Ke07
5-7	LIGHT OF THUNDER	91So05	88Ke08 91So05

Khatwah was forecast to go off at odds-on and although her claims were obvious, I wasn't interested at that sort of price and looking at the speed figures Exuding had at least as strong a chance. The trip was a question mark as she had never tackled it before, but her pedigree was encouraging enough in that regard and she was available at 5-1, so I was happy to have £50 on her.

However, everything went right for Khatwah as after a solid pace had been set by her stablemate Eponina, she picked up well and won going away. Exuding, who had been ridden cold in last place, made a brief effort but it came to little, and it appeared that she didn't stay.

The next contest was down at basement level, a 0-50 classified event over 1m4f.

7-30   JOIN RACING TV NOW CLASSIFIED STAKES (0-50) (6) 4-Y-O+
12f   Par = 101 13 runners

AW Form	Name	Highest	Last Six Ratings
408-56	DEBBONAIR	102Ne10	101Wo09 96Ke16 75Ke12 35Wo14 97Ke11 94Ke12
325-04	GLOBAL STYLE	106Ke07	97Ke08 101Ke07 90Li10 97Li10 91Li10 92Wo09
323-82	HANNALITE	106Li15	94Wo09 93Ch14 94Li15 106Li15 98Li15 95Ch13
08-986	SANTORINI SAL	96Ke12	87Li05 87Ke07 94Li08 92Ke11 95Li10 96Ke12
737-81	SAVOY BROWN	100Ke12	98Ch10 96Li12 90Li10 96Ch10 88Ke12 100Ke12
5-00-9	SCARLET RUBY	91Wo14	81Ke08 85Ch08 91Wo14 86Li10 82Wo09 88Ke12
64-866	TILSWORTH LUKEY	101Ch10	73Ch13 89Ch14 101Ch10 96Li12 85Ch13 96Ch10
83-807	TURN OF PHRASE	100Ch10	93Wo08 100Ch10 87Li12 95Wo14 88Li13 86Ke11
77-253	YORKTOWN	101Li12	93Li10 88Wo09 96Li10 101Li12 80Li10 89Ke11
0-4	I'M GRATEFUL	97Ke12	84Ch10 97Ke12
09-507	INTOXICATION	106Ke16	106Ke16 92Ke16 93Wo14 100Ke11 88Ke12 102Ke16
04217-	OWEN LITTLE	102Li15	67Ch10 75Ke08 89Ch08 96Ke12 101Ke16 102Li15
90-4-	SUPERSONIQUE	87Li12	86Ke07 76Ke07 87Li12

These aren't normally the type of races I like to get involved in, but I was here now and looking at the field there seemed to be quite a few who may have preferred another half-mile, including the favourite Owen Little. He was still one of the three I had narrowed the race down to, though, while Savoy Brown was an obvious contender after his win in a similar event over course and distance 11 days earlier, but I preferred the chances of Yorktown who, unlike several of the others, appeared to be running over his optimum trip. The gelding had performed even better than it looked when third at this track four days earlier, having been held up in a race where the winner, third and fourth were always up with the pace. He was available at 3-1 which made him just about backable to me, so I happily parted with my £50.

Given a fine waiting ride by Ross Coakley, Yorktown was able to deliver a telling turn of foot down the outside to comfortably beat Owen Little and Savoy Brown. My only regret was that having been fairly sure that only three horses really counted, I didn't invest in the trifecta which paid £55.20 to a £1 stake.

The last race was a modest handicap over 2m, but with my original selection Wemyss Point now a non-runner I was content just to watch the race before jumping in the car and heading home.

MONDAY, 28 FEBRUARY: WOLVERHAMPTON

Due to work commitments, it had now been 19 days since I had been able to actually go racing, so I was very much looking forward to this trip. A wet twilight meeting at Dunstall Park on a February Monday may not be everyone's cup of tea (and boy it was wet!), but I don't mind at all as it's a labour of love for me. The crowd was never going to be large, but in many ways that makes the whole experience more intimate. Besides, I had written the *Racing Post* Spotlight for six of the eight races on the card, which meant I felt an even greater responsibility to get things right. It certainly meant that no stone had been left unturned when it came to researching the races involved.

The first contest, a 0-65 amateur riders' handicap over the extended 1m1f, was one I had done the Spotlight for.

5-00   PLAY 4 TO WIN AT BETWAY AMATEUR JOCKEYS' HANDICAP (0-65) (6) 4-Y-O+

9.5f   Par = 101   12 runners

AW Form	Name	Highest	Last Six Ratings
9-0	KING'S CASTLE	96Ke08	88Wo12 96Ke08
44-225	CLASSY DAME	103Li10	98Li10 101Ch10 103Li10 101Li10 100Li10 98Li10
4/	CHORAL CLAN	97Ke08	97Ke08
355-41	SMOKEY MALONE	105So08	100So08 96So07 105So08 93So12 94So12 101Ch10
208-16	KINGSON	101Ne10	97Wo09 100Ne10 98Ch10 100Li10 101Ne10 96So11
3032-6	THE GAME IS ON	105Ch10	97Li10 97Li08 80Li08 105Ch10 100Wo09 92Wo09
87-337	GOLD STANDARD	106Li12	106Li12 94Wo09 100Wo12 100Wo12 100Li12 93Wo16
427-28	INTERNATIONAL LAW	105Wo09	100Ne10 103Ne10 99Wo09 96Ne10 100Ne10 99Wo09
7780-7	ONE TO GO	108Li08	98Ch10 96Wo09 93Ch08 97Wo08 100Wo09 90Wo08
	LEXINGTON BULLET		
8	BORN TO PLEASE	84So11	84So11
5667-0	HOMEGROWNALLIGATOR	99Wo08	99Wo08 90Wo06 89Ch06 87Li10 89Wo08

These races aren't usually high on the list for me from a betting point of view, but having researched the contest thoroughly I did like the look of Classy Dame, who was having her first start for Archie Watson after leaving Robert Eddery. The filly was still racing off her last winning mark and the form of her recent starts was working out particularly well (the winners of the last three races she had contested had been successful again at least once in the meantime). Her trainer also happened to be parked right next to me, but I don't necessarily subscribe to such coincidences.

The presence of top amateur Brodie Hampson in the saddle was another positive, so although odds of 11-4 would have been at the lower end of what I was prepared to take, I did invest £50 on her in the hope of getting the meeting off to a flyer and for much of the contest I was hopeful, with Classy Dame soon having established a nice prominent position.

However, I didn't feel quite so comfortable when the filly was sent for home rounding the final bend, quickly taking a couple of lengths out of her rivals. I know from previous experience that despite the final straight being relatively short (less than 2f) it can be a long way home from there. My fears were realised when despite trying hard, the combination was swamped on either side late on, with Kingson just holding on by a nose from King's Castle with Classy Dame a neck away in third.

I didn't dwell on the outcome for long as if you bet in races like these, you should know what you are getting and it's your choice as to whether you invest in them or not. I quickly turned my attentions to the second race, a 0-75 sprint handicap and another contest I had compiled the Spotlight for.

5-30   BETWAY HANDICAP (0-75) (5) 4-Y-O+
5.1f   Par = 103 11 runners

AW Form	Name	Highest	Last Six Ratings
24-524	ATIYAH	110Ne05	103Wo05 98Wo05 101So05 98Wo05 104So05 110Ne05
174-59	VANDAD	110Li05	108Li05 100Li05 104Ch05 107Li05 105Ch05 95So05
13424-	LILKIAN	104Ch06	103Li06 101Ch05 93Ke06 96Wo06 104Ch06 99Ch06
0-235-	SARAH'S VERSE	100Wo06	89Wo07 97Wo07 91Ke07 100Wo06 93Wo06 97Wo06
31-327	THE THIN BLUE LINE	108Ne05	93Ne06 100So06 101So05 101So05 106So05 108Ne05
335-37	BUY ME BACK	105Ne05	105Ne05 97Li05 101Li05 102Ch05 101Li06 99Ch05
9-2-68	SERAPHINITE	105Wo05	89Ch06 90Wo05 90Li05 105Wo05 96Wo05 98Ch05
8304-1	CUBAN BREEZE	105Ch05	95Wo06 96Ch05 99Ch06 89Ch06 101Wo05 105Ch05
-94362	SCALE FORCE	106Wo05	96So05 86Ne05 103So05 103Wo05 91So05 99So05
201-97	PERFECT SIGN	93Ne06	93Ne06 86Ne06 92So06 87Ke06 92Ke06
56-977	MUTABAAHY	107Wo06	98Wo05 101Wo05 102Ne05 93Ne06 95So06 98Ne05

Having dissected this event within an inch of its life, I was even stronger on Atiyah than I had been on Classy Dame. David Barron's filly had gained her two career wins over this course and distance and had run well when fourth at Newcastle last time (earning that big speed figure) where she had The Thin Blue Line over a length behind her in seventh. As I had mentioned in the Spotlight, the Newcastle performance was probably even better than it looked as she raced away from the other principals, more towards the far side of the track, yet was still beaten less than two lengths. I felt that her odds of 3-1 were fair enough so happily parted with my cash.

The race could hardly have gone any better for her (at least 99 per cent of it did) as she soon managed to get herself to the front and seemed to be controlling things for most of the contest. However, as I said before it can be a long way home from the home turn and although she gave her all, by the time they flashed past the post (I was stood right on the line) she had been joined by old rival The Thin Blue Line. Even before the result of the photo finish was announced, I knew what had happened (the freeze frame on the big screen on the inside of the track made sure of that). The filly had gone down to a short-head defeat, and I had waved goodbye to another £50. At least I knew my thinking was sound and that I couldn't have come much closer to winning, but I needed to see some money going in the other direction so that I had something tangible to show for it.

Perhaps the third race on the card, another 0-75 contest over 5f, albeit one for three-year-olds only, might produce the goods. I hadn't done the Spotlight for this race.

6-00 PLAY CORAL RACING-SUPER-SERIES FOR FREE HANDICAP (0-75) (5) 3-Y-O

5.1f   Par = 97   9 runners

AW Form	Name	Highest	Last Six Ratings
1-	DORA PENNY	101Wo06	101Wo06
138-	LOVELY MANA	95Wo06	94Wo05 95Wo06 87Wo06
213-43	POET	99So06	96Wo06 96Ke06 99So06 93Ke07 95Wo07
12-255	RESILIENCE	102Li06	92Wo06 93Wo06 102So06 102Li06 98Li06 95Ke06
46-936	DUSKY PRINCE	104Li05	95Wo05 93So05 89Ne05 104Li05 95Ne05
47	SHERDIL	97Ne05	95Ch05 97Ne05
152-	HOT DIGGITY DOG	102Wo06	94Ne06 89Ne06 102Wo06
37-222	FAIR AND SQUARE	105Li05	92Li05 97Li05 93So05 100Wo05 105Li05 101Li05
350644	COAST	98Li05	94So05 96So06 90So06 93So06 98Li06 95Wo05

I did like the look of Resilience, whose sole success had come over this course and distance, while he had faced an impossible task in his previous outing. He was now having his first start for Tony Carroll, which was certainly not a negative, but I just preferred the chances of Keith Dalgleish's Hot Diggity Dog, who had run well to finish second here in his previous start when pulling four lengths clear of the third horse. Unfortunately, the prices of the pair made backing them both unrealistic, so I just had £50 on the latter at 9-4.

The race was run in a monsoon, but I still watched the race next to the rail while the rather more sensible racegoers sought shelter (I just love being as close to the action as possible). I did end up getting very wet and also backed another loser, but not for the first time at this meeting I could have few complaints. Hot Diggity Dog was produced to hold every chance towards the inside of the track, but Resilience just had his measure by the time they reached the line, scoring by a neck. Having narrowed the race down to the pair beforehand, in retrospect I should have invested a few quid on the exacta (paid £11.90), but hindsight is a wonderful thing. Yet another case of 'close, but no cigar'.

I called the next two races correct in the *Racing Post* Spotlight, but both were returned at odds-on, so they didn't carry any of my money. At least it meant that I wouldn't have a complete blank in the Spotlight (there is nothing worse), but I was back in action in the sixth race, a very moderate middle-distance classified event.

7-30   BETWAY CLASSIFIED STAKES (0-50) (6) 4-Y-O+
12.2f   Par = 101   12 runners

AW Form	Name	Highest	Last Six Ratings
60-823	BEAU GESTE	106Wo09	86Wo09 90Wo08 96So08 97So08 96Wo09 99Wo12
638-04	FLEURSALS	98Wo12	93Ke16 98Wo12 97Wo12 85So11 91So12 96Wo12
-3938-	JENNY REN	102Wo14	97So11 83Wo12 90Wo12 78Wo12 90Wo12 93Wo14
042-57	KING CHRISTOPHE	99Wo14	94So12 63So08 99Wo14 94So12 96Ch10 83Wo14
54-812	MISS SLIGO	101Li12	101Li12 98Ch10 93Li10 91Ch10 91Ke11 95Li10
0-4	ROCKINOVERTHEWORLD	89Ke11	77Ke08 89Ke11
3-8074	TURN OF PHRASE	100Ch10	100Ch10 87Li12 95Wo14 88Li13 86Ke11 92Ke12
149-	DANCING MASTER	95Wo16	89Wo16 95Wo16 78So16
863-57	DEW YOU BELIEVE	99Wo08	82Wo09 91Wo08 93Wo09 95So12 91Ke12 91So12
87-008	MUSTANG KODI	95Wo12	93Ke16 90Li15 91Li12 92Li10 74So11 94Ch10
56-8	ONLY DEBRIS	95Wo09	89Ne10 95Wo09 61So12
8-06-4	TRIBUNA UFFIZI	97Ch10	87Wo08 84Ke08 78Li07 89Wo14 97Ch10

As with the earlier amateurs' contest, races like this don't normally float my boat, but I had done the Spotlight for it and had come down on the side of Beau Geste, whose four career successes included three over shorter trips at this venue. The gelding had been attempting this far for the first time when third in a similar event over course and distance three weeks earlier, so with stamina not appearing to be an issue then I felt 7-2 was a fair price for a horse who clearly enjoys himself around here. Also, the stable had already struck with Resilience earlier on the card, so I was happy to get stuck in.

Unlike with the earlier races, I never felt I was going to win this, as although Beau Geste plugged on into sixth, he never really looked a threat. At least I could console myself that the 20-1 winner Jenny Ren had come nowhere near making my shortlist, but fair play to anyone who did support her, especially if their name wasn't Jenny.

The penultimate race was little better, a 0-55 handicap for three-year-olds over 7f.

8-00   DUNSTALL PARK HANDICAP (0-55) (6) 3-Y-O
7.2f   Par = 95   12 runners

AW Form	Name	Highest	Last Six Ratings
65-5	ISLADAAY	92Wo08	77So05 90Ne07 92Wo08
780	VIVE LA REINE	90So07	82Wo07 90So07 86Ke07
22-131	STORM ASSET	100Wo07	92Ch06 91Ch07 93Ne0785Li07 100Wo07 95Wo07
9-2	SHABS	100Wo07	84Wo06 100Wo07
57-69	SAFETY FIRST	100Ke08	88Wo07 84Li07 100Ke08 85Wo07
907	TWILIGHT TONE	91So07	87Ke07 86Li07 91So07
798-31	BAILEYS EMINENCE	97Wo07	66Ke07
86Ch07	81Ch06	97Wo07	91Ch07
8008-8	THREE DONS	90Wo06	90Wo06 76Ke06 76Wo05 78So05 82Wo06 86Ke06
58-242	ARPINA	100Wo07	79Li06 86Ch07 88So06 100Wo07 92Wo07 90Ch07
00-379	MY NAME'S HOWARD	92Wo08	70Ke07 74Li07 81Li07 92Wo08 90Ke08
00-366	THE ORMER GATHERER	100Li08	67Wo06 58Ch07 84So06 100Li08 96Li10 85Ne08
00-896	SONNY BROWN	84So06	62Ke06 56So07 78Ch06 84So06 77Ke06

I hadn't enjoyed much luck at the meeting up until now, but that was about to change, albeit it was as much down to circumstance as to any clever thinking on my part.

When I had originally compiled the Spotlight, I was very keen on Shabs, who had been beaten a nose on his handicap debut over course and distance the previous month. In fact, I had been so confident over him in the Spotlight that I had napped him, but at that stage there were still 12 runners. With three having been taken out in the meantime, including Storm Asset who would probably have been vying for favouritism, we were now down to just nine runners and the size of the field wasn't the only thing getting lower, so were Shabs's odds.

The opening show on-course about him was 5-6, and with the best will in the world there was no way I was going to back him at that price. I still wanted some action, though, so had another look at what I had written in the Spotlight to see if there was something who might offer some each-way value. The one who caught my attention was Twilight Tone who hadn't shown much in his first three starts, but he was a half-brother to five winners so he could well show more now that he was switching to handicaps at a modest level. He was just about backable at 10-1 so I decided to have £25 each-way.

Shabs had every chance and kept on well despite coming off the bridle some way out, but he was comfortably picked off by Twilight Tone who did indeed take a major step forward. I had made a profit on the race but had been very fortunate to do so, as without the non-runners I would have just backed Shabs to win and would have had £50 on him, so would have done my money.

Things were about to get even better with the closing contest of the night, another 0-55 for older horses over the same trip. This was the other race I hadn't done the Spotlight for.

8-30   NEWBRIDGE HANDICAP (0-55) (6) 4-Y-O+
7.2f   Par = 101 12 runners

AW Form	Name	Highest	Last Six Ratings
2-4311	MILLION REASONS	107Ne06	92So08 103Wo07 100Wo07 106Ch07 96Li06 107Ne06
008-	LUCIA CHANGRETTA	90Ke06	84Wo06 59Ne07 90Ke06
702827	STREET POET	105Wo07	100So08 91Wo08 97Wo07 89Wo08 98Ch08 103So07
70-985	ELUSIVE ARTIST	102Ch10	99Li10 102Ch10 84Wo09 89So12 87Ke07 101Wo07
-1-465	MACS DILEMMA	103Wo07	91Du06 88Du07 98Wo07 99Ch07 103Wo07 96Wo07
5-9	APACHE CHARM	94Wo07	94Wo07 81Ch08
2556-8	TOMMYTWOHOOTS	103Wo07	91Ne06 103Wo07 88Wo07 100Wo07 91Ch07 96So07
/2550/	CAMACHO MAN	101Wo12	91Wo07 90Wo09 98Wo09 97Wo14 101Wo12 84Ne08
-31798	DUBAI ELEGANCE	102Wo07	98So07 101Wo07 99So08 98So08 96So08 93Ne08
7-59-7	CENTS IN THE CITY	94Ch10	80Ke07 91Wo07 89Wo09 94Ch10
/7960/	HEY PRETTY	103Du07	97Du08 97Du07 89Du08 78Wo07 96Ke07 83Ke07
-60-97	LUCKYANGEL	94Wo05	84Ne07 94Wo05 79Wo07 91Wo06 83Wo06

Everything pointed to Million Reasons and just by looking at the above card you don't need to be a genius to figure out why. The gelding was clearly coming into this on a high and, although he was back up in trip for his hat-trick bid, he had run well in both previous appearances over this course and distance. His latest win at

Newcastle had also put him on the Sandform Hotlist and he had a nice draw in stall two, so what was there not to like?

As the race approached my main concern was that he was so obvious that his odds would surely reflect that. Indeed, his opening price was 11-8 which was just about as tight as I would have expected, but then something strange started to happen, David Evans's gelding began to drift. The only question I now had was how long I was going to hold my nerve before steaming in.

Strength behind Macs Dilemma in the market may have been part of the reason, but probably a greater factor was a major late plunge on Elusive Artist, with Tony Carroll's gelding backed all the way in from 10-1 to 4-1 just before the off. To my utter amazement, Million Reasons was now available at 9-4 and this was an ominous drift on the face of it but having made sure he still had all four legs in each corner, I convinced myself it was well worth the risk.

I never really had a moment's worry as although Million Reasons only won by half a length, he looked likely to score from a long way out. Again, unforeseen circumstances had turned this race into a profitable one (or at least a *more* profitable one) and it meant that the long journey home on the motorways in the heavy rain and awful spray was a happier one than it would otherwise have been.

SATURDAY, 19 MARCH: WOLVERHAMPTON

Again, work commitments meant that it had been a while since the last meeting I had managed to attend. This was the week of the Cheltenham Festival, so there was plenty of freelance work available, and as I tend not to frequent that particular meeting anymore I was more than happy to step in. However, I would have much preferred to have been at this fixture in any case, not least because I had again done the *Racing Post* Spotlight for all eight races on the card, so I felt very much in tune with it. There looked to be some interesting punting opportunities during the evening so there was no way I was going to miss it!

The meeting was an unusual one, with all the races restricted to jockeys who had ridden 30 winners or fewer in 2021. There were plenty of apprentices with rides on the night, as you might expect, but I was surprised by the names of some of the senior riders who matched the necessary criteria for one reason or another. Still, this was a meeting I was determined to get stuck into and because of the extensive research I had done for the *Racing Post*, I decided to play the placepot alongside any others bets I was due to have. Unless I have a good reason for doing otherwise, I keep my total investment on the placepot to around the same amount as for my average bet (£50).

Having assessed the situation I felt that as the horses I was interested in for the placepot weren't likely to be big prices, I would push the unit stake upwards rather than have loads of lines to a smaller unit stake. After all, I had come up with a selection for all eight races in the Spotlight, so I put each of those into the placepot on their own, but the third race posed a bit of a question. The contest was a 6f novice which looked to be a match, and there were just the five runners, so rather than have just the one placepot selection I put in both of the market leaders, which meant that my placepot would consist of two £25 lines (£50 stake).

Originally the opening race, the first division of a 0-55 handicap over the extended 1m1f, was very much on my radar for a win bet as I thought I had unearthed one.

4-55   BETYOURWAY AT BETWAY HANDICAP (RIDER RESTRICTED RACE) (DIV I) (0-55) (6) 4-Y-O+
9.5f   Par = 101 12 runners

AW Form	Name	Highest	Last Six Ratings
-3-361	SAMMY SUNSHINE	101So08	82Ke08
97So08	90So12 101So08	96Ne08	85Ke11
-65258	PARIKARMA	106Wo07	98Wo09 94Li12 100Li13 94Ke11 93Ke12 100Li10
7/5/1/	SIMPLY SIN	97Wo07	77Ke06 86Ke06 92Ke06 97Wo07
071-30	COPAKE	98Ch10	92Ne08 84Wo07 98Wo08 96Wo09 98Ch10 89Ch10
4337-9	BOASTY	107Du10	103Du08 99Du08 102Du08 106Du10 98Du10 95Du08
6-5086	CITY ESCAPE	100Wo09	94Wo08 94Wo09 93Wo09 91Wo09 91Li10 97So08
-99035	PILOT WINGS	106Ke11	91Wo09 85Wo09 99Wo09 93Ke08 94Li10 96Li12
0-6672	RIVAS ROB ROY	103Wo07	87Ke07 89Wo08 97Li10 94So08 89Li10 98Li10
41-635	JUST ALBERT	97Ke08	86Ch10 94Wo08 86Wo09 94Ke11 97Ke08 95Wo09
93-70-	DESERT CAT	94Wo08	81Ke08 94Ch08 89Wo08 94Wo08 67Ne07 79Wo08
57-0-	JACK BEAN	81Ch08	75Wo08 76Ch08 81Ch08
8-4698	NEW LOOK	100Li10	93Wo08 90Ch08 99Wo09 96Ne10 91Wo09 92Wo09

The horse I was interested in was Boasty, a Kempton winner for Charlie Fellowes in October 2020 and, following 18 starts in Ireland without a win, he was now making his debut for Ivan Furtado. However, despite the barren spell his form on the Dundalk Polytrack as recently as the previous autumn looked good in the context of this race, while this modest grade was going to be something new for him (they don't have races catering for this lowly level in Ireland). He had joined a stable I have the greatest respect for when taking over horses from other yards, so what was there not to like?

I must confess to a serious error of judgement at this point. When perusing the betting for this contest the previous evening I saw that Boasty was available at 5-1 and I don't know why I would have thought this, but I felt that price was short enough and that he would be bigger on the day. Imagine my horror then when he was backed right into 6-4 in the minutes leading up to the race (he went off at 6-5). Clearly, some people were looking at him the same way I was, a Class 5 horse effectively taking on Class 7 opponents, but there was no way I was going to back him at those odds. He didn't win, going down by a neck to recent Kempton winner Sammy Sunshine, but he should have collected and probably would have done so had he not hung so wide off the final bend.

I had kept the £50 in my pocket, so it had worked out well but that's not the point. Had he won at such skinny odds after I had missed a juicy price the previous day, then I would have been annoyed to say the least. At least I was still in the placepot, alongside everyone else.

The second division was now coming up and hopefully I would soon be back on track.

5-30 BETYOURWAY AT BETWAY HANDICAP (RIDER RESTRICTED RACE) (DIV II) (0-55) (6) 4-Y-O+

9.5f   Par = 101   12 runners

AW Form	Name	Highest	Last Six Ratings
2-4766	LENNY'S SPIRIT	103So08	101Ne08 98Wo08 103So08 97Li12 95Ch08 91Li13
581-80	TENTH CENTURY	100Ke08	87So06 88Ch05 88Ch05 99Ke08 100Ke08 83Ke07
702-04	UTHER PENDRAGON	107Ke08	89Li10 92Li10 90Li12 89So11 90So12 94Li10
46-632	AMALFI SALSA	100Ke08	91Li10 89Wo09 96Wo12 80Li10 100Ke08 99Ch08
8-5321	STRATEGIC FORTUNE	100Ne08	89Ke07 97Wo07 96So07 99Ke08 100Ne08 99Wo09
58U7-	ROCKY SEA	90Ke08	87Li07 90Ke08 0Li08 88Ch06
28-415	QUOTELINE DIRECT	101Wo09	93Wo09 101Wo09 87Ne10 99Ne10 97Wo09 95Wo12
3-5054	NINE ELMS	101So08	87Wo09 88So11 101So08 89So12 89So11 96Wo09
-70459	CASARUAN	104Ch07	98Ch08 95So08 97So08 96Ke08 103So07 90Wo09
6870-8	AIR OF YORK	104Wo07	96Wo07 92Wo08 97Ke08 91Wo08 88Wo09 99Ke08
0-0-90	BEATRIX ENCHANTE	85So08	26Ne08 56Wo12 84Ke08 85So08
70-900	DYLAN'S RUBY	98Li10	89Ke07 77Ke06 98Ke08 81Ke08 98Li10

Like the first division, this wasn't a race that was going to take a lot of winning and the one who made the most appeal to me was Lenny's Spirit. True, he had gone 17 starts since his sole win, but there were still reasons to be interested in him. He had finished runner-up in a couple of 0-60 handicaps on Tapeta in December, including on this track where he looked unlucky not to go even closer. Apart from the fact he was 4lb lower in the weights now, two of his last three starts had been over trips he was never going to stay, so I thought his price of 3-1 was acceptable in the circumstances.

This was one of those races where everything went right. Jockey Ross Coakley always had the gelding in a great position and when asked to take the gap which opened up for him, he made no mistake. We were now up and running.

The next race was the aforementioned five-runner novice.

6-00   BETWAY NOVICE STAKES (RIDER RESTRICTED RACE) (5) 4-Y-O+
6.1f   Par = 103 5 runners

AW Form	Name	Highest	Last Six Ratings
5-1	ACRION	103Li06	92So07 103Li06
	GENERAL SAGO		
09-707	LEVENDI	100Ke08	96Li08 92Ch08 88Wo09 100Ke08 91Ch08 89Ch08
9	LEXINGTON BULLET	79Wo09	79Wo09
48	WESTERN MELODY	87Ne06	80So07 87Ne06

I had selected General Sago for the Spotlight as although he was 0-9 and making his debut for a new stable, he seemed a likely type on the surface with four of his five winning siblings successful on the All-Weather. However, despite appearing to travel well enough in front he eventually blew up with his 203-day absence seemingly taking its toll. That left market rival Acrion with the race at his mercy, albeit he only scraped home by a neck from 20-1 shot Western Melody.

The fourth race on the card was the highlight of the evening, a Class 3 conditions event over 5f.

6-30   BETWAY CONDITIONS STAKES (RIDER RESTRICTED RACE) (3) 4-Y-O+
5.1f   Par = 107 6 runners

AW Form	Name	Highest	Last Six Ratings
110-36	LORD RIDDIFORD	113Wo05	0Ch05 110Wo05 110Li05 97Li06 102Wo05 105Li05
1422-3	MAY SONIC	115Ke06	107Ne05 111Ch06 107Ch06 104Ch06 107Du05 93Ke06
71-351	TONE THE BARONE	115Ch05	108Li05 103Li06 109Wo05 111Li05 106Li05 109Li05
-21-35	HIGHFIELD PRINCESS	112Ch07	105Ch07 103De07 108Ch07 112Ch07 103Ch07 108Wo07
03/	ALLIGATOR ALLEY	102Du05	96Du06 102Du05
0-2753	WATER OF LEITH	109Wo06	100Wo0679Ne06 105Wo06 102Li0693So06 104Wo06

Tone The Barone looked almost too obvious to me. Not only did he have a wonderful strike rate of 7-12 on the All-Weather and 11-27 overall, arguably his very best performance had come just seven days earlier when humping top weight to victory in a warm handicap at Lingfield. These conditions weren't going to be a problem for him either, having finished first and second in two previous starts over today's course and distance. The only danger on the numbers as I saw it was Highfield Princess, who was 3lb well in with Tone The Barone on these terms, but she was down to the minimum trip for the very first time on her 24th start.

My only concern with Tone The Barone was that I felt sure he was going to be too skinny a price to back, probably odds-on. Therefore, I was surprised to see him put in at 11-8 the previous evening which I felt was generous. Thankfully I didn't make the same mistake as with Boasty, I felt the odds were very much in my favour so was more than happy to wade in.

As with the earlier winner, things couldn't have worked out better as once allowed to stride on by Ross Coakley at halfway, he was always doing enough to hold off the staying-on Highfield Princess. So far so good, but could I keep it going in the next race, a 0-85 handicap over the extended 1m1f?

7-00   BETWAY HANDICAP (RIDER RESTRICTED RACE) (0-85) (4) 4-Y-0+
9.5f   Par = 105 8 runners

AW Form	Name	Highest	Last Six Ratings
74-146	FOX POWER	117Wo08	101Li08 108Ke08 86Ne10 88Wo08 100Ne08 108Wo08
-36114	ATHMAD	109Wo08	96Wo09 81Ch10 95Li10 102Wo09 105Ne10 105Wo09
1-3	NANKEEN	103Ch08	90Wo08 103Ch08
423-42	PRECISION STORM	105Wo09	96Ke12 103Ke11 105Wo09 96Wo09 101Wo09 102Wo09
2-1104	LAMMAS	106So08	101Ke07 105Wo08 103So08 106So08 103Ke08 99Wo08
2-6550	STARRY EYES	107Li08	90Ke08 87Wo08 93Li08 89So08 101Li10 100Wo08
-1718-	LIBERATED LAD	100Ke12	79Ke07 92Li07 95Li10 86Wo09 100Ke12 88Ke12
24539	BROOMY LAW	102Wo09	96Ne08 102Wo09 100Wo09 88So07 94Wo09

This contest was posing something of a dilemma. Fox Power was the one who jumped off the page at me, especially after having run well to finish sixth of 12 runners in the Lincoln Trial (a 0-105 contest) over 1f shorter here a week earlier. He had won over that trip around here on his debut for Mick Appleby the previous month but had finished unplaced in all five starts over this far and further. There clearly was a stamina issue, but perhaps they wouldn't go a strong pace this time and given that he had so much in his favour otherwise, I didn't like the idea of him coming out on top without my money on him, so I had £50 on at 5-2.

The one thing you don't need with a horse who has even the slightest doubt over their stamina is to become embroiled in a disputed lead, and that is exactly what happened with Fox Power, the gelding being taken on by Nankeen for most of the journey. He showed his class by seeing that rival off, but it left him vulnerable when things got serious and the pair who had stalked the duelling leaders from the start, Lammas and Precision Storm, came sweeping past to fill the first two places with Fox Power back in third.

A resurgence was now required, and I thought I might get it in the next contest, a 0-90 handicap for fillies over 7f.

7-30   PLAY CORAL RACING-SUPER-SERIES FOR FREE EBF FILLIES' HANDICAP (RIDER RESTRICTED RACE) (0-90) (3) 4-Y-O+

7.2f   Par = 104 6 runners

AW Form	Name	Highest	Last Six Ratings
-31116	KHATWAH	111Ke07	96So05 104Wo06 103Wo07 101Ke07 111Ke07 100Ch07
225-61	NIGHT NARCISSUS	108Wo06	98Wo06 102Ke06 103Ke06 108Wo06 98So05 106Wo06
13-531	AMBER ISLAND	111Ke08	102Ch07 95Li07 103Li07 93Li08 111Ke08 109Wo07
46-435	CRY HAVOC	109Ch07	103Ke07 93Li07 97Ne07 88Ke07 99Wo07 103Ch07
77-	SEPARATE	102Ch07	102Ch07 91Li07
-40139	HOLD FAST	108Ke10	104Ch08 103Ke08 95Ke08 97Ke08 92Ke08 87Wo07

My old friend Amber Island was back for more and I thought she had a great chance, having only been put up 2lb for her win here 22 days earlier. There were doubts over the pair I considered to be her main dangers, with Khatwah now 12lb higher than when completing her hat-trick at Kempton the previous month and Night Narcissus having her first try at this longer trip. Amber Island was available at 7-2 and that was more than good enough for me.

My only slight concern was that Night Narcissus was notably strong in the market despite still having stamina to prove, but the reason she was so popular soon became obvious when she had no problem in picking off the front-running Khatwah and saw the trip out in such a way that it looked as though she had wanted it all her life. To be fair to Amber Island, she gave herself every chance and just bumped into a better one on the day.

The penultimate contest was the first division of a 0-65 handicap over the extended mile.

8-00   ALL WEATHER CHAMPIONSHIPS MILE HANDICAP (RIDER RESTRICTED RACE) (DIV I) (0-65) (6) 4-Y-O+

8.6f   Par = 101 11 runners

AW Form	Name	Highest	Last Six Ratings
504034	HARBOUR VISION	110Ch07	102So08 96So07 99Wo07 103So07 107Wo07 107Wo07
40-1-3	PERUVIAN SUMMER	99So08	82So08 96Ne08 86So07 88So07 97So08 99So08
9135-3	LOCAL BAY	105Ne07	86Du07 101Ne08 95Wo09 99Ne08 105Ne07
5-4353	MYTHICAL MADNESS	111Wo09	100Wo09 98Wo09 99Li10 100Wo08 101Li10 95Wo09
47-371	QUEEN OF BURGUNDY	102Ch07	94Li06 94Wo06 94Wo07 99Ke07 99Ne06 97Wo08
196-7-	ASTROMAN	99Wo12	80Ch07 88Ke07 99Wo08 83Ch08 98Ke12 99Wo12
29-634	HEADORA	103Wo08	72Wo08 103Wo08 95Wo09 94Li08 98Wo09 99Ke08
634625	DISTINCTION	108So07	100Ne07 99Wo07 98Wo08 97So07 107Wo08 98So08
89-767	RUSHMORE	102Wo14	102Wo14 91Wo09 88Wo14 100Wo09 91Li10 90Wo09
16279-	DEFILADE	101Wo07	99Wo07 101Wo07 97Ke07 96Wo08 97Wo07 94Wo08
-9763-	ZEFFERINO	104Ch10	97Li10 92Ch10 84Li10 95Ch08 97Ch08 97Ch08

Harbour Vision does stick out a bit like a sore thumb with those big speed figures for his last two outings around here (admittedly over a shorter trip). He had won over a mile at Chelmsford in the past, so I wasn't overly concerned about him seeing out the distance and there were other factors which made him so attractive. The first was that he had become well handicapped having dropped 7lb below his last winning mark and those last two starts in much better company had suggested that the wheels had certainly not come off. His appeal became even greater when I discovered that he had only contested two 0-65 handicaps before in his life and won them both, but you had to go back to January 2019 and August 2020 to find them.

Therefore, it's so important that you don't get totally bogged down in a horse's recent performances and try to look at their entire career in a tabulated format, otherwise things like this can be missed. Fortunately, my experience of doing *Racing Post* Spotlights has shown that, as one of my colleagues so succinctly put it, 'no stone is left unturned'. I invested £50 on Harbour Vision at 7-2 and this is all building up to a happy conclusion, isn't it? Well, this is what happened.

Harbour Vision has often made the running in recent months, but this time was understandably held up behind the leaders by Jack Duern with a couple of the others keen to get on with it. In fact, he was given a textbook ride by his jockey, and it is no fault of his that when he asked the gelding to gather stride once in line for home, he half thought about it, carrying his head to one side and losing concentration. He did stay on again and finished with quite a rattle but failed by a head to catch Headora. In my mind this was one that got away.

Still, there was the second division to look forward to.

8-30   ALL WEATHER CHAMPIONSHIPS MILE HANDICAP
(RIDER RESTRICTED RACE) (DIV II) (0-65) (6) 4-Y-O+
8.6f   Par = 101   11 runners

AW Form	Name	Highest	Last Six Ratings
3-3162	MAGICAL MILE	100So08	93Li07 96Ne08 99Ch08 100Ch08 82Ne08 100So08
7-2247	VOCATUS	102Wo08	100Ch10 93Ne08 100Wo08 100Wo09 94Wo09 94Wo09
728-14	CALONNE	107Ke08	100Wo06 102Wo08 100Wo09 90Ke06 102Wo08 107Ke08
7-5339	ONE STEP BEYOND	108Li08	94Ch06 96Wo07 99Li08 108Li08 100Ke08 100Li07
1-9945	UNIVERSAL EFFECT	105Wo08	99Wo08 100Wo08 89Wo08 97Ke08 102Ke08 105Wo08
6-5U86	GERTCHA	102Ch08	86Ch08 102Ch08 99Wo08 0So11 93So12 100Wo08
111160	BACK FROM DUBAI	104So08	101So08 104So08 101So08 100So07 98So08 87So08
0950-8	WELOOF	103Wo08	103Wo08 83Wo08 90Li07 99Li07 84Ke07 96Li08
6-2423	MAKAMBE	112So08	95Ke08 97Ke08 99So08 102Ke08 100So08 96Wo08
026-09	BOUNTY PURSUIT	102Ke07	88So06 85Ke06 97Li07 89Ch07 87Ke08 100So08
38-059	BERTOG	103Wo08	100Wo08 97Wo08 87Wo08 93So07 103Wo08 96So08

I was keen on Universal Effect in this, as not only had the mare fallen 3lb lower than for the latest of two wins over this course and distance early in 2021, but there had also been distinct signs that she was on the way back in her most recent outing (her fourth start since returning from almost a year off in January). She just had to be backed at 15-2.

Unfortunately, although she travelled well in midfield she travelled too well, pulling much too hard so that when she was produced with her effort those earlier exertions started to tell and she quickly flattened out. I made a note that I would be looking out for her the next time she ran, especially back here when it seemed likely there would be a good pace on.

It was possible to find the winner Weloof as not only was John Butler's gelding back off his last winning mark, his position in the market (11-2) indicated that he felt ready for this return from 75 days off.

I suppose I should have felt satisfied with my day's work – my Spotlight had yielded two winners, three seconds, two thirds and one horse unplaced from eight selections, but again I felt as though things could have gone more my way. At least I had won the placepot to a single line, though my expectations as regards the dividend weren't very high with five of the six favourites placed, three of them at very short prices. I thought the dividend would be titchy, perhaps barely covering my stake, so I was a bit surprised (pleasantly so) that it paid as much as £9.60 to a £1 stake, which for me was a bit of a bonus!

TUESDAY, 12 APRIL: WOLVERHAMPTON

The weather wasn't great in the lead-up to this fixture, but that wasn't going to put me off as having studied the meeting in detail the day before, this was a card I felt I could really get my teeth into. However, I nearly didn't make it as I endured the journey from hell and on a few occasions along the way I felt like turning back and coming home.

The problems started on the M40 when, on the approach to Banbury, I spotted the roadside message which said, '30 minute delay between junctions 11 and 12'. Unfortunately, it was too late for me to think of an alternative route to Wolverhampton, so I decided to just grin and bear it as I still had time on my side, or at least that's what I thought. After stopping and starting for what seemed an eternity, I finally arrived at a point where the three motorway lanes were funnelled into one. The central barrier had clearly taken quite an impact and was being repaired, hence the delay. It later transpired that there had been a serious accident here earlier in the day and although things had started to become physically uncomfortable for me, especially thanks to my bladder (resulting in quite a bit of Kenny Everett-style leg-crossing), I never forgot that someone could have been seriously hurt in that accident, which put any suffering I may have been experiencing into perspective.

Having made my way through that delay I then hoped that the rest of the journey would go rather more smoothly, but on reaching the M6 I was soon dissuaded of that notion. Again, I stopped and started for miles (coming to a complete standstill on occasions), but this was purely down to roadworks and volume of traffic and, although I eventually limped my way into the Dunstall Park car park, a journey that normally takes less than two hours had taken three and a half. I felt jaded and not a little stiff and having gone through the usual formalities of gaining racecourse entry, I proceeded to make my way to the gents' toilet like Usain Bolt. From that point on I was able to relax to a degree, partly with the help of the legendary

Wolverhampton beefburger and wedges, but I couldn't rest on my laurels as the first race was only half an hour away.

One of the main reasons I persisted in trying to reach the track was how attractive the fixture looked from a punting point of view and the opening contest, a 0-65 handicap 1m4f, was one of the races I was most looking forward to.

5-05   ·BETYOURWAY AT BETWAY HANDICAP (0-60) (6) 4-Y-O+
12.2f   Par = 101   11 runners

AW Form	Name	Highest	Last Six Ratings
01-721	STUDY THE STARS	102Ke12	88Wo09 88Ke08 78Ke08 100Ke08 102Ke12 100Wo12
6-47-7	AMSBY	107Li10	90Li08 77Li08 90Ke08 107Li10 90Ke11 86Wo09
45511-	WAY OF LIFE	102Li12	83Li08 92Wo09 83Li10 85Wo12 101Wo12 102Li12
702423	TERMONATOR	102Ne10	91Ne10 95Wo09 102Ne10 99Ne12 100Ne10 99Ne10
07-557	TOMMY R	102Wo12	85Ne12 35So12 102Wo12 99Wo12 96Ne10 94Ne12
22-468	KABUTO	105Li12	105Li12 93Ch10 93So12 96So12 86Ne12 88So12
7-2844	INTERNATIONAL LAW	105Wo09	99Wo09 96Ne10 100Ne10 99Wo09 91Wo09 95Wo09
11-052	AUTONOMY	101So12	91Wo12 101So12 96So12 80Ne12 94Ne12 100Ne12
80-	SHAMADAAN	89Ke07	89Ke07 84Wo07
9-4266	HAVEN LADY	98Wo12	91Ne08 98Wo12 96So11 95Wo09 96Wo09 96Ne10
57-0-8	JACK BEAN	88Wo09	75Wo08 76Ch08 81Ch08 88Wo09

The red-hot favourite was Study The Stars who had been successful in an amateur riders' event over the same course and distance three days earlier and had a 5lb penalty to carry as a result. I'm not someone who overplays the penalty factor if a horse is clearly at the top of their game as I feel that is of greater significance than an extra weight burden, but in my mind, there were other reasons I was keen to take him on. Firstly, his skinny odds made it worthwhile in trying to find reasons to oppose him, and another was as a result in having some meaningful speed figures to hand. It can clearly be seen that his ratings didn't suggest he was any quicker than most of his opponents, so the only question was which one was I going to side with?

The obvious candidate was Way Of Life, who had ended 2021 in fine form, winning over this course and distance and then at Lingfield. There was a question over how fit he would be after a 132-day absence, but you could argue that the favourite also had similar questions to answer in returning to the track so quickly. When it came down to it the pair were the most likely winners, but one was 8-11 while the other was 6-1. A no-brainer surely.

Happily, this was a theory which worked out just fine, with Way Of Life always travelling like a winner, and although he did cross the favourite once in front it made absolutely no difference to the result. The meeting had started off just as I had hoped.

The second race on the card was a 5f seller – thanks but no thanks. Sometimes a bet can be found in races like this (the same goes for claimers) but I tend to leave them alone and most of the punters would probably have wished they had done the same here when the favourite unshipped his rider soon after exiting the stalls.

The third race on the card, a 0-75 handicap over 5f, was a race I was keen to get involved in.

6-15   PLAY 4 TO WIN AT BETWAY HANDICAP (0-75) (5) 4-Y-O+
5.1f   Par = 103 9 runners

AW Form	Name	Highest	Last Six Ratings
968-55	OUTRAGE	110Ne05	110Ne05 97Li06 101So05 98Li05 101Ne05 98Ne05
112251	INTERVENTION	108Wo06	94Wo06 95So06 104Li07 104Wo07 97Li06 108Wo06
-43241	MICK'S SPIRIT	104Li05	98Li05 101Li05 95Li05 103Wo05 101Ch05 104Li05
436274	SCALE FORCE	106Wo05	103So05 103Wo05 91So05 99So05 98Wo05 90So05
199543	RED WALLS	105Wo05	99So05 87So05 98Wo06 95Wo05 99Wo06 103Ch05
3185-7	BRAZEN BELLE	105Wo06	92Ch05 97Ch06 89Li06 85Wo05 98Li06 99Wo06
234365	TATHMEEN	111Ne05	104Ne05 99Ne05 101Ne06 97Ne05 94Ne06 103Ne05
977964	MUTABAAHY	107Wo06	93Ne06 95So06 98Ne05 97Wo05 89Wo06 104Ne05
226343	AMAZING AMAYA	106Wo06	98Wo05 103Wo05 98Ne05 96Wo06 104Wo05 106Wo06

Although they were genuine players on the speed figures the first two in the market, Mick's Spirit and Intervention, had questions to answer, the former having been raised 9lb for his win in a 0-65 contest at Lingfield the previous month. As I said before, I'm not overplaying the rise in his mark (in terms of physical weight he was only carrying 3lb more), but it did mean he was taking on better rivals this time and as he was hovering at around the 9-4 mark, he did look vulnerable in my eyes.

Intervention had been in fine form all year, including five wins on All-Weather surfaces, but they were all between 6f and 7f and this was only the second time in 34 starts that he had tackled the minimum trip. With those two out of the way I was even more confident that Amazing Amaya was going to offer some value. Admittedly she had gone 12 starts without a win but had been running really well in defeat and also given the impression she was ready to take advantage when things went her way. I felt she would be around the 6-1 mark, so I was somewhat surprised (and a little perturbed) when the on-course bookies were offering 10-1. I now had a choice to make as I was originally going to back her win-only but was so convinced that she was likely to place at the very least I couldn't help but back her each-way at those odds.

The mare does have a habit of starting slowly (that is just her) and she did that again this time, but after having had to weave her way through between rivals she only failed by a short head to catch Red Walls. It was painful to watch in real time and even more so when watching the replay on the monitors – so near but so far. At least my late decision to back her each-way meant there was a small profit coming my way, but it felt like scant consolation.

The next race was a three-year-old novice over 1m4f and originally it wasn't a contest I was intending to get involved in.

6-45   WATCH RACING FREE ONLINE AT CORAL RESTRICTED NOVICE STAKES (FOR HORSES IN BANDS C AND D) (GBB RACE) (5) 3-Y-O
12.2f   Par = 98   8 runners

AW Form	Name	Highest	Last Six Ratings
	ASGOODASSOBERGETS		
21	CHARLES ST	97Li10	97Li10 93Wo12
32	GRIMSBY TOWN	101Ne12	82Du10 101Ne12
	MOSTLY SUNNY		
02-	CITY STREAK	94Ke08	83Ke08 94Ke08
	SNOOZE LANE		
7-	LA BELLE VIE	91Ke08	91Ke08
75	ROSELEA GIRL	94Li10	92Li07 94Li10

If I had done the placepot (which I hadn't this time mainly due to lack of time after reaching the track) I would probably have included Grimsby Town based on his latest speed figure, and the French import Asgoodassobergets. The problem with bets like the jackpot and placepot is that you can't wait to see what the horses look like in the paddock, which is crucial in events contested by lightly raced types like these. Asgoodassobergets had won a conditions event on turf in France five months earlier and it was likely he was going to play a part in this race purely on form, but how ready was he?

The answer, when finally seeing him in the flesh, was that he looked magnificent. In fact, if this contest had been based purely on looks, he was already past the post (not that I like that phrase). As I said I wasn't going to get involved in this race and the colt was now a best-priced 11-8, which was short enough for a horse trying a new surface on stable debut after a layoff, but I just couldn't get it out of my head how well he looked. Surely, I was in a better position than those punters off-course and felt I should at least try and capitalise on this situation, so I parted with my £50 at those odds.

It wasn't exactly easy, and he did drift left late on as he got tired, but he did enough to win by half a length so at least my instinct proved justified, as did the value of paddock inspection. Grimsby Town finished back in sixth.

The fifth race on the card was the feature contest, a 0-90 handicap over the same trip.

7-15 BETWAY HANDICAP (0-90) (3) 4-Y-O+
12.2f Par = 107 5 runners

AW Form	Name	Highest	Last Six Ratings
11-232	DESERT EMPEROR	**115Li12**	100Wo12 103Wo12 103Wo12 91Ne10 115Li12 104Li12
3-1114	OLD PORT	**108Wo09**	94Ke0696So07 106Wo08 108Wo09 107Ke11 97Li10
115713	PERCY WILLIS	**105So12**	97Ne12 96So12 100So12 105So12 101Wo12 89Wo12
32-1	WHITE WILLOW	**99Ne08**	99Ne08 90Ne08 89Wo09
4-59	CASTING VOTE	**98Ke12**	98Ke12 94Wo09 96Wo09

I was very keen on Desert Emperor, a three-time winner over course and distance late the previous year and running consistently well at other tracks in the meantime. He was only being offered at 6-4, but he had so much going for him in my view that I decided to back him nonetheless.

However, although he had run well when attempting to make all in the past, I'm not convinced that those tactics truly suit him (last year's wins had all been gained when getting a lead) and he soon found himself bowling along in front here. Although taken on by Old Port a long way out, he stuck to the task for as long as he could but could never quite get back on terms with his rival, going down by three-quarters of a length at the line. In what turned out to be rather a messy event, it was probably significant that the winner had proved himself so effective over shorter trips.

The penultimate contest was a 0-75 handicap for three-year-olds over 6f.

7-45   CORAL PROUD TO SUPPORT BRITISH RACING HANDICAP (0-75) (5) 3-Y-O
6.1f   Par = 98   7 runners

AW Form	Name	Highest	Last Six Ratings
	WATCHYA		
231-	KAPE MOSS	**91Ch06**	89Ne06 91Ch06 79Ne06
2-24	EBTSAMA	**105Li06**	87Ke07 85So07 105Li06
43-163	TRUE JEM	**99So06**	92Ne06 97Wo07 99So06 99So06 97Ne06
7-4211	SIR HENRY COTTON	**107Li06**	89Ch06 95So07 98Wo06 98Wo06 107Li06
152-22	HOT DIGGITY DOG	**102Wo05**	94Ne06 89Ne06 102Wo06 102Wo05 98Ne05
6	ETERNAL GLORY	**84Li07**	84Li07

I was drawn to Sir Henry Cotton on account of that big speed figure for winning at Lingfield 12 days earlier (with Ebtsama back in fourth), but he had proved himself over this course and distance the time before. The gelding was available at 5-1 and that seemed more than fair to me, but there were signs that he might find himself up against it. Adam Kirby had come here to ride in just the last two races, and this was probably the main reason he was here, with Watchya being trained by his guvnor Clive Cox. Despite making his All-Weather debut after 198 days off, the colt was sent off at just 9-4 and all these factors added together suggested he was going to run a big race.

He did just that, always being up with the pace and winning with a fair bit in hand at the end. Sir Henry Cotton ran on well to finish third, having not enjoyed a completely trouble-free passage, but he would never have troubled the winner in any case. He had at least again shown that he was effective around here, but perhaps just not quite as effective as at Lingfield.

The final contest was a 0-75 handicap over the extended 1m, and this was another race I felt quite confident about.

8-15   ALL WEATHER CHAMPIONSHIPS MILE HANDICAP (0-75) (5) 4-Y-O+
8.6f   Par = 103 9 runners

AW Form	Name	Highest	Last Six Ratings
-11164	THAPA VC	**108Ch08**	108Ch08 103Wo07 100Wo07 103Ke07 101Ke07 103Li07
115-85	ARCADIAN NIGHTS	**110Wo08**	95Ke08 95Wo08 110Wo08 98Wo09 102Wo07 91Wo09
217243	VISIBILITY	**110So08**	105So07 88So08 88So08 110So08 106So07 99Wo08
66-27	HANDEL	**102Ke08**	86Wo09 88So07 93Wo07 102Ke08
70-86-	YANIFER	**96Ch07**	87Li08 83Li07 82Wo07 91Wo08 96Ch07
434447	ABNAA	**113Ne07**	97Ne08 113Ne07 100Ne08 106Ne08 99Ne08 101Wo07
403424	HARBOUR VISION	**110Ch07**	99Wo07 103So07 107Wo07 107Wo07 99Wo08 100Wo09

| -6-313 | PLUMETTE | 107Wo08 | 99Wo07 100Wo08 79So07 107Wo08 105Wo07 101Wo09 |
| 0-3900 | ROCK CHANT | 102Wo09 | 90Du12 102Wo09 94Ke08 96So08 96Wo07 |

Plumette had been off for over a year before rejoining trainer David Loughnane in February, but her three outings in the meantime had suggested she had lost none of her ability. Quite the opposite; she had run well over an extra furlong here a fortnight earlier and won over 7f at this track the time before, but I felt that this trip (over which she had been successful at the end of 2020) was her true optimum. The warm favourite was Thapa Vc, the second of Adam Kirby's mounts and no doubt combined in doubles with his previous winner. However, despite three of his four wins having been achieved around here, all of his successes had been over 7f, and this was the longest trip he had ever attempted. That only served to increase my faith in Plumette, so I was happy to back her at 7-2.

This was one of those races where I felt confident the whole way around as the mare always appeared to be going well within herself and when Richard Kingscote asked her for more, the response was immediate. She ended up winning with any amount in hand and what had started off a difficult day had ended on a high, with three winners and an each-way return from six bets on the card. The journey home certainly proved a lot easier than the one up to the track earlier in the day.

WEDNESDAY, 18 MAY: KEMPTON

As I have said on many occasions, the winter season on the All-Weather can produce a star of the future, not just on four legs but also on two, and many a successful career has flourished in those cold winter months. Every year I'm on the lookout for an emerging talent, either a jockey or a trainer or both, and usually there are a couple of names I make a note of to see how they develop. I know I'm not alone, as after a while you can be sure that the mainstream racing broadcasters (ITV, Racing TV or Sky Sports Racing) will also focus on an individual. How long will it be before you hear that a horse is being ridden by the 'the apprentice find of the winter'? When I hear this said, I just pray that it isn't the kiss of death for said person.

At the start of 2022 one trainer and one apprentice jockey had made their way into my notebook as ones to monitor and the reason I'm raising the point here is that the jockey in question was due to ride at this fixture and the trainer was also represented, so now is as good a time as any.

The rider was Harry Davies (mentioned earlier on in this diary) who was certainly bred to be a jockey. His father Stephen was attached to Sir Henry Cecil's yard and won the apprentice title back in 1994, while his mother Angie was assistant trainer to Hugo Palmer. Harry himself had been crowned pony racing champion jockey in 2018 and 2019 and was attached to Andrew Balding's yard, for so long a renowned source of riding talent. I happened to be at Southwell on 11 January when he had his first ride under rules aboard a horse name Battered, and three days later at Lingfield he rode his first winner when giving Coolagh Magic an absolute peach of a ride to come from well behind and get up right on the line. I must admit I had backed him that day and the jockey was certainly a lot cooler than I was!

Just three days after that he doubled his tally when riding Desert Lime to victory at Wolverhampton, and it was this success that really brought him to my attention, as to my eyes he just looked the part. Sometimes you get apprentices who just don't look like apprentices, and he was one of them. A month later he was entrusted with the ride aboard Charlie Appleby's Tranquil Night at Kempton, and I thought if that wasn't a vote of confidence, I don't know what is. Earlier on that day I had tweeted:

'Harry Davies has only had 12 rides (3 wins) and is already being entrusted with a red-hot favourite for Godolphin. Good to see.'

He won of course, and tidily too.

The trainer to catch my eye was Kevin Philippart De Foy, who was in fine form on the All-Weather during February 2022, winning with six of his 11 runners between the third and 22nd of that month. I wrote in my blog published on the 20th:

'One stable which I notice has had a fine time of it during the past few months is that of Kevin Philippart De Foy (four winners with his last nine runners at the time of writing).'

A steady stream of winners followed and his career moved up a notch when his Vafortino beat 26 rivals to land the Victoria Cup at Ascot in May, so we were left in no doubt that this was a stable going places.

As far as this Kempton meeting was concerned, Harry Davies had a fancied ride in the opener, a 0-75 apprentice handicap over a mile.

5-30   UNIBET 3 UNIBOOSTS A DAY APPRENTICE HANDICAP
(LONDON MILE SERIES QUALIFIER) (0-75) (5) 3-Y-O
8f   Par = 99   8 runners

AW Form	Name	Highest	Last Six Ratings
12214	SUBJECTIVE VALUE	109Wo08	103Wo08 97Ke08 105Wo07 109Wo08 104Wo08
822	TWO TEMPTING	105Ke08	81Wo08 105Ke08 93Ke08
74-	FIORINA	94Ke08	86Ke07 94Ke08
351	WENDELL'S LAD	96So08	83Li10 87Wo12 96So08
3-	HAKU	102Ke08	102Ke08
5-852	VOLOS	99Wo08	94Ke08 93Ch07 98So07 99Wo08
863-	BLUE COLLAR LAD	99Ke08	91Li07 99Ke08 99Ke08
45-	GEOPOLITIC	92Ch10	92Wo08 92Ch10

He was aboard Fiorina, a filly making her handicap debut after six months off, and her prominent position in the market suggested she was fancied, albeit not by me. The one I liked was Subjective Value, not just because of his good speed figures but because, as far as I could make out, he was the only likely pace angle in the field. He was being offered at 9-2 and I felt that was far to big for the reasons I have given, so I happily stepped in.

Unfortunately, I knew my fate quite early as Subjective Value wasn't left alone in front, being repeatedly hassled up his inside by the hard-pulling Geopolitic, so it was inevitable that he would be vulnerable when the closers arrived. Under the circumstances he did well to hold on to third, albeit beaten five lengths at the line. The finish was fought out between Harry Davies's mount Fiorina and the favourite Two Tempting, and it took a while to sort out who had prevailed in the photo. In fact, I was right alongside Harry next to the horse-walk when the result was announced. He looked down at his saddlecloth number (number three) as the judge delivered her verdict, 'First number two, Two Tempting.'

It was at this point that I heard a loud crack and as I looked around, I realised that Harry had whacked his left boot with his whip in frustration. Clearly this was an example of what dedication is all about. No one likes to lose, especially by such a narrow margin.

The second race on the card was a competitive 0-85 handicap over the same trip of 1m.

6-00   UNIBET HORSERACE BETTING OPERATOR OF THE YEAR HANDICAP (LONDON MILE SERIES QUALIFIER) (0-85) (4) 4-Y-O+

8f   Par = 105   14 runners

AW Form	Name	Highest	Last Six Ratings
-51111	DEMBE	109Wo07	95Li07 92Ke07 100Ke07 109Wo07 106Li08 95Li10
49	PINWHEEL	100Ke07	100Ke07 96Li07
16-353	ARCTICIAN	106Ke08	103Wo07 105Wo07 96Ke07 106Ke08 102Li07
-46543	UZINCSO	113Ke08	86Ke08 113Ke08 95Li10 109Ke08 94Ke08 102Ke08
2-2	BEARAWAY	100So08	100So08 95So08
26-125	LAFAN	105Ke08	101Ch08 101Wo08 99Wo08 105Ke08 105Ke08 101Ke08
11/08/	FIRST VIEW	105Ke08	87Ke08 105Ke08 88Me08 85Me09
31	ENCOURAGED	109So07	102Ke07 109So07
45-	EMINENT HIPSTER	100Ne08	83Wo07 100Ne08
70-6-2	NEWTON JACK	106Ch08	89Ke06 88Wo06 94Ch07 69Ke08 100Li07 106Ch08
15-514	ROGUE FORCE	105Ke08	99Ke07 102Ke07 96Ch07 103Ke07 105Ke08 104Ch08
148-55	PRIORITISE	103Ke08	91Wo08 97Wo08 95Ke08 81Wo08 103Ke08 99Wo08
-23748	HECTOR'S HERE	107Wo09	102Wo09 100So08 107Wo09 98Wo09 98So11 94Wo09
657/	TYPICAL MAN	96Li07	94Wo06 96Li07 87Ne07

Originally there were meant to be 14 runners, but the draw plays a big part in races over this trip around here so I for one was far from shocked when the pair due to start from stalls 12 and 14 were withdrawn. I did like Encouraged on many levels, but the two negatives were that he had never attempted this far before and was due to go off cramped odds given the competitive nature of the race. I preferred to back Newton Jack who was available at 14-1 and appeared to offer some each-way value at that price.

I can have few complaints over the ride Newton Jack was ridden, as he held a great position throughout but just never picked up. The race duly went to Encouraged, though he had to dig deep to get the better of First View.

The next two races on the card were an older-horse novice and a two-year-old fillies' novice, neither of which made much appeal to me. Kevin Philippart De Foy had a runner in the latter contest called Mai Alward who ran well to finish third, stepping up considerably from her debut. I noted her as one to watch and she duly won at Lingfield the following month at odds of 5-2.

The next race I was determined to have a bet in was the fifth on the card, a 0-90 handicap over 1m4f.

7-30   TRY OUR NEW PRICE BOOSTS AT UNIBET HANDICAP (LONDON MIDDLE DISTANCE SERIES QUALIFIER) (0-90) (3) 4-Y-O+

12f   Par = 107   10 runners

AW Form	Name	Highest	Last Six Ratings
0/	DUBAI HORIZON	101Ke11	101Ke11
411-00	SKY POWER	109Ch10	97Ke11 103Ke12 86Li10 109Ch10 98So11 92Ke11
5-4625	DEAL A DOLLAR	108Ch14	101Wo12 94Li12 87Li10 106Li12 90Li12 89Ch14
85110-	THUNDERCLAP	104Ke08	94So08 86So08 94Li08 101Ke08 104Ke08 103Ke08
22-17-	VINO VICTRIX	98Li08	98Li08 98Li08 95Ke16 96Ke12
	JASMINE JOY		
-13-33	YEAR OF THE DRAGON	110Ke08	99Ke07 101Ke07 97Li08 110Ke08 102Ne08
	EAGLE COURT		
42311-	SPRING GLOW	103Ke12	95Wo12 101Wo12 98Ke12 100Ke12 103Ke12 102Ke11
323/	HEART OF SOUL	104Wo12	97Li10 101So12 104Wo12

This turned out to be a race in which I couldn't work out the betting market at all. The favourite turned out to be Jasmine Joy, despite the filly having no previous All-Weather experience. Admittedly she had won on turf, and I can only think that because the stable had already struck at the meeting there were liabilities in doubles, etc. Whatever the reason this did work to my benefit as I had presumed that the one I liked, Heart Of Soul, was going to be short enough in the market. After all, what wasn't there to like?

The gelding had won at Hamilton ten days earlier, but as that was an apprentice event, he had avoided a penalty and was 5lb well in compared to the mark he was due to race off the following Saturday. The only real question was the different surface, and this is where being able to view a horse's entire career record at a glance proved so useful. You had to go back to the spring of 2019 to find his three runs on the All-Weather and he had performed well in each of them, so any doubts over his ability to handle the conditions could be well and truly put to bed, so why was he being offered at 13-2? I don't suppose I'll ever know the true reason, but I didn't waste much time dwelling on it. I just parted with my £50 with great enthusiasm.

I should mention at this stage that the gelding was due to be partnered by Harry Davies who was probably still smarting from his earlier reverse, but I just hoped it might inspire him to gain quick compensation. I also must admit that things didn't look good when the rider started to push along rounding the home bend and especially when the combination started to hang left up the home straight. Fair play to the jockey, though, as not only did he manage to straighten the gelding up quickly he also managed to gain enough forward momentum to just prevail in a three-way photo. I was happy and so was my wallet!

Perhaps I should have had even more on, as the horse had been sent off at much longer odds than he should have been.

Race six was a 0-85 handicap over 7f.

8-00 UNIBET EXTRA PLACE OFFERS EVERY DAY HANDICAP (JOCKEY CLUB GRASSROOTS MILE SERIES QUALIFIER) (0-85) (4) 4-Y-O+
7f Par = 105 12 runners

AW Form	Name	Highest	Last Six Ratings
982-68	CORVAIR	108Wo06	100Li07 79Je07 97Wo07 108Wo06 101Wo07 81Ke07
7-32-4	LITTLE BOY BLUE	105Ke06	101Ke06 103Wo06 97Wo06 102So06 104So06 104Ke06
-15088	OSTILIO	104Li07	95Wo07 104Li07 103So07 97Ne07 97Li07 91Ch07
1533-1	IVASECRET	106Ke07	103Ke06 100Li07 95Li07 106Ke07 101Li07 104Li07
50-57	REPARTEE	103So07	103Wo06 70Ne06 103So07 96Ke06
4-9675	BOWMAN	110Li08	104Li07 98Ke06 98Li06 110Li08 108Li07 103Li07
2262-4	BILLY MILL	113Wo07	96Li06 113Wo07 105Ch07 99Wo07 107Ke08 104Ke07
32351-	WONDER ELZAAM	109Du06	106Du08 109Du08 109Du06 107Du07 102Ke07 101Wo06
6-71-	BIGGLES	97Wo08	93Ke07 97Wo08 91Ke06
-11225	GOT NO DOLLARS	109Ch07	99Ch07 102Ke07 103Ch06 103Ke07 109Ch07 94Ke07
77-847	EVASIVE POWER	109Li06	98Ke07 103Ke08 99Ke08 107Ke08 97Li07 96Li07
6-2785	HANDEL	102Ke08	86Wo09 88So07 93Wo07 102Ke08 98Wo08 98Li08

The one who took my eye was Got No Dollars who had shown on several occasions that he liked it around here, including two course wins. His below-par effort at this track on his previous start had been down to a lack of pace, but looking at the opposition here I didn't think that would be an issue. To be fair to jockey Sean Levey, he appeared to deliver the gelding with a race-winning challenge but having got there in good time his finishing effort was weak, albeit he held on for third. The race went to the unexposed Biggles, who made it three wins from seven starts on his return from a 286-day absence.

The last race on the card was a moderate 0-55 handicap over a mile and a half and as nondescript a race as you could possibly imagine, or was it?

8-30 RACING TV HANDICAP (0-55) (6) 4-Y-O+
12f Par = 101 14 runners

AW Form	Name	Highest	Last Six Ratings
12275-	THUNDER FLASH	99Li12	99Ch10 99Ch10 95Wo12 88Ch10 95Wo12 99Li12

-80612	ILHABELA FACT	**115Ke11**	92Li12 77Ke12 84Wo09 96Ke12 84Ke12 92Ke11
7-7097	BREGUET BOY	**104Li12**	99Ne10 81Li10 96Li08 98Li10 104Li12 78Ke12
531426	YORKTOWN	**101Li12**	80Li10 89Ke11 94Ke12 92Li13 83Ke12 90Ch14
0-28-4	LUCKY DRAW	**102So12**	76Ke07 92Ke12 85Wo12 100Ne12 81Ke12 102So12
67-	FOR LOVE OF LOUISE	**93Wo12**	93Ke12 93Wo12
3238-3	BUG BOY	**101Li08**	94Ke08 95Ke12 100So11 85Ke12 90So12 97So12
-52513	PLACATED	**102So12**	94Wo08 96Ch10 81Li10 89Ke11 92Li12 102So12
131652	SAVOY BROWN	**108Li12**	100Ke12 93Ke12 101Li12 97Ke12 106Li12 108Li12
	I DOUBT THAT		
4850-6	SETTLE PETAL	**106Li13**	60Ch10 94Ke11 97Ke08 106Li13 85Ke11 87Ke11
813-46	GRANDSCAPE	**102Ch14**	87So14 90Ch14 88Wo12 92Wo14 87Wo12 88Wo16
0-0-	PATRIOCTIC	**79Ke07**	79Ke07 45Ch08
0798-8	FAMOUS DYNASTY	**106Li12**	102Ch10 90Ke11 93Li10 73Li10 95Li10 89Li10

I was very keen on Savoy Brown, whose last two speed figures looked impressive in the context of this race. Admittedly a record of 2-28 wasn't great, but this was that type of race and at least one of his two wins had come over this course and distance, so why was he being offered at 7-1? The reason why he and all the others were bigger prices than might have been expected was an extraordinary gamble on I Doubt That.

Despite not having finished within 16 lengths of the winner in four Flat starts and two over hurdles when trained in Ireland, the gelding had been backed in from 33-1 to 11-4 (he was even showing 2-1 on one of the boards as I walked past) so someone clearly knew big improvement was forthcoming. He had even joined a stable that had gone 925 days and 95 runs without a winner, so I watched in fascination once the race started, not just at my selection but also the gamble, and the latter was much more interesting as he was ridden prominently from the start and always seemed likely to win, whereas Savoy Brown never really did.

As they passed the line and commentator Mark Johnson exclaimed 'gamble landed', I knew that I had just witnessed a successful touch at first hand. I don't like losing under any circumstances, but there is something fascinating about doing so in a race that you know will be talked about for a while yet. Still, it had turned out to be a winning night, so I was content enough.

SATURDAY, 3 JULY: CHELMSFORD

I wish I could get to Chelmsford more often than I do, but it's a long way away from home. On the other hand, it's a straightforward journey as it's mainly motorways and dual carriageways and, provided things aren't too bad on the M25, I can do the journey in around two hours. I had certainly picked a good meeting to attend as well, with the fixture featuring a £100,000 Listed contest for fillies and mares, plus a Class 2 sprint handicap. All in all, this was a meeting I was very much looking forward to.

The first contest on the card was a 0-65 nursery over 7f.

1-35   RACING WELFARE NURSERY HANDICAP (0-65) (6) 2-Y-O
7f   Par = 92   6 runners

AW Form	Name	Highest	Last Six Ratings
5	ALEXA'S PRINCESS	84Ne05	84Ne05
35	QUEEN OF ROMFORD	89Li06	82Ch06 89Li06
	CANDY RAIN		
	SWEAR		
6	JILTED	**86Ke06**	86Ke06
	PRINCESS NAOMI		

I must admit this wasn't a race I was originally going to play. For one thing there was precious little form to go on (let alone All-Weather form) and I do normally have an issue with Class 6 nurseries. Handicaps at this level for any age group aren't easy to dissect at the best of the times, but for youngsters it becomes even more complicated. However, I had looked deeply into each of the six contenders to see if anything emerged that might produce a bet. Once I had done so I had a bit of a rethink.

These types of contest are indeed difficult races to fathom, but more so as the year progresses when there is more evidence that these two-year-olds are as limited as their presence in such a contest might indicate, but here we were at the start of July with the nurseries only having just started to appear in the calendar. Therefore, with all due respect to the BHA handicappers, they were working with very limited information (each of the sextet in this field had raced just three times), but not only that none of them had raced over this far before, so there remained the possibility of improvement.

The likely favourite was Alexa's Princess and despite the modest speed figure for her Newcastle outing and that all three starts so far had been over 5f, I could see why she might be popular given her stamina-laden breeding. However, she wasn't alone in the extra distance possibly bringing about some improvement. The bottom weight, Princess Naomi, also had a pedigree which suggested she might appreciate going up in trip and she had shown a degree of ability in her latest outing, yet she was receiving upwards of 7lb from her five rivals.

A glance at the market revealed that she was the complete outsider of the field, but she was starting to attract some support. The opening 12-1 had all gone, but I decided that 10-1 was still big enough, so got stuck into her at that price (she would eventually return at 15-2). Alexa's Princess was heading the other way in the market and wasn't even sent off favourite, that position going to Queen Of Romford even though it was rather hard to see quite why.

Despite a slow break and having to come from behind, Princess Naomi powered her way through between rivals up the home straight and ultimately won with a good deal in hand, so I was naturally very pleased to have got involved in this race having not originally intended to. Alexa's Princess didn't appear to handle the bend very well while Queen Of Romford never looked like winning. The perfect start to what I hoped would be a highly successful day.

The second race was a 0-85 fillies' handicap over the same trip of 7f.

2-10   BRITISH EBF FILLIES' HANDICAP (0-85) (4) 3-Y-O+
7f   Par = 102   6 runners

AW Form	Name	Highest	Last Six Ratings
-43533	CRY HAVOC	109Ch07	97Ne07 88Ke07 99Wo07 103Ch07 106Wo07 99Li07
7-1	ADELAISE	97Ke07	93Ke08 97Ke07
961-	CYGNETURE	100Wo07	84Ke06 95Ke07 100Wo07
18	RIBBON ROSE	94Ke07	94Ke07 93Ke08
2-11	LILA GIRL	103Ch07	96Ch07 103Ch07 103Ch07
621	ETERNAL GLORY	102Wo06	84Li07 102Wo06 100Wo07

The betting market was very one-sided with Lila Girl, who was bidding for a course-and-distance hat-trick, finally being sent off odds-on at 4-6. Her speed figures for her two wins certainly made her a major player, both being above par for this type of contest, but I don't like taking such a short price about any horse (let alone in a handicap) and I preferred the chances of Cry Havoc in any case. She had gained two of her three wins at this track, had become very nicely handicapped and, despite returning from 79 days off, was proven fresh. She was available at 5-1 and that seemed fair enough to me.

Once the race was under way, I could have had no complaints over the position Cry Havoc soon adopted, travelling nicely behind the leaders against the inside rail, but when the field straightened up for home I became worried. To be fair to Adam Kirby he had no option but to challenge on the inside given where he was positioned, but although the mare was given every chance she just faded towards the finish, beaten a little over length into fourth at the line.

I couldn't help but feel that had she been able to challenge wider (where the main action was unfolding) she may have gone very close to winning. In this situation you often need to take something from the race that may well benefit you in the future. Therefore, at the same time as waving goodbye to my £50, I also made a note that Cry Havoc's performance should be marked up so that when she reappeared, I would likely give her another chance. The race duly went to the red-hot favourite Lila Girl, but only by a head and I hope those who took the skinny price about her enjoyed the white-knuckle experience.

The third race was a 0-75 handicap, again over 7f.

2-45 MARK ELKS 70 YEARS YOUNG CELEBRATION HANDICAP (0-75) (5) 3-Y-O+
7f Par = 103 10 runners

AW Form	Name	Highest	Last Six Ratings
212-6-	BEAUTY CHOICE	107Wo07	91Ke07 99Ke06 106Ch07 100Wo07 107Wo07 107Wo07
021-31	G'DAAY	106Li07	87Ch07 83Ke06 91Li06 102Ch07 103Wo07 106Li07
650879	GLOBAL WARNING	108Ne06	98Ne06 100So06 103So06 98So06 101Ch06 92Li07
2583-3	FORD MADOX BROWN	106Wo08	92Ke07 96Li07 106Wo08 104Li08 102Ch07 99Li06
	DAMAAR		
5-23	WAY TO WIN	106Wo07	85Ch06 106Wo07 102Ke07
59-177	DYNAMIC TALENT	101Ke07	94Ch07 96Li08 101Ke07 92Ne07 92Ne07
278508	HANDEL	102Ke07	93Wo07 102Ke08 98Wo08 98Li08 102Ke07 93Li07
13-525	BAILEYS ACCOLADE	101Ch07	90Ne06 98Ch06 97Wo06 101Ch07 98Li06
3354	TAKE A STAND	95Li07	82Ke07 86Ke07 90Wo07 95Li07

The one I liked was Beauty Choice and the reasons for liking him were similar to those that had drawn me towards Cry Havoc in the previous contest. He had become well handicapped (4lb below his last winning mark) and was down in class, so his price of 11-2 looked more than reasonable to me.

However, the similarities with Cry Havoc continued as he travelled well behind the leaders on the inside and made his effort one off the rail as an inviting gap opened, but although he didn't have a great deal of room to play with there was still enough of a gap for him to make his effort in good time. He also ended up finishing fourth, beaten around a length and a half behind the All-Weather debutant Damaar. I concluded that where he was forced to make his challenge had compromised his chance, especially as the first three all made their efforts down the centre of the track. This was though no fault of David Probert as he had no choice but to challenge where he did.

It was now time for the day's feature, the fillies' Listed race which was once again to be run over 7f.

3-50   LOUIS ROEDERER QUEEN CHARLOTTE FILLIES' STAKES (LISTED RACE) (IRE INCENTIVE RACE) (1) 4-Y-O+

7f   Par = 108   8 runners

AW Form	Name	Highest	Last Six Ratings
3-2194	AROUSING	109Ke06	100Ch07 103Ch07 109Ke06 101Ke06 101Ne07
	BOUNCE THE BLUES		
1-4195	FAUVETTE	106So06	103Li06 101Ch06 106So06 104Ch07 105Wo07 98Ne07
5-	IMPROVISED	96Wo06	96Wo06
11-172	INTERNATIONALANGEL	107Ne07	106Ch07 100Ch07 107Ch07 107Ne07 106Wo07 107Ne07
1-437-	MISHAL STAR	103Ch06	94Ke06 103Ch06 100Ke06 100Ke06
2-2-	SHE DO	105Wo07	105Ch06 105Wo07
110-0	SOFT WHISPER	100Me07	100Me07 99Me08 71Me09 97Me08

I had narrowed the race down to three possible winners, but Bounce The Blues had never run on an All-Weather surface before and neither had Soft Whisper, even though she had won twice in the dirt at Meydan. That just left Internationalangel for whom there was no doubt over the conditions, having won four in a row over course and distance at the end of 2021. She had also proved herself at this level when second in another Listed race at Longchamp in her previous start, so what was there not to like? I had availed myself of some of the 5-2 on offer earlier in the day so was expecting a big run, but it all went wrong from the very start.

After having become edgy in the stalls, she completely missed the break and in trying to come from last place in a slowly run race she never had a prayer. The winner Soft Whisper, on the other hand, was able to boss things from the front and kept more than enough in reserve to see it out. This was just a case of pure bad luck, and it could never have been foreseen, so I just dusted myself down and switched my attention to the forthcoming 0-105 handicap over 6f.

3-55   BETSI HANDICAP (0-105) (2) 3-Y-0+
6f   Par = 109   9 runners

AW Form	Name	Highest	Last Six Ratings
3341-7	ABOVE	111Ke06	109Wo06 111Ke06 110Li06 104Ke06 109Ch06 100Wo06
-33605	AYR HARBOUR	113So08	113Wo07 96Li08 113So08 107Wo07 92Ne08 103Ne06
111343	STRONG POWER	114Li05	109Li05 114Li05 103Li05 111Li05 103Li05 104Li05
6-71	PRINCESS SHABNAM	104Ch06	99Ke06 100Ch06 104Ch06
139276	MOHAREB	112Ch07	109So06 100So07 105So06 98Ke06 101Ke06 98Ke06
	TOLSTOY		
242322	CRIMSON SAND	113Ch06	107Ch05 107Li06 107Li05 96Li06 113Ch06 106Ch06
1-12	SHANKO	102Ch05	98Ch06 102Ch05 99Ke06
326-64	EL HADEEYAH	101Li06	101Li06 94Ch06 97Wo06 85Ne06 56Ne05 97Ch06

Crimson Sand was a horse I liked in general, not just for this race but because he was a real trier. He had made the frame in all nine starts since his latest win, while his record at Chelmsford read 124222. Clearly the conditions were no problem, but his consistency wasn't earning him any respite from the handicapper, so he needed just that something extra to enable him to turn those near misses into a win. I felt that he might get that here as he was due to be ridden by Harry Davies for the first time and that his 5lb claim might just be that missing catalyst.

Crimson Sand did endure a wide trip (about five-wide) on the bend, but he was produced with his effort in plenty of time and looked the most likely winner until gunned down late by Tolstoy, who like Damaar was an All-Weather newcomer from the Gosden yard. I couldn't have it both ways, as having put earlier defeats on the card down to racing on the unfavoured inside of the track I wasn't prepared to put this one down to going too wide, especially as some earlier winners had taken a similar route. It was yet another near miss for Crimson Sand, but this looked just pure bad luck rather than anything more sinister.

The sixth race on the card was a 0-60 handicap for three-year-olds over a mile.

4-30   SARCOMA AWARENESS HANDICAP (0-60) (6) 3-Y-0
8f   Par = 98   9 runners

AW Form	Name	Highest	Last Six Ratings
6-625	PUNDA MARIA	96So08	79Ke07 93Li08 93Wo08 96So08
-12523	MCQUEEN	106Li08	85Ch08 103Ke08 91Ke08 103Ke08 95Wo08 106Li08
2741-6	MUVERAN	96Ke08	94Ne07 95Ne07 96Ke08 83Ne08 89Ne08

5	LORDMAN	94Wo07	94Wo07
8-70	SHIFTER	92So07	76Ke07 92So07 81Li08
7-4	PLANTATREE	96Li07	91Ke08 96Li07
7-	BELISA DE VEGA	85Li08	85Li08
7067	RAVI ROAD	88Wo09	87Wo08 88Wo09 84Li08 86Li07
0039-	TAKEUSTOTHEMOON	89Ch07	87Ke08 71Ke08 89Ch07 87Ke08

McQueen looked to have plenty going for him, not only being a previous course and distance winner but also having three speed figures well in advance of anything his rivals were able to muster. The outside stall wasn't ideal over this trip around here given that they meet a left-hand bend quite early, but with everything else in his favour his price of 3-1 looked tempting enough for me.

Despite not getting the best of starts, the colt travelled well behind the two leaders under Ray Dawson and when the gap opened between the pair and he quickened through, the winner Shifter made her effort widest of all.

All that was now left on the card were two divisions of a 10f novice, both of which contained a short-price favourite. Neither contest appealed to me for betting purposes, but I decided to stay and watch the two races before starting the long journey home.

It had turned out to be a winning day for me, albeit not thanks to the horses I thought might yield me a profit. It was only relatively late that I had decided to invest in the opening nursery, and it was a good job I did. The fact that I was unable to add to that success was disappointing, but I felt it was more down to bad luck rather than poor judgement.

WEDNESDAY, 3 AUGUST: NEWCASTLE

As previously mentioned, Newcastle is an awfully long way from home, but I was determined to fit at least one fixture into the diary and this one fitted in perfectly with work commitments, even though it meant staying locally for the two nights either side of the meeting. Even that is always a pleasure, though.

It also helped that I approached this fixture with plenty of confidence, having studied the card in detail the previous evening, and one of the most appealing bets of the afternoon was due to run in the very opening contest, a 0-55 apprentice handicap over 1m2f.

1-30   SKY SPORTS RACING SKY 415 APPRENTICE HANDICAP (0-55) (6)
3-Y-O+
10.2f   Par = 101   9 runners

AW Form	Name	Highest	Last Six Ratings
90455-	HOT TEAM	102Li10	93Wo09 87Wo09 91Wo09 102Li10 95Wo09 100Ne10
48	WAUD HOUSE	94Ne12	94Ne12 90Ne07
U7-056	TOP ATTRACTION	102Ne08	97Ne08 0Ne08 87Ne10 91Ne10 98So08 92Ne08
853098	TURBULENT POWER	99Ne10	78Ne08 85Ne08 99Ne10 92Ne10 87Ne10 98Ne10
84-678	CHANNEL PACKET	106Ch10	102Ch10 97Ke08 94Wo09 77Ch10 93Wo09 85Ch08
6304	CARACRISTI	98Ne07	74Ne08 98Ne07 86Ne06 84Wo08
47-0	BUACHAILL	93Wo07	88Ke07 93Wo07 81Ke07
070-	MAD ARTYMAISE	88Ne05	82Ne07 85Ne06 88Ne05
0-7	OSCAR DOODLE	93Wo07	89Wo06 93Wo07

Hot Team hadn't run on the All-Weather since the previous September and it's fair to say that his first few starts on turf after reappearing in the spring had left plenty to be desired, but he had performed much better when third at Hamilton four days earlier. His effort there had made a bit more of an impression on me than would usually have been the case as I had done the analysis and close-ups for the *Racing Post*, so was aware that this was an improved performance. It was also the first time he had dropped into a 0-55 since winning at Hamilton in May 2021, while his last win had come in a 0-70 at that track in September.

So here he was, 4lb lower than for his last win and still contesting a 0-55. He certainly had the All-Weather form to be competitive at this level too, so what was there not too like? I fully expected him to be available at around the 9-4 mark when betting commenced, certainly no bigger than 5-2, so imagine my delight when he was being offered at 7-2 when the on-course bookies began to put their prices up.

That would have been more than good enough for me, and I started to take a few steps forward to place my bet, only to notice that the next board was offering 4-1. Then I noticed that a couple of bookmakers further down the line were showing 9-2, and it was at that point that I began to get a little concerned. This is a situation all of us who like to have a bet will have come across – the horse you like starts to take a dramatic drift in the market. What do you do? Still make the investment with the possibility that the horse will flop badly, and you will then be cursing yourself because the market told you so, or give the race a miss and watch your selection win without you having a penny on it. In this situation I decided to go with it. All my research had told me that Hot Team was one of the bets of the day, if not the week, and any doubts I may have had disappeared when I saw one board going 5-1. I was there in a flash!

The race itself was a very interesting one and it nicely brought together a few different subjects covered in this book. Firstly, just to describe the race in pure hard facts, Hot Team was given a waiting ride before being delivered with this effort halfway up the home straight, and having hit the front he pulled right away, eventually bolting up by an eased-down three lengths. Of course, I was delighted to have backed a winner, especially at such a generous price, while the success vindicated all the study that had gone into the race, but among that delight was a realisation that *the way* he went about the victory could also have great significance for the rest of the meeting.

The field in that first race had made straight for the centre of the track after turning for home (nothing unusual in that), but jockey Conor Planas had made a positive manoeuvre to come closest to the stands' rail and the way he picked off his rivals was like seeing a car in the outside line of the motorway whizzing past those in the slower lanes. Apparently coming so wide had been the plan, so was this a sign of a potential track bias? After just one race it wasn't possible to say, but it did give me another angle to digest so now I might need to approach the remaining six races in a slightly different way. Certainly, I would need to pay extra special attention as to what was going on.

The second race on the card was a two-year-old novice over 6f.

2-00   AT THE RACES APP EXPERT TIPS/IRISH STALLION FARMS EBF REST' NOVICE STAKES (QUAL/GBB) (IRE INCENTIVE) (5) 2-Y-O
6f   Par = 94   14 runners

AW Form	Name	Highest	Last Six Ratings
	MOUNTAIN WARRIOR		
	TRIBAL HUNTER		
	HOUGOUMONT		
	KNIGHTS ARTIST		
	OAHU		
	STAR START		
	HEART OF SOFIA		
	MAM'ZELLE DUPONT		
	PRINCESS SAVANNAH		

SOPHIA'S STARLIGHT
ZERBINETTA
GREYCIOUS ANNA
SPURN POINT
TECHNO LADY

It wasn't a betting race for me as none of the 14-strong field had run on an All-Weather surface before. In fact, some hadn't run at all but it's still a race that deserves a place in the diary. In races like these I may try to find another angle such as the horse's pedigree, including the sire stats shown in each of the racecourse chapters. The one with the best credentials was Mountain Warrior, who had made a promising debut when fourth at Ayr and whose three winning siblings had all been successful on an All-Weather surface. The problem was he was being offered at around the 5-4 mark (he was sent off at 11-8), which was short enough in a race full of unknown quantities, but potentially a bigger turnoff was that he was drawn in stall one. If there was indeed a track bias in operation, then his draw meant that he was in the worst possible place, so I watched his performance with keen interest.

The action duly unfolded centre-to-nearside, but although the winner Hougoumont passed the line in the centre of the track it was only because he hung that way late on. The runner-up Tribal Hunter was only beaten a short-head having stuck limpet-like to the nearside rail, while the fourth horse, 33-1 newcomer Oahu, went straight into the notebook as he made his effort furthest from the stands' rail yet was battling for the lead half a furlong from home before fading late on. The favourite Mountain Warrior only managed fifth, having raced wide from his low stall and on the face of it was a disappointing favourite, but not from where I was standing. He had a valid excuse as far as I was concerned so was more than happy to give him another chance.

The third race was another 0-55 handicap, again over 6f.

2-30   QUINNBET HANDICAP (0-55) (6) 3-Y-O+
6f   Par = 101   12 runners

AW Form	Name	Highest	Last Six Ratings
365945	TATHMEEN	111Ne05	97Ne05 94Ne06 103Ne05 94Wo05 96Ne06 97So06
P-055	SLAINTE MHATH	91Ne05	0Ne06 43Ne08 89Ne07 91Ne05
3067-7	ZAMJAR	108Wo05	88Wo05 101Li06 90Wo06 95Ne06 84Ne06 91Wo07
5-372-	ARNOLD	101Ne06	98Ne06 98Ne05 94Ne06 99Ne05 94Ne05 100Ne06

8-38	DIRTY LEEDS	**93Ne06**	82Ne06 93Ne06 85Wo07
6	LINCOLN PRIDE	**97Wo07**	97Wo07
0-14-2	BILLY WEDGE	**105Ne06**	75Ne06 99Ne07 86Ne07 105Ne06 97Ne06 99Ne06
30-520	BIRDIE BOWERS	**101Ne06**	97Ne06 101Ne06 98So07 96Ne06 90Wo06 83So06
80-	STORM MASTER	**73Ne06**	73Ne06 18Ne06
22-249	EMBLA	**105So06**	87Ne06 93Ne06 102Ne06 100So07 105So06 80Ch07
9/	SEE MY BABY JIVE	**81Ne06**	81Ne06
2500-7	CHEESE THE ONE	**92Ke06**	77Wo08 92Ke06 91Wo07 88Li07 91Ch07 89Ch05

The one I liked was Billy Wedge, a course regular who had a clear chance based on the speed figures. My confidence was further boosted by the fact he was drawn in stall 11 in a 12-strong field, so I also had the evidence of my own eyes on my side. I could back him at 15-2 which I was more than happy to do, but despite holding a good position early he dropped right out and finished last. There were no excuses forthcoming afterwards, but in my view for whatever reason the gelding failed to give his true running.

The race was another fascinating one to witness, though, as the winner Lincoln Pride stuck to the nearside rail like glue and put in a smooth and sustained finishing effort very much in similar style to Hot Team. He had started from stall ten, the runner-up Arnold came from stall seven and the third Slainte Mhath from stall 12. I had suspected there was a golden highway next to the stands' rail, now there was no doubt about it.

How much significance that would make in the next race, a 0-70 fillies' handicap over 1m4f, was hard to say as like the opener it would be run on the round track, so the route the horses took up the straight would be purely down to the jockeys.

3-00 DOWNLOAD THE AT THE RACES APP FILLIES' HANDICAP
(0-70) (5) 3-Y-O+
12.4f   Par = 100   8 runners

AW Form	Name	Highest	Last Six Ratings
0/4/	EAST END GIRL	**95Ke11**	73Ke08 95Ke11
06-0-	BATTLE ANGEL WORLD WITHOUT LOVE	**90Du08**	89Du07 90Du08 88Du08
2-5	DELPHINUS	**101Ke11**	91Ch10 101Ke11
55	GOLD CHARM	**97Li10**	97Li10 92Li12
6-	QOYA VON DER LEYEN	**90Li08**	90Li08
683-5	LITTLE EMMA LOULOU	**91Wo09**	87Ne06 86Ne07 91Wo09 89Wo12

As you can see, there wasn't a great deal to go on form-wise, but I felt I had discovered a potential angle. World Without Love hadn't run on an All-Weather surface before, but her pedigree was interesting as not only was she closely related to the stable's Ascot Gold Cup winner Subjectivist (also successful on Polytrack), her sire Ulysses was 2-3 with his runners at Newcastle. She was available at 7-1 which I felt was most generous.

I can have no complaints over the ride Ben Curtis gave her. He attempted to make all on the filly, and she eventually ended up against the stands' rail after the whole field had come nearside after turning in, albeit that was mainly due to her hanging that way. She fought back gamely after being headed by East End Girl but was always being held, and although she didn't win, I felt the bet was the right one.

The fifth race was the first division of a 0-65 handicap, and this was a race which left me in a real quandary.

3-30   DOWNLOAD THE QUINNBET APP HANDICAP (DIV I) (0-65) (6) 3-Y-O+
7.1f   Par = 101   11 runners

AW Form	Name	Highest	Last Six Ratings
-5154-	TURBO COMMAND	108Du08	97Du07 103Du08 102Du08 94Du07 108Du08 100Du07
281161	MOSTALLIM	109So06	109So06 107So07 101Ne06 99Ne06 104So07 105Wo07
0-3611	ROCKET ROD	107Ne07	94Ne07 94So07 98Ne08 107Ne07 101Ne08 96Ne08
-36-53	KATYUSHA	100Ne10	82Wo08 98Ch08 99Ke08 98Ch07 100Ne10
3-7312	BURABACK	103Li07	97Li07 94Ke08 82Li07 91Li07 89Li07 103Li07
6-5565	MUTARAAFEQ	105Ch10	101Ne08 102Wo09 95So12 101Wo09 99Ke07 102So08
745149	VIVENCY	104Ke07	103So06 94Wo07 97Wo07 93Ch07 98Ch07 93Wo08
6-	WABA DABA DO	94Ne07	94Ne07
	BASTILLE		
	KRAKEN FLORIDA		
	MADAME HELEN		

I was keen on Mostallim for a few reasons, the main ones being his recent good speed figures and the fact that he had been successful on his last two visits here. There was only one negative, but it was a big one, he was drawn in the lowest stall.

So once again I had to do some thinking. Even with the non-runner he would be ten horse-widths off the nearside rail and my eyes had been telling me all afternoon that was going to be a problem, even for a top jockey like Ben Curtis. I could have just left him alone and watch a horse who had so much going for him otherwise possibly win unbacked by me or go with him in the hope that he would be able to overcome this major obstacle.

In the end I decided on a compromise. I backed Mostallim at 9-2, but also decided to take out insurance. My second choice was Rocket Rod, a gelding who had won his last two starts over 1m here, while he had no problem with this trip judging by that good speed figure three starts back. He was the 2-1 favourite, which was short enough, but was better drawn in stall six and if Mostallim couldn't overcome his draw, he was the one most likely to benefit.

As it turned out, once again Ben Curtis gave his mount the best possible chance despite the handicap of the number-one stall and ended up finishing second, while Rocket Rod was given an identical ride to Lincoln Pride, sticking to the stands' rail, and winning with loads in hand. It wasn't the result I had hope for as Mostallim was the bigger price, but I still made a profit on the race because of having my eyes open. However, I did tell myself off for not doing the exacta (paid £11.20 to a £1 stake).

I had no strong opinions on the second division, so waited patiently for the closing 0-70 fillies' handicap over 6f.

4-30 FREE TIPS DAILY ON ATTHERACES.COM FILLIES' HANDICAP (0-70) (5) 3-Y-O+
6f   Par = 100   8 runners

AW Form	Name	Highest	Last Six Ratings
465-54	DANDYS GOLD	108Ne06	102Ne06 70Ne08 93Ne06 101Ne06 87So07 102Ne07
1-4	TROIS VALLEES	94Ne06	94Ne06 92Ne06
5257-2	LADY CELIA	99Ne06	97Ne06 90Ne06 98Ne05 95Li06 99Ne06 83Ne05
5-2	ROSHAMBO	100Wo06	
	87Ne06 100Wo06		
1-8	SWEET GLANCE	92Wo05	92Wo05 91Ch05
	MISS BRITAIN		
659/	SOLLER BAY	93Ne07	88Wo06 93Ne07 78So08
3-	KITTYBREWSTER	86Ne06	86Ne06

Dandys Gold had much to recommend her. Admittedly she was an eight-year-old mare taking on seven less exposed rivals, five of them three-year-olds, but it was hard to get away from her superiority on speed figures and she also had plenty of good form here, including a course-and-distance success. Her draw in stall three wasn't perfect, but in a field of this size she was still berthed closer to the stands' rail than Mostallim had been, so I was happy to back her at 11-2.

Once again, although I didn't win, I can have no complaints as Jonny Peate (successful earlier aboard Rocket Rod) did everything right in attempting to make all on her, but she was just unable to withstand the late flourish of the unexposed Roshambo. One thing I did do straight away was to make a note of the winner, because she had to switch left to get past Dandys Gold, thereby ending up in the centre of the track, yet she still won comfortably. She only won by half a length and would be handicapped on that, but this was a performance that could be marked up.

So, it did end up being a winning day, even though it could have been even better. One thing it did achieve, though, was to demonstrate the appearance of a major track bias as it happened.

TUESDAY, 9 AUGUST: LINGFIELD

I do miss Lingfield. At one time I spent just about every Saturday there during the winter months even if there was a bigger jumps meeting closer to my home, such was my affection for the place. Unfortunately, after I moved further west a few years back the journey there became significantly greater and, with the complications already posed by the M25, it became a bit too far.

Apart from attending the All-Weather Championships every year I was able to (it didn't happen in 2020 and was held behind closed doors in 2021) I didn't get down there very often. I will have to do something to change that, and I was determined to include a meeting in this diary. This was the only one that fitted in with my workload and, although it wasn't the classiest meeting in the world, I was delighted to be back there and managed to see some old familiar faces. Before describing the action from a punting point of view, I just wish to touch on another slightly different (yet connected) subject.

This was a minor meeting and, although I don't know if this is intended policy, fixtures like this can see the blooding of new racecourse commentators. I have been racing in a few countries around the world and have no hesitation in stating that we have the best commentators. Everyone will have their favourites of course, but many of our commentators are knowledgeable, clear, easy to understand, don't sound like robots and don't talk down to you. I have the honour of knowing many of them personally and know the hard work they put it, so I have the utmost respect for them. Today it was the turn of Alex Fussey, a new commentator whom I had heard a couple of times before, but this was the first time I had heard him on the racecourse. I have to say he was most impressive and if this is sign of things to come, then the future of racecourse commentary looks bright.

The first race on the six-race card was a 0-50 apprentice classified stakes over 1m5f, not a race that made any appeal to me whatsoever.

1-30   RACING LEAGUE ON SKY SPORTS RACING APPRENTICE CLASSIFIED STAKES (0-50) (6) 3-Y-O+
13f   Par = 101   11 runners

AW Form	Name	Highest	Last Six Ratings
80-0	ALJASRA UNITED	79Wo09	79Wo09 74Wo08 75Ch08
8808-7	DOUBLE LEGEND	109Ke12	97Ke12 98Wo12 89Li12 91Ke11 79Ke12 98Li12
708/0/	LONGVILLE LILLY	93Wo09	57Wo09 84Wo08 89So07 83So08 93Wo09 87Wo09
60-0-	NEMINOS	84Ch07	84Ch07 83Ch07 74Li06
2-9009	PARTY PLANNER	108Ne10	96Wo16 81So14 94Wo14 74Li13 89So14 94Wo12
99-03-	PUMP IT UP	96Li10	89Ch06 80Li07 84Ke07 90Wo07 96Li10
613778	TULANE	108Ke16	95So12 108Ke16 99Ke12 107Ke16 101Wo16 99Ke16
600-9	COULDN'T COULD HE	91Li10	89Ch08 78Li10 86Ke08 91Li10
758	GOT CARTER	93So12	83Li08 79Ne10 93So12
57	HERMONIE	90Ke12	90Ke12 47Wo12
0-5	JUST AN INKLING	87Ke07	80Li07 87Ke07

I didn't have a bet but looking back I may have missed a trick and gave myself a good telling off. After all, this was the lowest grade of race imaginable and the horses contesting it were hardly known for their consistency, but perhaps I was too quick to write off the contest. At this level any sort of edge can make all the difference and what was the point in being armed with speed figures if you don't use them? I should have had a few quid on Double Legend for merely being the top rated and had I done so I would have backed a 22-1 winner, probably at longer odds. However, it proved to be even worse (much worse) than that as Party Planner finished second and Tulane third (just look at those highest speed figures!). The exacta paid £334.50 to a £1 stake and the trifecta £3,141.80.

I didn't have much time to admonish myself before the second contest, a two-year old fillies' novice.

2-00   BRITISH STALLION STUDS EBF FILLIES' NOVICE STAKES (GBB RACE) (4) 2-Y-O

5f   Par = 93   8 runners

AW Form	Name	Highest	Last Six Ratings
	LADY JANE GREY		
	AIRA FORCE		
2	APACHE SPARK	90Ke06	90Ke06
	HOOF IT HOOF IT		
	REFINE		
	SHAWASHA		
	SO SLEEPY		
	TEPHI		

This provided a completely different conundrum to the opener, and I was determined to play this race in some form or other. It wasn't so much that there was a horse taking part that I wanted to back – it was more that it contained a horse I wanted to take on. Admittedly Apache Spark had run well to finish second at Kempton on her second start and the winner had gone on to finish second in a Group 3, but this was going to be a completely different ball game, and this is where knowledge of each of the All-Weather tracks comes in handy.

Kempton is a galloping track while Lingfield is tight and the 5f around here is mostly on the turn, so although she was dropping a furlong on the face of it, given the nature of the two venues she was almost dropping 2f! The market didn't seem to care, though, as she was being offered at around the 4-5 mark. I had to take her on, but with what? In such a situation I don't force myself into trying to find one horse to back against her and in any case, I couldn't narrow it down to just one. I laid her to £50 at those odds (I rarely lay a horse at odds against) with a view that the track would beat her rather than the opposition and I was proved right.

She was slow to break (albeit the winner So Sleepy was even slower) and she could never summon the pace to mount a challenge, eventually finishing fourth. I initially felt that perhaps I should have laid her for a place, but it would have been annoying had she sneaked into third so just contented myself with the fact that my analysis of the situation had proved correct.

The third race was an older-horse fillies' novice over 1m, and this wasn't a contest I had originally intended to get involved in, but again the betting proved to be the catalyst for a punt.

2-30   AT THE RACES APP MARKET MOVERS FILLIES' NOVICE STAKES (GBB RACE) (5) 3-Y-O+
8f   Par = 100   6 runners

AW Form	Name	Highest	Last Six Ratings
	SEA TSARINA		
	AL AGAILA		
	KHAMSIN LADY		
5-	LADY SHOTGUN	86Ke07	86Ke07
-52322	MINWAH	100Li07	99Me07 95Me07 98Me08 85Me09 97Je07 100Li07
	PINK HAZE		

The top two in the list dominated the betting based on their turf form and I couldn't argue with that, but I felt they were the wrong way round as Al Agaila was sent off at 5-6 and Sea Tsarina 6-4. The latter had a 7lb penalty for her win which may have had something to do with it, but her turf form was superior to her rival's and the key to me having a bet was her pedigree. Not only was she a sister to an All-Weather winner, but her dam had also been successful on an artificial surface so in what was basically the toss of a coin, I was content to take 6-4 about Sea Tsarina.

She had to come from behind, but I was very happy when Tom Marquand delivered her down the centre of the track and I knew she was always going to get there. These last two races had proved that although speed figures are invaluable, if you don't have many to go on there are still other tools available to help find a selection.

There was no shortage of speed figures for the fourth race, a 0-65 handicap over 7f.

3-00   AT THE RACES APP FORM STUDY HANDICAP (0-65) (6) 4-Y-O+
7f   Par = 101   10 runners

AW Form	Name	Highest	Last Six Ratings
8/	AFTA PARTY	92Wo08	92Wo08
3-4	ANGEL AMADEA	98Ke07	95Li08 98Ke07
9-8431	HEALING POWER	106Wo07	96Wo08 90Ch08 87Ch08 92Ch08 100Li07 104Li07
5-749-	DRAGON'S FIRE	100Ke08	90Ke06 95Ke08 100Ke08 96Ch07
2504-5	BLAME CULTURE	106Ch08	102Ch06 99Ch07 101Ch07 95Wo07 100Ch07 96Ch07
524116	SILVER DOLLAR	101Ke06	91Ch06 66So06 94Wo06 99Wo06 101Ke06 94Ke06
-25164	INCLEMENT WEATHER	103So06	96Wo06 103So06 102So06 99Ke07 96Ch07 97Ke07
694396	SIR SEDRIC	109So07	101Wo06 94Wo06 97Li07 98Li07 84Ke08 97Li07
882264	CAPPANANTY CON	109Wo05	98Li06 100Li07 101Li07 103Li06 95Li07 98Li07
766552	CATCH MY BREATH	107Li08	97So08 93Li08 84Ch10 100Li08 97Ke08 101Li07

I was very keen on Healing Power, as apart from having won in good style over course and distance the previous month, the gelding was the only likely pace angle should his rider decide the go forward, albeit he hadn't led early last time. I wouldn't suggest that his odds of 3-1 were generous, but still big enough for me to invest and I did like him.

Unfortunately, he had to do quite a bit of running to secure the early advantage and although he did his best, he couldn't quite maintain the gallop, fading late to finish third behind Silver Dollar. I had no complaints about the performance and just hoped things might pan out a bit better in the next contest, a 0-85 handicap for three-year-olds over the same trip.

3-30   HAPPY BIRTHDAY JILL HUMPHREY HANDICAP (0-85) (4) 3-Y-O
7f   Par = 102   8 runners

AW Form	Name	Highest	Last Six Ratings
12	ANOTHER ROMANCE	106Wo07	106Wo07 102Ch07
13	SPRING IS SPRUNG	102So06	101So06 102So06
12	ARCHIANO	96Wo06	94Li06 96Wo06
	OUTSIDE WORLD		
2-	BAILEYSGUTFEELING	100Ch07	100Ch07
2-422	SECRET STRENGTH	104Ke06	90Ne05 98Wo06 104Ke06 103Ke06
322371	LITTLE PRAYER	101Wo06	101Li06 99Li06 99Li06 101Wo06 94Wo06 98Li07
1-158	GOLD MEDAL	102Li06	99Wo06 102Li06 100Ke07 90Ke06

This was another race where I felt an air of confidence as I thought Another Romance had a great chance. Her turf form was OK, but once you stripped that away her credentials became clearer, and I was more than hopeful that the return to an All-Weather surface would help her return to winning form. The betting public was of the same opinion as the best price I could see available was 2-1. That was plenty short enough, but again I liked her claims so backed her anyway.

I shouldn't have done so, though, as she met plenty of trouble and ended up third behind Baileysgutfeeling, but I wasn't convinced that getting an interrupted run was the difference between victory and defeat. I thought she was just plain disappointing.

So now we came to the final race on the Lingfield card, a 0-55 handicap over 1m2f.

4-05   SKY SPORTS RACING SKY 415 HANDICAP (0-55) (6) 3-Y-O+
10f   Par = 101   11 runners

AW Form	Name	Highest	Last Six Ratings
-051-4	POINT LOUISE	97Ke08	87Ke07 90Ke07 72Ke07 97Li07 96Wo08 97Ke08
-57963	VILLEURBANNE	108Ke08	103Li08 99Ke08 91Li08 60Ke11 94Li10 97Li10
14-548	MORANI KALI	101Li08	97Ch10 85Ke12 91So12 94Li12 101Li08 96Li10
01-175	TAWTHEEF	100Wo09	85Ch07 75Ke07 100Wo09 96Li10 91Li10 94Li10
294455	TOO SHY SHY	106Ke08	100Li12 91Li12 92Li10 94Wo09 93Li10 94Li10
888954	AGENT OF FORTUNE	108Li08	96Ke08 100Li08 89Li07 95Li07 100Li08 98Li10
0-0072	BLAIRLOGIE	99Ch10	89Li08 95Ch08 97Li08 83Ke07 92Li10 98Li10
0-4-58	SUPERSONIQUE	91Ke12	86Ke07 76Ke07 87Li12 91Ke12 82Ch10
-42437	RITA RANA	99Li12	89Wo08 96Li10 90Wo12 97So11 89Ch13 99Li12
890	GLENISTER	90Ch07	81Ch07 90Ch07 79Ch07
0-87	DON BEKAR	94So12	86Wo07 71Ke07 94So12

I wouldn't have chosen to have ended with a race like this, but despite a record of 0-16 I decided that Villeurbanne might be a bet at 10-1 based on the speed figures, so backed her accordingly. Her run was all right, but she could manage only fifth of the ten runners behind Glenister, thereby becoming a 17-race maiden! Sometimes you get what you deserve.

The winner was a handicap newcomer trained by Sir Mark Prescott and the speed figures wouldn't have been much help in finding him, but his pedigree strongly suggested the longer trip would suit and strong market support was another indication. As stated earlier there are lots of factors that can put you on to a winner, but there was no way I was going to back him at 13-8. Of course, I was happy for those who did.

Now it was time for the long journey home. By the time I had reached Amen Corner on the M25 (that's what I call the stretch between junctions ten and 16 because before you reach it you are already praying) I had begun to analyse how things had gone during the diary and tried to work out if I could have done anything different. Of course, I could have done but that would be with the benefit of hindsight, and at least I had made a profit. The secret is to try and avoid the mistakes before they happen, though one or two will be inevitable. The main thing was that during these ten meetings I had an awful lot of fun.

SUMMARY OF BETS

DATE	TRACK	HORSE	STAKE (£)	ODDS	POSITION	PROFIT/LOSS	TOTAL
3 Feb	Southwell	Love Your Work	50 win	5-4	Won	+62.50	+62.50
		Griffin Park	50 win	3-1	Won	+150.00	+212.50
		Dark Enchantment	50 win	5-1	2nd	-50.00	+162.50
		Brazen Arrow	50 win	5-1	2nd	-50.00	+112.50
		Sweet Aroma	50 win	10-1	8th	-50.00	+62.50
		Donya	50 win	3-1	2nd	-50.00	+12.50
		Batocchi	50 win	5-4	Won	+62.50	+75.00
6 Feb	Kempton	Equitation	50 win	7-2	3rd	-50.00	+25.00
		Tranquil Night	50 win	Evens	Won	+50.00	+75.00
		Precisely	50 win	6-1	4th	-50.00	+25.00
		La Tihaty	50 win	5-4	Won	+62.50	+87.50
		Uzincso	25 ew	11-1	5th	-50.00	+37.50
9 Feb	Kempton	Flaming Dawn	50 win	7-4	Won	+87.50	+125.00
		Deacs Delight	50 win	10-1	8th	-50.00	+75.00
		Sicilian Vito	25 ew	14-1	3rd	+45.00	+120.00
		Amber Island	50 win	4-1	3rd	-50.00	+70.00
		Exuding	50 win	5-1	3rd	-50.00	+20.00
		Yorktown	50 win	3-1	Won	+150.00	+170.00
28 Feb	Wolverhampton	Classy Dame	50 win	11-4	3rd	-50.00	+120.00
		Atiyah	50 win	3-1	2nd	-50.00	+70.00
		Hot Diggity Dog	50 wins	9-4	2nd	-50.00	+20.00
		Beau Geste	50 wins	7-2	6th	-50.00	-30.00
		Twilight Tone	25 ew	10-1	Won	+300.00	+270.00
		Million Reasons	50 win	9-4	Won	+112.50	+382.50
19 Mar	Wolverhampton	Lenny's Spirit	50 win	3-1	Won	+150.00	+532.50
		Tone The Barone	50 win	11-8	Won	+68.75	+601.25
		Fox Power	50 win	5-2	3rd	-50.00	+551.25

Date	Course	Selection	Stake	Odds	Result	P/L	Total
		Amber Island	50 win	7-2	2nd	-50.00	+501.25
		Harbour Vision	50 win	7-2	2nd	-50.00	+451.25
		Universal Effect	50 win	15-2	6th	-50.00	+401.25
		Placepot	2 x 25	-	Won	+190.00	+591.25
12 Apr	Wolverhampton	Way Of Life	50 win	6-1	Won	+300.00	+891.25
		Amazing Amaya	25 ew	10-1	2nd	+25.00	+916.25
		Asgoodassobergets	50 win	11-8	Won	+68.75	+985.00
		Desert Emperor	50 win	6-4	2nd	-50.00	+935.00
		Sir Henry Cotton	50 win	5-1	3rd	-50.00	+885.00
		Plumette	50 win	7-2	Won	+175.00	+1060.00
18 May	Kempton	Subjective Value	50 win	9-2	3rd	-50.00	+1010.00
		Newton Jack	25 ew	14-1	6th	-50.00	+960.00
		Heart Of Soul	50 win	13-2	Won	+325.00	+1285.00
		Got No Dollars	50 win	9-2	3rd	-50.00	+1235.00
		Savoy Brown	50 win	7-1	6th	-50.00	+1185.00
3 Jul	Chelmsford	Princess Naomi	50 win	10-1	Won	+500.00	+1685.00
		Cry Havoc	50 win	5-1	4th	-50.00	+1635.00
		Beauty Choice	50 win	11-2	4th	-50.00	+1585.00
		Internationalangel	50 win	5-2	8th	-50.00	+1535.00
		Crimson Sand	50 win	3-1	2nd	-50.00	+1485.00
		McQueen	50 win	3-1	3rd	-50.00	+1435.00
3 Aug	Newcastle	Hot Team	50 win	5-1	Won	+300.00	+1735.00
		Billy Wedge	50 win	15-2	12th	-50.00	+1685.00
		World Without Love	50 win	7-1	2nd	-50.00	+1635.00
		Rocket Rod	50 win	2-1	Won	+100.00	+1735.00
		Mostallim	50 win	9-2	2nd	-50.00	+1685.00
		Dandy Gold	50 win	11-2	2nd	-50.00	+1635.00
9 Aug	Lingfield	Apache Spark	50 lay	4-5	Correct	+62.50	+1697.50
		Sea Tsarina	50 win	6-4	Won	+75.00	+1772.50
		Healing Power	50 win	3-1	3rd	-50.00	+1722.50
		Another Romance	50 win	2-1	3rd	-50.00	+1672.50
		Villeurbanne	50 win	10-1	5th	-50.00	+1622.50